A Companion to
Dharmaśāstra

A Companion to Dharmaśāstra

by

Sures Chandra Banerji

PRINTWORLD
Publishers of Indian Traditions

Cataloging in Publication Data — DK
[Courtesy: D.K. Agencies (P) Ltd. <docinfo@dkagencies.com>]

Banerji, Sures Chandra, 1917-2000, **author.**
A companion to Dharmaśāstra / by Sures Chandra Banerji.
pages cm
"First published in India in 1998" – Title page verso.
Includes bibliographical references.
ISBN 9788124600986

1. Dharma. 2. Hindu law – Sources. 3. Law – India – History – To 1500 – Sources. I. Title. II. Title: Dharmaśāstra.

LCC KNS123.B36 2024 | DDC 294.594 23

ISBN: 978-81-246-0098-6
First published in India in 1998
Second impression in 2024

Printed and published by:
D.K. Printworld (P) Ltd.
Regd. Office: *Vedaśrī*, F-395, Sudarshan Park
(Metro Station: ESI Hospital), New Delhi – 110015
Phones: (011) 4172 2626, 98713 94815
e-mail: indology@dkprintworld.com
Website: www.dkprintworld.com

Preface

WHEN the texts of many works on a branch of knowledge become available, studies in them grow in bulk, and new horizons of it are discovered; then the need for reference books is felt. The sociology of ancient and medieval India has drawn the attention of many scholars. Aspects of it are still being avidly studied. For such studies, works on *dharmaśāstra* or *smṛti* are a repository of materials.

The present work has been designed to provide brief accounts of the important works on *dharmaśāstra* and their authors with short bibliographical notes. At first, we have given a rapid survey of the milieu — political, social and religious, in which this vast literature, spanning about one thousand five hundred years, originated and developed.

Besides texts on old and new *smṛti*, we have taken into account the sociological matters contained in our work, entitled *Smṛti Material in the Mahābhārata*.

A chapter has been added on important aspects of the society revealed in the works concerned. Finally, we have given a glossarial index of *smṛti* literature keeping in view particularly those who are not familiar with the technical terms without a knowledge of which ancient and medieval sociology of India cannot be fully understood.

As many as twelve appendices have been added. In three of them, we have dealt with the relation of *smṛti* to the *Mahābhārata*, Purāṇa and Tantra. An appendix dwells on the different schools of neo-*smṛti.* The theory of creation, according to Manu, forms the subject of one appendix. Taking the *Manu-smṛti* as the basic text, we have noted information about flora, fauna, geographical material, names of tribes and races contained in it. The concluding appendix deals with Manu's influence abroad.

The monumental *History of Dharmaśāstra* by P.V. Kane, has been of immense help. For the dates of the authors, we have taken Kane as the principal authority. R.C. Hazra's *Studies in the Purāṇic Records*, etc. have provided very useful information. In our account of the background of *smṛti* literature, R.C. Majumdar's *Advanced History of India* has served as an authoritative work.

The author feels encouraged to compose this work by the readers' warm appreciation of his works, *A Companion to Sanskrit Literature* (now running the second edn.), *A Companion to Middle Indo-Aryan Literature* and *A Companion to Indian Philosophy*.

The author's labour will be amply rewarded if this humble work goes some way in smoothening the path of those who are interested in ancient and medieval Indian sociology, particularly of those who have no access to the original works of the area of their interest. It is hoped that it will serve as a handbook to those who find Kane's above work forbidding both in bulk and erudition.

All said and done, the author's feeling is similar to that expressed in the *Raghuvaṃśa* of Kālidāsa:

titīrṣur-dustaraṃ mohādu-ḍupenāsmi sāgaram ।

S.C. Banerji

Contents

Abbreviations

ABORI	:	*Annals of Bhandarkar Oriental Research Institute*, Poona.
AIOC	:	All-India Oriental Conference.
ASS	:	Ānandāśrama Sanskrit Series, Poona.
BBRAS	:	Bombay Branch of Royal Asiatic Society.
Bib. Ind.	:	Bibliotheca Indica Series, Asiatic Society, Calcutta.
BORI	:	Bhandarkar Oriental Research Institute.
BSOAS	:	*Bulletin of School of Oriental and African Studies*, London. (Formerly: *BSOS - Bullten of School of Oriental Studies*.)
BSS	:	Bombay Sanskrit Series.
CSS	:	Chowkhamba Sanskrit Series, Varanasi.
GOS	:	Gaekwad's Oriental Series, Baroda.
HDH	:	*History of Dharmaśāstra* by P. V. Kane.
IA	:	*Indian Antiquary*.
IHQ	:	*Indian Historical Quarterly*.
IO	:	India Office, London.
JOR	:	*Journal of Oriental Research*.
MS	:	*Manu-smṛti*.
NCC	:	New Catalogus Catalogorum, Madras.

NIA : New Indian Antiquary.

Notices : *Notices of Sanskrit Manuscripts.*

NSP : Nirṇayasāgara Press, Bombay.

PO : *Poona Orientalist.*

SBE : Sacred Books of the East, Oxford.

TSS : Trivandrum Sanskrit Series

YS : *Yājñavalkya-smṛti.*

Important Dates

[Entries in English alphabetical order.]

Alexander's Invasion of India	327-326 BC
Arthaśāstra of Kauṭilya	Generally assigned to 4th century BC
Buddha	*c.* 563-483 BC
Caitanya	AD 1486-1533
*Dharmasūtra*s	*c.* 600-100 BC
Gupta Age	*c.* AD 320-510
Lakṣmaṇasena (King of Bengal)	Accession AD 1178
Mahābhārata	Date of origin unknown. Present form *c.* between fourth century BC and fourth century AD
Mahāvīra	d. 468 BC. According to others, 528 BC
Megasthenes' visit to India	302 BC
Pāla dynasty of Bengal and Bihar	*c.* AD 750-1155 (in Bengal), -1199 (in Bihar)
Purāṇa	Purāṇic literature appears to have originated before fifth or sixth century BC. Earliest extant Purāṇa probably dates back to a period before the seventh century AD

Rāmāyaṇa	Date of origin unknown. Present form finalised *c*. second century AD
Ṛgveda	Generally believed 1200-1000 BC
Sena dynasty of Bengal	*c*. AD 1095-1245
Tantra	Time of origin unknown. Original Tantras, believed by some to date back to a period after the fifth or sixth century AD

1

Introduction

The Land and the People

WE shall deal with the *dharmaśāstra* literature of India; we mean the undivided subcontinent in the pre-Independence period or the British India comprising the present India, Bangladesh and Pakistan. This country has a society which is multi-racial, multi-religious and multi-lingual. The population is predominantly Hindu. There are the followers of other religions, e.g., Muslims, Buddhists, Jains, Christians, Sikhs, etc. There are several sects and sub-sects of the different religious faiths. For example, the Hindus, with the four castes and sub-castes, are divided into various sects like *Śāktas*, *Vaiṣṇavas*, *Śaivas*, *Pāśupatas*, *Gāṇapatyas*, etc.

An analysis of the Indian population reveals the following principal ethnic groups:

1. ARYAN OR INDO-ARYAN

They are the Hindus of the upper classes. They are tall, fair-complexioned with sharp noses, speaking a language of Sanskritic origin.

2. DRAVIDIAN

Most of them are south Indian, with physical features different, in certain respects, from those of the Aryans. They speak languages, called Tamil, Telugu, Malayālam and Kanārese;

these are not derived from Sanskrit, but some of them have incorporated a few loan-words from Sanskrit.

3. ABORIGINAL

Like Kol, Bhil, Muṇḍā. They live in hills and forests. Their general physical features are: short stature, dark complexion, snub-nosed. Their languages are totally different from those mentioned above.

4. MONGOLOID

Their general physical features are as follows: no beard, yellow complexion, snub-nose, flat face, high jaw-bone. Most of them live in the Himālayas and the hilly tracts of Assam.

Dharma — Meaning and Source

Some people think that *dharma* is an albatross round the neck of India, hindering her progress; it makes the Indians blind to the advanced ideas developing in the world at large. In this scientific age, they aver, *dharma* is retrograde, keeping people in the straitjacket of antiquated, and sometimes superstitious, ideas. Those, who have an iconoclastic bent of mind, advocate a total effacement of *dharma* which, as they hold, gives rise to fissiparous tendencies in the society by preaching casteism, untouchability, etc.

The following observations of Khusvant Singh (Calcutta daily, *Telegraph*, 16.12.1996) sum up the general attitude to religion at present:

> Religion seems to be fast losing its hold among the advanced nations. Its only bastions remain among the poor and illiterate of West Asia and the far East. Religion has become a stumbling block to progress, prosperity and peace. If any evidence was needed to prove the negative rôle of religion in the present-day society, it is provided by the Cable News Network. Every hour there

> is a clip with Anita Pratap commenting on the destruction of the Babri Masjid by Hindu fanatics. This is an example of the CNN's efficiency and objectivity in covering the world. I wish we could organise a conference of champions of religious fundamentalism — the *āyātollāhs*, the *taliban*, *mollāhs*, Sikh *jathedars*, preachers of *Hindutva* — and leave them to fight it out. I would pray they all lose so that we could have a world society based on common sense and ethics. I would convert places of worship to more profitable uses like schools, hospitals, colleges, and places of tourist interests.

Before categorically castigating *dharma* as an unmixed evil, it is worth our while to understand the precise connotation of the term *dharma*. The word 'religion' does not convey all that is meant by *dharma*. According to the *Concise Oxford Dictionary* (1993), religion is "the belief in a superhuman controlling power, esp. in a personal God or gods entitled to obedience and worship", "a particular system of faith and worship". Let us see the connotation of *dharma* since Vedic times.

Dharma, derived from root *dhṛ* (to hold), etymologically means that which upholds. In a few passages of the *Ṛgveda* (e.g., I. 187.1; X.92.2), it is used to denote upholder, sustainer. In some passages (e.g., *Ṛgveda*, I.22.18; IX.64.), however, the meaning is religious injunction or rite. In the *Atharvaveda* (XI.7.17), the word *dharma* appears to mean merit accruing from the observance of religious rites. The *Aitareya Brāhmaṇa* (VII.17) seems to take *dharma* to mean the entire body of religious duties. The *Chāndogya Upaniṣad* (2/23), perhaps for the first time, clearly spells out the full implication of *dharma* as follows:

> There are three aspects of the word *dharma*. Of these, one consists in sacrifice (i.e., *yajña*), study and charity (to be practised in *gārhasthya āśrama* or the stage of householder). The second is marked by austerities

applicable to the *vānaprastha* or the stage of hermits. The third is that practised in the stage of *brahmacarya*; a *brahmacārin* has to stay in the house of the preceptor for a fixed period or for the whole of his life.

Jaimini, the propounder of *Pūrva Mīmāṃsā* philosophy, defines (I.1.2) *dharma* thus—*codanālaksaṇo'rtho dharmaḥ*; *dharma* is a beneficial act, indicated by Vedic injunctions. According to the *Vaiśeṣika-sūtra* — *yatobhyudaya-niḥśreyasa-siddhiḥ sa dharmaḥ*; that is *dharma* which results in the attainment of prosperity and salvation.

The *Āpastamba-dharmasūtra* (I.7.20) declares — *yat tu āryāḥ kriyamāṇaṃ praśaṃsanti sa dharmaḥ*; that practice or observance, which the Āryas praise, is *dharma*; Ārya means respectable, noble or honourable.

According to Manu (II.1), *dharma* is that which is observed by learned men, and heartily approved by those who are honest and free from hate and attachment. From *Manu*, I.2, it is clear that *dharma* is what has been narrated in the *Manu-smṛti* as the duties of all the castes and sub-castes. The duties of the castes, of course, include those of the four stages of life (*āśramas*). The comphrehensive import of *dharma* is more explicit in the following expression of the *Yājñavalkya-smṛti,* I.1: *varṇāśrametarāṇāṃ dharmān*. *Varṇa* means caste, *āśrama* stage of life, *itara* indicates sub-castes.

From the foregoing descriptions of *dharma*, it is clear that *dharma*, in its wider sense, comprehends all rules and regulations pertaining to all the walks of life, domestic, social and political. So, those who decry *dharma* as teaching narrowness, making people believe in old-world dogmas and doctrines, are not aware of the real meaning of *dharma* which means much more than what is conveyed by religion. *Dharma* means a way of life, and not merely a set of rites and rituals. To discard *dharma* is to give a go-by to civilised life. Even religion, which is comprised in *dharma*, can be given up only at the peril of civilisation. Even a scientist of the eminence of Einstein is reported to have remarked that science without religion is lame and religion without science is blind.

As regards the sources from which one can learn *dharma*, Yājñavalkya mentions (I.3) the following:

> *Purāṇa*, *Nyāya* (logic), *Mīmāṃsā* (philosophy), *Dharmaśāstra* (also called *Smṛti)*, *Aṅga* (six accessories of the Veda, viz. *Śikṣā, Kalpa, Vyākaraṇa, Nirukta* or Etymology, *Chandas, Jyotiṣa)*, the Vedas (four in number).

The sources of *dharma*, according to Manu (II.12), are Veda, *smṛti*, *sadācāra* (the conduct of the wise) and *svasya priyam* (*ātma-tuṣṭiḥ* or self-satisfaction).

Here, *sva* (own) does not mean anybody and everybody; it means one with a cultured mind. Manu's injunction is to do what is pure to one's mind (VI.46). Kullūka comments *pratiṣiddha-saṃkalpa-śūnya-manasā*, i.e., with a mind devoid of prohibited resolve. It may be added that, in the *Abhijñānaśakuntalam* (I.20), the king, being in doubt as to whether or not Śakuntalā is fit for being married to him, decides that she is certainly fit as his *ārya manas* (cultured mind) is eager for marriage with her.

It may be noted that, in Sanskrit literature, *dharma* has been used also to indicate the occupation, even if reprehensible to the cultured men, of a class of people. For example, in the *Bhaṭṭikāvya*, (II.33, 34), when Rāma accuses the demon Mārīca of killing innocent and poor hermits, the latter defends himself by saying — *dharmohyayaṃ nijo naḥ;* this is our own *dharma.*

General Remarks

The *Ṛgveda* (*c*. 1500 or 1200 BC) is the earliest work of not only the Indo-Āryans, but also of the Indo-Europeans. It was followed by the other three Vedas. The four Vedic texts, along with the *Brāhmaṇas*, e.g. *Aitareya Brāhmaṇa*, *Śatapatha Brāhmaṇa*, etc., constitute what is called Veda. The Vedic hymns are believed, by orthodox *Brāhmaṇas*, to have been seen, not written, by the sages with whose names these are associated. In other words, the Vedic hymns were revealed to them. Originally, these hymns are believed to have been orally transmitted to successive generations; hence it is called *śruti* (from root *śru* — to hear).

In course of time, the need was felt for works facilitating the comprehension of the Vedic texts. In those times, great emphasis was laid on rites and rituals; various sacrifices came to play an important rôle in the religious life. In the performance of rites, even the minutae were insisted upon.

The result was the composition of ancillary works of two kinds, viz., Exegetical and Ritualistic; these were called *Vedāṅgas*. The ritualistic works, written in the mnemonic aphoristic style, were collectively known as *Kalpasūtras*. These were divided into four kinds, viz., *Śrauta-sūtra* (dealing with Vedic rites), *Gṛhya-sūtra* (dealing with domestic rites to be performed by householders), *Śulva-sūtra* (dealing with the measurement of the sacrificial altar, etc.) — *Śulva*, meaning measuring string, is directly attached to *Śrauta-sūtra*); and *Dharma-sūtra* (containing rules of conduct, education, law, etc.).

Smṛti literature can be divided into two broad classes: *prācīna* and *navya*.

A. PRĀCĪNA SMṚTI

1. *Dharma-sūtras*

The *Dharma-sūtras* were the earliest works of *Prācīna Smṛti*.

As time rolled on, the society expanded, population increased, and the complexities of life multiplied. The necessity was felt for rules and regulations relating to the different spheres of life —

domestic, social and political. The social and political leaders as also the law-makers tried to spell out their injunctions and prohibitions more clearly than the terse *sūtras*.

2. *Metrical Smṛti*

The result was *dharmaśāstra* composed in more explicit verses. The principal authors of such works are named as follows in the *Yājñavalkya-smṛti* (I.4-5):

> Manu, Atri, Viṣṇu, Hārīta, Yājñavalkya, Uśanas, Aṅgiras, Yama, Āpastamba, Saṃvarta, Kātyāyana, Bṛhaspati, Parāśara, Vyāsa, Śaṃkha, Likhita, Dakṣa, Gautama, Śātātapa and Vaśiṣṭha.

It is significant that Manu heads the list. He is not only the earliest among the authors of *dharmaśāstra*, but also the most authoritative. He and his work have been highly extolled by such observations as *manvartha viparīta yā sā smṛtir-na praśasyate* (that *smṛti*, which runs counter to what Manu means to say, is not commended) and *manur-vai yat kiṃcāha tad bheṣajam* (whatever Manu said is medicine). Next in importance is Yājñavalkya. The *Manu-smṛti* has been looked upon as the standard work in respect of social and familial rules and regulations; the *Rājadharma* portion of the work throws a flood of light on politics and statecraft in the days of yore. The *Yājñavalkya-smṛti*, discussing the topics of *smṛti* in general, assumed great importance in the sphere of law. In fact, its *Dāyabhāga* portion, interpreted in Vijñāneśvarā's *Mitākṣarā,* formed the basis of the Hindu law of inheritance and succession in vogue in the Indian subcontinent, excepting Bengal. The aforesaid portion of the *Yājñavalkya-smṛti*, as interpreted by Jīmūtavāhana, was the foundation of the Hindu law of inheritance and succession prevailing in Bengal.

The contents of *dharmaśāstra* or *smṛti* can be broadly divided under the following heads: *ācāra* (rules of conduct in general), *prāyaścitta* (expiation), *vyavahāra* (law) and *rājadharma* (politics and statecraft).

B. NAVYA SMṚTI

Smṛti Digests and Commentaries

The society was controlled by the Brāhmaṇas who belonged to the intellectual class. The Brāhmaṇa scholars vied with one another in interpreting the *dharmaśāstra* texts. Of the commentators of Manu, the earliest is Medhātithi; his commentary is extensive and erudite. Govindarāja also seems to have been another renowned commentator; Kullūka, author of the brief but lucid commentary on the *Manu-smṛti*, often refers to his views besides those of Medhātithi. In course of time, the elaborate *dharmaśāstra*s and their recondite commentaries became unwieldy. Moreover, there were many conflicting views of the writers of *dharmaśāstra*. Again, different customs obtained in the different regions. These factors were responsible for short-cuts dealing with particular topics like *vivāha*, *śrāddha*, etc. In these works, generally known as *nibandha*s (digests), attempts were made to interpret the *dharmaśāstra* texts in the light of *mīmāṃsā* rules of interpretation, and also to reconcile the divergent texts on a particular topic. Regional customs also found place in them. These regional works gave rise to different schools of *Navya-smṛti*, which have been dealt with in an appendix. *Navya-smṛti* includes also the authoritative commentaries like those of Medhātithi, Vijñāneśvara, etc.

2

Political, Social and Religious Background of Dharmaśāstra

Political Conditions

THE political condition moulds the society of a country to a considerable extent; the society, in its turn, plays an important rôle in shaping the literature, religious and profane. We shall set forth a rapid survey of the political, social and religious background of the *dharmaśāstra*s.

As we have seen, Indian civilisation is older than the Vedas by several millennia. Unfortunately, nothing about the political condition of the pre-Vedic period is known. In the Vedic age, the patriarchal family was the nucleus of the society and politics. A study of the Vedas, particularly the *Ṛgveda*, reveals that the political hierarchy comprised the *grāma* (village), *viś* and *jana*, each succeeding unit superior to the preceding one. The works, called *Brāhmaṇa*s, inform us that there were also regions beyond the Āryan settlement. In this connexion, the following verse is worth quoting:

aṅga-vaṅga-kaliṅgeṣu saurāṣṭra-magadheṣu ca ।
tīrtha-yātrāṃ vinā gacchan punaḥ saṁskārama-rhati ॥

One, going to the following regions except for pilgrimage, should undergo the sacrament (of *upanayana*) again:

Aṅga, Vaṅga, Kaliṅga, Saurāṣṭra, and Magadha — (for the identification of these regions, see *infra*).

From some ancient texts, we come to learn that the Aryan settlement extended from Uttarakuru (nothern Garhwal in the Himālayan region) and Uttaramadra (Media in Persia) to the land of the Sātvatas (and Bhojas) south of the rivers Yamunā and the Cambal, and from the land of the Nīcyas and Apācyas in the west to the territory of the Prācyas in the east. The precise location and extent of the Nīcya and Apācya regions have not been determined. The Prācyas were the people of Magadha and the neighbouring provinces. Manu mentions parts of the territory, occupied by the Aryans. In II.22, he describes Āryāvarta as the vast stretch of land lying between the Himālaya and Vindhya mountains, and bounded by the eastern sea (Bay of Bengal) and the western sea (Arabian Sea). The commentator, Kullūka explains the meaning of the term Āryāvarta as *āryā atra āvartante punaḥ punaru-dbhavanti*; here the Aryans are born again and again (i.e., from generation to generation). Manu names Brahmāvarta (II.17) lying between the rivers, Sarasvatī (rising on Siwalik in the Himālayan range, and emerging at Ād-Badri in Ambālā) and Dṛṣadvatī (probably the modern Citraṅg, Cautaṅg or Citaṅg which runs parallel to the Sarasvatī). It is stated to be *deva-nirmita* (made by God). The next verse states that the traditional canons of conduct of the castes and sub-castes, prevailing there, are designated as *sadācāra* (righteous conduct or conduct of the righteous). Obviously, it was within the habitation of the Aryans. Beyond the above Brahmāvarta lay the regions called Kurukṣetra (Thāneśvar, formerly comprising Sonepat, Amin, Karnāl and Pānipat), Matsya (Jaipur which included the whole of the present territory of Alwar with a portion of Bharatpur), Pañcāla (Rohilkhaṇḍa, originally, Pañcāla was the region north and west of Delhi, from the foot of the Himālaya to the river Cambal), and Śūrasena (a kingdom of which Mathurā was the capital): these regions are stated to have formed parts of Brahmarṣi-deśa. *Manu,* II.20 directs all men to learn their respective rules of conduct from the Brāhmaṇas of Brahmarṣi-deśa. This direction and the name of the country leave no doubt about its inclusion in the area inhabited by the Aryans. From the context, it is clear that Madhyadeśa, stated to be lying between the Himālaya and the Vindhya, up to east of Vinaśana (the place of the disappearance of the river Sarasvatī in the sandy desert of district Sirhind, i.e., Pāṭiālā), was also within the Aryan habitation. Manu specifies (II.23), as fit for sacrifice, that (unnamed) country where the species of deer, called *Kṛṣṇasāra* (the spotted deer or blackbuck — *Antelope cervicapra*) roams at will (not driven by force). The land, fit for sacrifice, must have been suitable for the Aryans. The same verse declares that the region, beyond what has been mentioned, is Mleccha-deśa or the country of the *mlecchas*. From some ancient texts, e.g., *Gautama-dharmasūtra,* IX.17, *Vaśiṣṭha-dharmaśāstra,* VI. 41, etc., and commentaries thereon, we learn that *mleccha* may denote the Persians and the like or those who live in Ceylon and such other places as are devoid of the caste-system and the four stages of life. In this connection, it may be noted that the Persians made incursions into the north-west India as early as the middle of the sixth century BC. The Indus Valley, as far as the desert of Rājpūtānā, was a satrapy under Darius (522-486 BC), a great Persian emperor. Persian domination continued till the advent of Alexander who crushed (333 and 331 BC) the Persian sway, and established Greek domination. After Alexander's invasion of India (327 BC), Greek principalities were established. In his commentary, *Bālakrīḍā* on *Yājñavalkya,* III. 256, Viśvarūpa (*c.* ninth century, first half) explains *mlecchas* as *pulindas* (name of a tribe) and *tājikas* (Arabs). Kullūka (before AD 1100), in his commentary on *Manu,* X.45, in which the term *mleccha* occurs, states that all those among the members of the four castes, who became outcastes owing to the non-performance of their respective duties, whether speaking Aryan or *mleccha* language, came to be called *dasyus* (demons). From this, it appears that *mleccha* indicated a people speaking a particular language (and not belonging to a particular region).

In the post-Vedic Brāhmaṇical and Buddhist works, we come across the following places: Kaliṅga (Orissa), Avantī (in Mālavā), Surāṣṭra (Kāṭhiāwāḍ) and Sindhusauvīra (lower valley of the Indus).

In ancient Buddhist literature, we find the names of the following great *janapadas*:

> Aṅga (East Bihār), Magadha (South Bihār), Kāśī, Kosala (Oudh), Vṛjji (North Bihār), Malla (Gorakhpur district), Cedi (in between the rivers Yamunā and Narmadā), Vatsa (Allāhābād), Kuru (Thāneśvar, Delhi and Meerut district), Pañcāla (Bareily, Badāun and Fārūkhābād districts), Matsya (Jaipur), Śūrasena (Mathurā), Aśmaka (on the banks of the river Godāvarī), Avantī (Mālavā), Gāndhāra (Peshawar and Rāwalpiṇḍi district), Kāmboja (to the south of Kashmir and part of Kāfiristān).

These were, perhaps, independent principalities; but what sort of administration (monarchical, oligarchical or dictatorial) prevailed in them is not known. We do not know the extent of the kingdom about which we read in the *Rāmāyaṇa*. According to many scholars, the whole of the *Rāmāyaṇa* is a fiction. Some think that the epic symbolises the domination of the Aryan culture, represented by Rāma, over the Dravidian of which Rāvaṇa was the representative.

As regards the Great War, described in the *Mahābhārata*, there are exaggerations and supernatural elements. Scholars, by and large, think that stories of various sorts have been woven round a war that actually took place. As a result of excavations, archaeologists claim to have found some evidences of the civilisation of the age of the above epic.

In about the middle of the sixth century BC, the tract, in the west of the Indus, was annexed to the Persian Empire. Gradually, Persian sway extended up to the desert area of Rājpūtānā (Rājasthān).

There is no evidence to prove that the whole of India had ever been under one king since the Vedic times. In course of time, Magadha, referred to above, developed into a powerful kingdom. In it, the Haryaṅka dynasty was followed by the Śiśunāgas (sixth and fifth centuries BC).

The Nanda Kings of Magadha were very powerful. Mahāpadmananda, the founder of the dynasty, is known to have been son of Mahānandin by a Śūdra woman. Candragupta dealt a death-blow to the dynasty, and founded the Maurya dynasty in *c*. 324 BC. Tradition has it that he was born of a Śūdra female slave or attendant, named Murā; accordingly, the dynasty was called Maurya.

In 327 or 326 BC, Alexander invaded India, and established Greek sway over the north-west India from where the Persians were driven away. Candragupta rid the Punjab and Sindh of the foreign yoke, and annexed the regions to his kingdom. The greatest emperor of this dynasty was Aśoka (reign *c*. 273-232 BC) who embraced Buddhism, and adopted various measures to propagate it not only in India but also in such far-off lands as Burma (Myānmār), Ceylon (Śrī Laṅkā), Sumātrā, etc.

The post-Aśoka period saw the decay and eventual disintegration of the Maurya Empire. Seizing this opportunity, the Greeks once again invaded the north-west, and, perhaps, infiltrated into the capital at Pāṭaliputra.

Puṣyamitra, the Brāhmaṇa General of the last Maurya ruler, dethroned him, and founded (*c*. 187 BC) the Śuṅga dynasty, and ruled up to about 151 BC. After Puṣyamitra, this dynasty declined and eventually fell to Vāsudeva who founded the Kāṇva dynasty in *c*. 75 BC. Both these dynasties were short-lived, and were effaced from the political map of India within a short span of ten years (*c*. 40-30 BC).

Then came to the throne a king of the Sātavāhana dynasty in the reign of which the kingdom of Kaliṅga became powerful; Khāravela of uncertain date was the greatest monarch of the kingdom. He carried his victorious arms far into the south beyond the Godāvarī.

The Tamil or Draviḍa land of South India was parcelled out into small kingdoms of which noteworthy were the Cola, Pāṇḍya and Kerala. The political instability and the absence of a power to reckon with attracted the greedy eyes of the Greeks who again brought under their control the north-west India, particularly the Punjab and Sindh. They were, however, repulsed in the first century of the Christian era, by the successive waves of invasion by the Śakas, Pahlavas (or Pārthians) and the Kuṣāṇas. Of these foreign invaders, the Kuṣāṇas gradually became powerful enough to initiate the administration of the region under their occupation. The greatest Kuṣāṇa ruler, Kaniṣka introduced the Śaka era probably in AD 78 ; and chose Peshawar as the capital. After Kaniṣka, the proverbially fickle goddess of royalty embraced the Nāga dynasty which fell to the Guptas by the middle of the fourth century AD.

The Guptas of Brāhmaṇical persuasion founded their dynastic rule in the first quarter of the fourth century. The Gupta Age saw the efflorescence of Indian culture in its varied aspects of literature, architecture, sculpture, painting, etc. Kālidāsa, the greatest poet of ancient India, and one of the greatest ever born in the world, most probably belonged to this period. This dynasty began to crumble with the end of the reign (*c.* AD 467) of Skandagupta. The tottering edifice of this empire somehow survived till the reign of Budhagupta (476-95); portions of the western frontier, however, passed into others' hands. After this ruler, the mighty Hūṇas made inroads into the interior of the country. The alert and energetic ruler of Mālavā crushed the Hūṇa power even before AD 533-34.

In the mid-sixth century AD, the Maukharis of the Gangetic

Valley and the Cālukyas of the south became extremely powerful. In Kanauj, Harṣavardhana (606-46 or 647) assumed power, and subjugated the whole of north India. Having been converted to Buddhism, he tried, in various ways, to propagate it. The passing away of this powerful personality resulted in a political vacuum. In the same century, however, Kāśmīr figured as a mighty kingdom on the political map of India. In the seventh-eighth centuries, the kingdom of Gauḍa (west and north-west Bengal) emerged as a formidable rival of Kannauj and Kāśmīr. The noted king of Gauḍa, Śaśāṅka died sometime between AD 619 and 637. This was followed by anarchy in Bengal; the people became restless, and elected one Gopāla as their king. Thus was founded the Buddhist Pāla kingdom of Bengal. Towards the end of the Pāla rule, a section of the population, called Kaivartas, revolted, amassed immense fortune, and acquired considerable power. In the regime of Dharmapāla, around AD 836, the Pratihāra kings, ensconced in Kannauj, gradually extended their sway up to Pāhārpur in north Bengal.

In the heyday of the Pratihāras, they resisted the Arabian invaders. By the end of ninth century, the Hindu kings of the Shāhīya dynasty, with their capital at Udabhāṇḍapura (modern Ohind), defended their country against the growing power of the Muslim state of Ghazni, and ruled over the land from Kābul to river Indus. In course of time, this kingdom extended from East Afghanistan to the Punjab and farther south up to Multān.

In South India, the Pallava, Cālukya and Rāṣṭrakūṭa kings became powerful. The ports on the western coast allured the Arabians. In about AD 637, an Arabian army reached Thāne near Bombay (Mumbai). By the middle of the seventh century, they brought south Afghanistan and Baluchistan within the ambit of their influence. The next important event was their conquest of Sindh.

Turning to Bengal, we find that one Vijayasena, belonging to a south Indian family, ousted the last Pāla ruler, and founded the Sena dynasty (*c.* AD 1095-1245). The Senas were of Brāhmaṇical persuasion, and brought about the revival of this religion which supplanted the Buddhist faith of the Pālas. They were patrons of Sanskrit learning. Ballālasena himself was a Sanskrit scholar to whom several *smṛti* works are attributed. Under the patronage of Lakṣmaṇasena flourished a galaxy of scholars, the most brilliant among them being Jayadeva, author of the universally acclaimed lyric *Gītagovinda*.

The last Sena King, Lakṣmaṇasena was dethroned, at the end of the twelfth century or in the beginning of the thirteenth, by an ambitious Muslim, Muhammad Khalji who declared himself as Governor of Bengal under Shihābuddin Muhammad Ghuri, founder of the Muslim rule in India and of the Delhi Sultanate.

Shihābuddīn was succeeded by Qutbuddīn who founded the Slave dynasty, which was followed by the Khalji dynasty. Alāuddīn of this dynasty invaded Rājpūtānā (Rājasthān), and extended his power also in south India. This dynasty was succeeded (1398) by the Tughlaks. The Tughlak regime saw the devastating depredations (1320) of Timur or Tamerlane who forcibly reduced a large number of men and women to slavery.

The above dynasty was followed successively by the Saiyad and Lodi dynasties.

Taking advantage of the weakness of the central government, the maverick rulers of Bengal, though legally owing allegiance to Delhi, virtually became independent. Similarly, Jaunpur, Mālavā, Gujarāt, Kāśmīr, etc., also almost shook off the Delhi yoke.

In the south, several Muslim principalities and the Hindu dominion of Vijayanagara, etc., became prominent in the political scenario.

In the wake of the establishment of Turko-Afghan rule in Delhi, commerce and industry developed to a considerable extent. The accounts of Āmir Khusrau (*d.* 1324 or 1325), Mauhān (Bengal visit 1406), Barthema (Indian sojourn 1503-8), etc., testify to the high quality of the merchandise during the fifteenth and sixteenth centuries.

Maritime trade brought India into contact with several parts of Europe, besides Malay Archipelago, China and the littoral areas of the Pacific Ocean. There were industrial relations of India, through land-routes, with Central Asia, Afghanistan, Persia, Tibet, Bhūṭān, etc. From the *Masālik-ul-absār* we learn that pure gold was continuously imported from various countries; different kinds of forest-products were exported. Among the imported things were chiefly luxury goods, horses and mules. Exported items included various agricultural products, clothes, opium, indigo-pellets, etc.

So far as the standard of living is concerned, we find that the rich rulers and high-ranking royal employees rolled in luxury, while the cultivators languished in penury and destitution.

The rural areas of the medieval age were, by and large, economically self-supporting. The villagers led a simple and contented life far from the madding crowd of the city with political intrigues, rebellion, disputes, etc.

The Sultāns and Āmirs used to maintain both male and female slaves who were employed in various kinds of manual work. There were provisions of manumission under certain circumstances. Besides Indian, particularly Assamese slaves, there were also those from China, Turkestan and Persia.

Women generally used to live in seclusion at homes. On the Gujarāt coast, excepting a few cities, both Hindu and Muslim females were accustomed to *purdah* mainly for security in the wake of the invasions of foreigners like the Mongols. Though usually engaged in household chores, the women of the upper echelon of the society cultivated arts and science. *Satī* (*suttee*)-*dāha* or burning of widows prevailed among certain classes of people. Moral life was usual, but there are evidences of immoral sexual relations and other vices.

The Mughal-Afghan feud for supremacy in India began in AD 1526. The first stage of the contest was marked by the subjugation of the latter by the former, and the defeat of the Rājpūts under the leadership of Rāṇā Sāṅgā.

In 1530, Bābur founded the Mughal Empire. Akbar (1556-1605) was the greatest monarch of this dynasty. His reign was marked by tolerance towards all religious systems, cessation of discriminatory treatment against the Hindus, patronage of literature and fine arts. There were Hindu women too in the royal seraglio. The emperor married also a Rājpūt woman.

The decline of Mughal power started after Akbar. Jehāngīr (reign 1605-27), however, defeated the Rājpūts of Mewār, but lost control over Kaṇḍāhār. Himself a painter, the emperor extended patronage to literature and arts.

He was succeeded by Shāhjahān (reign 1628-58) to whose glorious architectural achievements the Āgrā Mosque, Diwān-i-ām, Diwān-i-khās, Jāmā Masjid, the renowned peacock-throne, and, above all, the Tāj Mahal, one of the wonders of the world, stand as mute witnesses. In his reign, the Deccan and Gujarāt were plagued (1630-32) by severe famine. We have it, on the authority of Bernier (Indian visit 1656-68) that, as a result of the misrule of the provincial rulers, most of the agriculturists and craftsmen were deprived of the bare necessities of life. The huge financial burden, involved in maintaining the behemoth of bureaucracy, a leviathan army and in realising the architectural dreams of the emperor, had to be borne by the farmers and factory-owners. The national financial crunch, that followed, continued till the time of the next monarch, Aurangzeb (reign 1659-1709), and precipitated the fall of the empire. A historian has aptly remarked that Shāhjahān's India was, in many respects, like France under Louis XIV.

Aurangzeb's religious bigotry, oppressive treatment of the Hindus, suspicious nature, neglect of painters, etc., and wrong policy resulting in the hostility of Jāṭs, Sikhs, Rājpūts and others, coupled with the complicated situation in the Deccan and the rise of the Marāṭhās under Śivājī, brought the empire to the brink of disaster which took place in the beginning of the second decade of the eighteenth century.

The fall of the Mughal empire led to the rise of self-governed small states in India.

Taking advantage of this condition, the foreigners, who came in droves for trade and commerce, established the power of their respective countries in the regions, frequented by them. Of them, prominent were the British, French and Portuguese. Of them, the British became the most powerful. Having received various commercial facilities from the provincial rulers, they exerted power at different places, particularly in Bengal. The commercial power of the British people was gradually transformed into imperial power. The battle of Palāsī (1757), in which the British inflicted a crushing defeat on the then Nawāb Sirāj-ud-daullā of Bengal, facilitated the foundation of the British Rāj, destined to rule India for nearly two centuries. India shook off the shackles of bondage in AD1947.

Social and Religious Conditions

Broadly speaking, Indian society passed through the following periods: Pre-Vedic, Vedic, Age of *sūtra*s, Epic-Purāṇic as well as the age of *dharmaśāstra*s.

PRE-VEDIC AGE

The relics of the Indus Valley Civilisation testify to a highly developed urban civilisation in which people used to live in brick-buildings. There was a developed drainage system. Besides a public bath, there were swimming pools. There were broad and straight public roads. Things, made of terracotta, include those with figures of animals and humans, inscribed seals, etc. Female figurines in terracotta probably represent mother-deities thus hinting at *śakti* (female energy) as underlying creation. A male figure, appearing to be seated in a yogic posture, surrounded by animals, seems to be the precursor of the later Śiva-Paśupati, the great *yogin*. The three-faced figure with a head-dress and one horn-like thing on each side represents, according to some, the trident of Śiva. Some stone-pieces are like the Śiva-phallus. It is inferred that such natural things as trees, stones and animals used to be worshipped.

Food probably consisted of wheat, barley and dates. Necklace, ring, bangles, etc., were used as ornaments by both the males and the females. Waist-chain, nose-ring, earring, anklet were for the females only. There was the use of gold, silver, copper, ivory, jewels, etc. Painted pottery was in use. Iron, however, is conspicuous by its absence. Handloom, needle, etc., for domestic use prevailed. The implements, axe, chisel, knife, sickle, fishing hook, razor were made of copper or bronze. Mace, bow and arrow, etc., were some of the means of self-defence. Toy-carts and chairs were, perhaps, in use. Pieces of dice have been discovered.

Some seals and stone images of Harappā bear witness to the considerable development of sculpture.

Agriculture played the greatest part in the economic life. Bull, buffalo, sheep, elephant, camel, etc., were the main domestic animals. The ubiquitous dog is also met with.

The Indus Valley society had potters, weavers, carpenters, masons, blacksmiths, glodsmiths, ivory-workers, stone-cutters and others. That metallurgy was developed, to a considerable degree, can be surmised from evidence of the use of moulds and alloy.

The remains indicate trade and commerce even with foreign countries. It seems tin, copper, precious stones, etc., used to be imported. Certain similarities between the civilisation of India on the one hand, and Sumeria and Mesopotamia on the other have led some scholars to consider India as the borrower. There may have been commercial contacts of India with those countries; but who the borrower was cannot be definitely ascertained, and there is nothing to preclude the possibility of independent development.

The script, found in the seals of the Indus Valley, is still undeciphered. Their decipherment is expected to throw more light on the state of civilisation in this area.

VEDIC AGE

We do not know precisely the part of India occupied by the R̥gvedic people; the *R̥gveda* is deemed as the earliest of the Vedic *Saṃhitās*. From certain references, e.g. *Sapta-sindhu* (X.67.1) *Nadī-stuti* (*R̥V*, X.75), the Vedic Aryans appear to have first settled, according to Hopkins (*JAOS*, XIX.19-28), around Ambālā in the Punjab between the rivers Sarasvatī and Ghaggar; it is believed that most of the R̥gvedic hymns were composed (revealed!) in this region. Hertel's view (*Indo-German Forschungen*, 41, 1923, p. 188) that the oldest parts of the *R̥V* were composed in Iran has not been supported by scholars like Winternitz. That, in the earliest Vedic period, the Aryans did not spread far in the east seems probable from certain facts. First, the river Ganges, which played such a prominent rôle in the cultural life of the Indians of the later times, hardly appears to be referred to in the *R̥V*. The Vedic people of these times do not reveal familiarity with the tiger which lords it over in the jungles of Bengal. Rice, the staple food in north-east India and the main agricultural product, seems to be unknown.

A study of the *R̥gveda* reveals that the Aryans, who are generally believed to have migrated to India (*c*. 1500-1200 BC), clashed with the primitive Indians. Those who surrendered to them lived side by side with them, while the defiant were forced to live in the hilly regions. In this connexion, the following line of the Ṛgvedic stanza II.12.4 is relevant: *yo dāsaṃ varṇamadharaṃ guhākaḥ*.

The *ṚV* is the earliest record of the Vedic Aryans. The picture of the Vedic society is briefly given below. The date of this *Saṃhitā* is highly controversial, and scholars differ not by centuries, but by millennia. While D. Frawley (*Glory of India*, a quarterly journal on indology published by Motilal Banarsidass, Delhi, Vol. V, Nos. 3-4, 1981) assigns the origin of the Veda to about 12,500 BC, some would bring down the lower limit of the Ṛgvedic hymns to 1000 BC. As Winternitz aptly says, the prudent course is to guard against the extremes of a stupendously ancient period or a ludicrously modern epoch. It should be noted that the Vedic hymns originated verbally, and were transmitted orally for a long time before they came to be written; hence the term *śruti* (that which is heard). The time-lag between the first appearance of the hymns and their assumption of the written form cannot be determined with certainty. Winternitz is of the opinion that the Vedic age began in about 2000 or 2500 BC. Some scholars are inclined to assign the *Ṛgveda* to about 1,500 BC.

It is now almost universally admitted that the different Books (*Maṇḍala*s) of the *ṚV* came into being in different periods. The tenth *Maṇḍala* is regarded as very late. It is in this part (X.90) that we get the earliest reference to the clear division of the society into the four castes; there is, however, no reference to the four stages (*āśrama*s) of life which are well-defined in the later works. Vedic civilisation was mainly rural; cities also were there. Unlike the Indus Valley Civilisation, agriculture appears to have been the principal occupation of the people. In the Gambler's Lament (*ṚV*, X.34), the penitent gambler, who has squandered whatever he had, has been advised to take to agriculture (*kṛṣimit kṛṣasva*). The term *pañcakṛṣṭi* (*ṚV*, IV. 38.10) has been interpreted by some modern scholars as the rotation of five kinds of crops grown on the same land or the growing of them in different pieces of land. There are references to *lāṅgala* (plough), *phāla* (ploughshare), *yuga* (yoke), etc. We meet also with the cattle-rearer, merchant, usurer, barber, garland-maker, sewer, weaver, blacksmith, goldsmith, labourer, physician, tanner, distiller, potter, actor, wood-cutter, etc.

Besides music and dance, dicing, chariot-race, etc., were some of the means of amusement.

The Vedic family was patriarchal. The people appear to have been life-loving. Their craving was for worldly happiness. They desired good houses with servants, good issues, etc. Regarding the importance of money, it has been stated that it makes even an uncouth person look beautiful (*R̥V*, X.27.12).

We find, in the *R̥V*, references to foodgrains like wheat and paddy. Milk, ghee and meat were also consumed. An intoxicating drink, called *soma-rasa*, was used in sacrifices. This drink was, perhaps, confined to the upper classes.

It has been justly remarked that the *R̥V* is anything but a textbook on morals. We have already referred to gambling. Among other immoral practices were illicit relations between men and women (e.g., I. 134.3), theft (II.23.16), robbery (III.29.9), cheating (II.23.5), disobedience of son (II. 29.5), conjugal infidelity (IV.5.5), incest (VI.55.4), unchastity (VII.76.3), illegitimate child-birth (II.29.1), blatant usury (VIII.66.10), etc. Judging by the frequency of references, theft and robbery appear to have been very common. VI.28.3.7 refer to cow-stealers. Besides ritual drinking, it seems to have been a common vice (e.g., I.116.7, I.191.10; VI.39.1, 40.1, 43.1; VI.37.2, 39.1, 40.1, 43.1; VII.59, 86.6; VIII.2.12; IX.53.4, 68.3, 69.3, 7, 78.4, etc.). From the above references as well as from X.107.8-9 wine and women seem to have been looked upon as objects of pleasure. The love-overtures of Yamī toward her brother Yama (*R̥V*, X.10) appear to hint at the vogue of incest.

Underlying the Vedic people's conception of gods there were three main factors. One was the sense of awe and wonder at the sight of various aspects of nature, e.g. sun, forest, ocean, rivers, etc. Secondly, an element of fear, caused by natural calamities, fierce animals, robbers, enemies, etc., led them to seek the protection of mighty gods. Thirdly, craving for material prosperity, long life, good sons, a happy household, freedom from disease, poverty, etc., urged them to pray to gods. The very names of the deities like *Duḥsvapna-nāśana* (I.120.12), *Sapatnī-dhāvana*, *Alakṣmīghna*, *Rājayakṣmaghna*, *Sapatnaghna* (*sapatna* denotes enemy) reflect the sentiments underlying their conception.

The Vedic pantheist was polytheistic. In some hymns (e.g., *ṚV*, X.121), there is a henotheistic attitude; the deity, worshipped for the time being, was regarded as the Supreme. Towards the end of the Ṛgvedic period, a monotheistic trend is discernible : *ekaṃ sad viprā bahudhā vadanti, agniṃ, yamaṃ*, etc., *ṚV*, X. 164.46. The words *ekaṃ sat* seem to foreshadow the later Upaniṣadic conception of *Brahman* as the sole reality.

It is noteworthy that certain abstract matters like *śraddhā*, *manyu*, etc., are also deified. Even such things as were useful for sacrifice and agriculture, etc., were looked upon as gods. It is interesting to note that all the deities in the *ṚV* are not conceived as benign. For example, the goddesses Kṛtyā (e.g., X.85.28 ff) and Nirṛti (e.g., I.38.6, X.114.2 ff.) are conceived as causing various kinds of mischief, even death.

Besides deities, ancestors were also worshipped. Some of the popular beliefs and practices were as follows.

Agni was supposed to carry a dead person to the other world, and impart immortality to him (*ṚV*, X.16.1-4). The deities Pūṣan and Savitṛ were supposed to guard the way of the departed one to the other world (X.17.4).

Traces of totemism are found in some passages. For example, the names of some persons hint at their origin from animals or plants. Thus, Kaśyapa is supposed to have originated from *kacchapa* (tortoise). A sect of priests is called *Gotama*; *go* indicates their origin from cows.

Several passages of the *Ṛ̥V* (e.g., I.35.10; VII.104.15 ff.; X. 14.9, 10, 12, etc.) reflect belief in ghosts, spirits and demons.

There are instances of belief in miracles and magic. It was believed that, through divine grace, a blind person could see and a lame one could walk (II.15.7; IV.19.9; I.112.8; II.13.12). A person is stated to have been cured of blindness and his barren land made fertile (VIII. 91). Viśpalā, a lady with a broken leg, was given an iron leg by the divine physicians, Aśvins (I.112.10). The leprosy of another woman, Ghoṣā, was cured by them (I. 117). Rejuvenation, caused by the Aśvins, is referred to in I.117.3, 118.6; V.74.5; X.39.4, etc. Rejuvenation through the grace of Ṛ̥bhus (a class of minor deities) is mentioned in I.20.4, IV. 33.3, etc.

Certain mystic syllables like *phaṭ* (X. 87.13) seem to suggest that they were believed to have magical significance. A mischievous magical practice was to invoke an evil force for causing miscarriage of women (X.122). In some hymns (e.g., X. 159.4), we find belief in the magical power of the sacrifice in destroying enemies. Some passages, e.g. X.49.5, testify to the belief in *vaśīkaraṇa* (bringing others under control). In X.145, we find the use of a creeper as a means of winning over the husband and co-wife.

As regards diseases, certain rivers were supposed (VII. 50.4) to cure *śrīpada* (filaria). *Soma* was believed to heal incurable diseases (VIII.48.11). In X.164, 163, we find the priest healing diseases by *mantras*. The curious belief in transferring human diseases to other creatures and objects is reflected in I.50.12. The disease, called *harimāṇa* (jaundice?), is stated to be transferable to the parrots and to turmeric.

There was the belief in demons intent on causing various kinds of mischief including diseases. The words *muradeva*, *sahamūla* (III.30.17) seem to reflect the belief that demons assumed the forms of some roots for malevolent purposes.

In I.191.2, we find reference to a drug believed to kill invisible poisonous creatures infecting people. I.191.10 refers to *Madhuvidyā* (certain *mantra* so-called?) turning poison into nectar. The recitation of the names of ninety-nine rivers was supposed to counteract poison (I.191.13). Certain prayers were supposed to destroy the effect of poison (VII.50.1, 2, 3).

Bad dreams were so dreaded (VIII.47.15) that, as already stated, a deity, called *duḥsvapna-nāśana-devatā*, was conceived and invoked (X.164).

The cry of the bird, Kapiñjala (Francoline partridge?) was believed to be ominous (II.42.3). Pigeons were regarded as agents of the maleficent deity Nirṛti (X.165.1-3), referred to earlier. The owl was looked upon as an agent of Yama, God of Death (X.165.4).

Some information about women can be gathered from the *ṚV*. The mention of female seers (*ṛṣis*) like Apālā, Ghoṣā, Viśvavārā, etc., testifies to the fact that women, as a class, were not relegated to a position lower than that of men. The female deities, however, appear to have been inferior to the male ones. The prevalence of the custom of polygamy is clear from references to *sapatnī* or co-wife. That co-wives were at loggerheads with one another is obvious from references to the *sapatnī-dhāvana-devatā,* mentioned earlier. Though the prevalence of divorce, as a legal measure, is not clear, yet there is reference to a man forsaking his wife. Apālā is stated to have been deserted by her husband. Among material possessions, which were very much prized, were beautiful women of a good number. Women were keen upon the love of their husbands. A woman, in separation from her husband, appears to have lived in fear. Women used to pray to God for averting the painful condition of widowhood. The ideal of chastity of a woman was her attachment only to her husband. There is, however, reference to a widow embracing her younger brother-in-law in bed. From *Ṛ̥V*, 185.3, it seems that *kṣetraja* son (i.e., son begotten by one person on the wife of another) was recognised. *Ṛ̥V*, III.31 tends to testify to the custom of *putrikāputra*, i.e., the son of the daughter of a sonless man appointed to be his son (*asyāṃ yo jāyate putraḥ sa me putro bhaviṣyati*). At one place, it is stated that the love of women is transient; their hearts are hard as that of a wolf (cf. *na vai straiṇāni sakhyāni santi, sālāvṛkāṇāṃ hṛdayānyetā* — *Ṛ̥V*, X. 96.15).

Ṛ̥V, X. 27.12 appears to hint at the self-choice, by women, of their husbands from amongst many suitors. Negotiated marriage, however, seems to have been common (X.68.2). It appears that a girl was not given away in marriage with an undesirable person. We find references to women living with their fathers even up to an advanced age presumably for want of suitable grooms. Princess Ghoṣā gives vent to her passionate yearning for a suitable husband.

The wife appears to have enjoyed an exalted position in the family, controlling the in-laws like *samrājñī* or empress (*Ṛ̥V*, X. 85.46).

Ṛ̥V, II.17.7 seems to indicate that a girl, living with her parents permanently, was entitled to a share of the patrimony.

Coming to the *AV*, we find a spurt in magical practices, particularly *abhicāra* (black magic), use of charms, amulets and talismans, etc. The contents of an entire section of this Veda are designated as *ābhicārika*; it deals with curses and exorcisms against demons, wizards and enemies. There are increasing beliefs in ghosts and spirits. The Ṛ̥gvedic Nirṛti and Kṛtyā have become more prominent. The Brāhmaṇas particularly the priests assumed great importance. For example, from *AV*, IV.13, it appears that many diseases were believed to be cured simply by the healing touch of the priest. Snake-bite seems to have been of common occurrence. Various means were devised to counteract snake-poison. VI.56 was used for shutting the mouth of a snake for ever; its recitation was believed to render beds, houses and fields free from serpents. It is curious that *AV*, V.13, which is a charm against snake-venom, contains certain terms of non-Aryan origin; e.g., *Āligi, Viligi*, (both in V.7), *Urugulā, Asikni* (both in V.8), etc. These words are believed, by some scholars, to have been borrowed from foreign lands, possibly Sumeria. It was Tilak's conjecture that, before the second millennium BC, the Vedic Aryans came into contact with the Assyrians as neighbours or traders. It is also suggested that a prehistoric colony of Indian horse-dealers was set up near the land of the Hittites and Mitannians. Commercial relations between India and West Asia appear to have been established in the period of the Indus Valley Civilisation.

Divination or skilful forecast of unknown happenings by supernatural means is common in this age.

From certain passages, e.g. *Kauśika-sūtra*, II. 8, 9, it is clear that ordeals (*divya*) were resorted to for proving the guilt or innocence of an accused person.

As regards women, the *AV* reflects their position as inferior to that of men. In VI.11.3, the birth of a daughter has been deprecated. I. 11.6 and III. 23.2 reflect a strong desire for a male issue. A brotherless girl was looked down upon as devoid of protection and support (I.17.1).

Agriculture and cattle-rearing got added importance in this age. III.17 provides for the invocation of *sītā* (furrow) to give bumper crops. VI.50 is for the exorcism of the creatures which are harmful to grains in the field.

VI.72.72, II.32 (*Kauśika-sūtra*, 27.21-26), VI.59.3, VII. 75.1, II. 26.2, IV. 3 — these indicate that the people set much store by their cattle.

This Veda reflects a clearer view about hell of which no detailed description is found in the *Ṛ̥V*.

EPIC AND PURĀṆIC AGE

There can be no clear line of demarcation between the epic and Purāṇic periods. The epics, *Rāmāyaṇa* and the *Mahābhārata*, had their origin in the hoary past which cannot be determined in terms of centuries. It is, however, pretty certain that their nucleus originated long before the Christian era. They arose in the form of ballads sung particularly by two classes of people, viz., *sūta*s or bards living in royal courts and *kuśīlava*s or travelling singers resembling, to a great extent, the troubadours, the medieval French lyric poets. It is not known when these ballads, which circulated and were transmitted orally from generation to generation, assumed written form. Even after being reduced to writing in manuscript form, the literary common property of the people or the national literature of the country, they became a curious blend of the genuine and the spurious. Modern scholars are applying scientific methods for separating the wheat from the chaff.

The chronological relation between the *Rāmāyaṇa* and the *Mahābhārata* is still a matter of controversy. According to tradition, the former is the earlier. But, some scholars assign the latter to a period earlier than that of the former. Some of their arguments cannot be summarily dismissed. For example, it is pointed out that the grammar of Pāṇini of *c.* fourth century BC, which, to some extent, reflects the contemporary society, mentions some characters of the *Mahābhārata* in the rules *vāsudevārjunābhyāṃ vun* (IV.3.98) and *gaviyudhibhyāṃ sthiraḥ* (VIII.3.95); but nowhere does Pāṇini refer to any character of the *Rāmāyaṇa*. This tends to point to the earlier date of the *Mahābhārata*. Polyandry in this epic is another pointer to its earlier age. It is argued that the *Rāmāyaṇa* is written in a more ornate style while the *Mahābhārata* retains the old ballad form; thus, it introduces a speech with words like *arjuna uvāca*. It is further stated that the *Mahābhārata* reflects a more warlike society which is a sign of its earlier date. Taking all features into consideration, the fact seems to be that the nucleus of the *Mahābhārata* was earlier than that of the other epic, but, in their present forms, the *Rāmāyaṇa* is earlier. Winternitz, in his *History of Indian Literature*, vol. I, holds that if the *Mahābhārata* had its present form completed by the fourth century AD, the *Rāmāyaṇa* assumed the present form a century or two earlier.

Both the epics have regional recensions. It should be noted that neither of the epics is the work of a single author or of a particular period.

The term *purāṇa* occurs, perhaps for the first time, in the *Atharvaveda* (XI.7.24; XV.11-12). It should be noted that originally *purāṇa* denoted *itihāsa*. Some other works of the later Vedic literature also refer to *purāṇa*. The *Āpastamba-dharmasūtra* (II. 9.24.56) of pre-Christian age names as *Bhaviṣyat Purāṇa*. But, among the extant Purāṇas, none is earlier than the third century AD. The dates of the *Mahāpurāṇas*, available hitherto, range between *c.* AD 200 and sixteenth century AD. It should be noted that parts of particular Purāṇas were composed or compiled in different periods.

The *Rāmāyaṇa* bears the impress of mainly two distinct cultures, the Aryan and non-Aryan, the former represented by Rāma and the later by Rāvaṇa, hostile to the Aryans. The simian culture, represented mainly by Hanumat, was favourable to the Aryans. The people of this type, as suggested by some, may have used monkey as a totem.

Both the epics uphold the ideal of *varṇāśrama-dharma*. The *Rāmāyaṇa* contains the example of filial piety, fraternal love, conjugal fidelity, and the triumph of good over evil. Rāma is not only an exemplary son, but also an ideal king. He renounced royalty in honour of his father. In order to please his subjects, he forsook Sītā, his wife dearer to him than his life.

The *Mahābhārata* seeks to inculcate the lesson that, despite temporary reverses, *dharma* is sure to triumph over *adharma*. The epic betrays quite a few departures from the traditional Brāhmaṇical religion and practices. For instance, contrary to the cherished ideal of one woman one husband, Draupadī has as many as five. There are examples of relaxation of the rigidity of the caste-system. Kṛṣṇa, originally a Kṣatriya, was later deified. Vidura, son of a *dāsī*, was highly respected by the people of superior classes due to his exemplary character and conduct.

The Purāṇas were composed at a time when the conventional Brāhmaṇical religion was imperilled mainly by two factors, viz., Buddhism and Tantrism. In the post-Vedic period, women were denied the right to Vedic study and many of the rites and rituals which were the exclusive preserves of the menfolk. The Śūdras were reduced to abject servility under the upper classes, particularly the Brāhmaṇas. They had right neither to religious practices nor to property. Long periods of neglect and indifference bred, in them, a simmering discontent. They sought escape from the domination of males and the Brāhmaṇa community. At this juncture, females and Śūdras embraced Buddhism in droves; this religion gave them considerable liberty in religious practices. An attractive feature of Buddhism was that it preached the middle path avoiding the extremes of luxury and self-abnegation. It set greater store by ethics than ritual practices. Tantra raised the status of women to a great extent, so much so that a woman was considered as an indispensable partner of a man in Tāntric *sādhanā*. The mother was regarded as the best *guru* of one seeking Tāntric initiation. The worship of virgin girls was considered to be a pious act. Unlike the Brāhmaṇical scriptures, Tantra did not advocate asceticism and physical mortification as means to the attainment of the highest goal.

As a result of the tremendous popularity of Buddhism and Tantra, the leaders of the Brāhmaṇical society found it difficult to stem the tide of efflux of women and Śūdras. Extremely brainy as they were, they devised the Purāṇas. These gave women and Śūdras the right to the observance of Purāṇic *vrata*s and performance of certain *pūjā*s with the recitation of Purāṇic *mantras*. A network of *vrata*s was introduced. The very names of some of the *vrata*s betray the motive of attracting people by the prospects of material well-being as the acquisition of a son, escape from widowhood, etc., e.g., *āśūnya-śayana*, *pati-saubhāgya-vardhana*, *kalyāṇa-saptamī*, etc. The Brāhmaṇas, whose main source of income was *yājana* (officiating as priests of others) and *pratigraha* (acceptance of gifts), were in economic distress due to the depletion of the pious males and females, caused by conversion. This was why in *vrata*s gifts of various things, including even the bare necessities of life like cloth, umbrella, etc., were emphasised as conducive to great merit. *Vitta-śāṭhya* (deceitful economy) on the part of one observing *vrata*s was severely condemned; this means that they were required to spend as much as they could for the articles to be received by the priests.

Gradually, the Purāṇas became very popular. They were publicly recited highlighting, by means of attractive stories, the power of Brāhmaṇas and the glory of the Brāhmaṇical religion. In accordance with the predominance of one or the other of the Trinity (viz. Brahmā, Viṣṇu, Maheśvara or Śiva), the Purāṇas were mainly divided into three classes.

In course of time, besides the *Mahāpurāṇa*s with which we have dealt above, there arose a number of *Upapurāṇa*s which belonged to different sects, *Śaiva, Śākta, Vaiṣṇava, Gāṇapatya, Saura,* and *Pāśupata*, etc.

3

Authors

Anantadeva II

AUTHOR of the huge digest, entitled *Smṛtikaustubha*.

From the account, given by the author himself, we learn that he compiled this work at the command of Bāj Bahāduracandra of Almora and Nainital (AD 1638-78) for pleasing whom the work was undertaken.

The author was the great great grandson of Ekanātha; grandson of Anantadeva I, and son of Āpadeva II (author of *Mīmāṃsā-nyāya-prakāśa* or *Āpadevī*). Our author was elder brother of Jīvadeva (*Aśaucanirṇaya*), and *guru* of Raghunātha Navahasta (*Prayoga-ratnabhūṣā, Prāyaścitta-kutūhala*, etc.).

He also wrote tracts on *Mīmāṃsā* and the procedure (*prayoga* or *paddhati*) of certain rites.

Besides the *S. Kaustubha*, he wrote also *smṛti* digests like *Nirṇayabindu, Prāyaścitta-pradīpikā*, etc.

P.V. Kane is inclined to assign Anantadeva to the third quarter of the seventeenth century.

Aṅgiras

One of the twenty traditional writers of original *smṛti*. An *Aṅgiras-smṛti* and a *Bṛhad-aṅgiras-smṛti* exist. References are found to a *Madhyama-Aṅgiras*. Date uncertain. There is also an *Aṅgiraḥ-saṃhitā*.

Some Manuscripts of *Aṅgiraḥ-smṛti* are available in two parts, *Pūrvāṅgirasa* and *Uttarāṅgirasa*.

Aniruddha Bhaṭṭa

A famous *smṛti* writer of Bengal, mentioned by Vallālasena, King of Bengal (twelfth century), as his *guru*. Belonging to the Campāhaṭṭīya section of the Vārendra Brāhmaṇas of Bengal, he was *dharmādhikaraṇika* (Judge) of the above king. His native place was Vihārapāṭaka on the Ganges.

He mentions Bhojadeva, Govindarāja and the work, *Kāmadhenu*.

Author of the *smṛti* digests, *Hāralatā* and *Pitṛdayitā* (also called *Karmopadeśinī-paddhati*). A *Cāturmāsya-paddhati* is also attributed to him (*vide* Pro. Asiatic Soc. of Bengal, Calcutta, 1869). He assisted the above king in the compilation of the *Dānasāgara* (q.v.), dated AD 1169.

Aparāditya

Another name of Aparārka (q.v.).

Aparārka

Also called Aparāditya, he appears, from his work, to have been king of the northern Koṅkaṇ Śilāhāra line, born in the family of Jīmūtavāhana of the Vidyādhara race. There are inscriptions of him; their dates fall between AD 1115-30. According to Maṅkhaka's *Śrīkaṇṭha-carita*, XXV.109-11, he sent an embassy to King Jayasiṃha of Kāśmīr (AD. 1129-50).

Author of a voluminous commentary called *Aparārka-Yājñavalkyīya-dharmaśāstra-nibandha*, popularly known as *Aparārka*, on the *Yājñavalkya-smṛti*.

Probably flourished in the first half of the twelfth century.

Āpastamba

One of the twenty traditional writers of original *smṛti*. The school of Āpastamba is supposed to have originated in south India.

The *Āpastamba-dharmasūtra* is assigned, by P.V. Kane, to some period between 600 and 300 BC.

Asahāya

Appears to have written a *bhāṣya* on the *Nārada-smṛti*. According to P.V. Kane, he flourished between AD 600 and 750.

References are available, in some later works, to his commentaries on *Gautama-dharmasutra, Manusmṛti, Likhita-smṛti* and *Śaṃkha-smṛti*.

Atri

One of the traditional writers of original *smṛti*.

Besides an *Ātreya-dharmaśāstra*, there are several works, styled *Atri-smṛti* or *Atri-saṃhitā*. Two works, called *Vṛddhātreya-saṃhitā* and *Laghu-atri*, are also known. As he is mentioned in the *Manu-smṛti* (III.16), Atri must have been older than that work.

Bālakṛṣṇa

Same as Bālambhaṭṭa (q.v.).

Bālambhaṭṭa

Bālambhaṭṭa or Bālakṛṣṇa Pāyaguṇḍa, son of Vaidyānātha and Lakṣmī, was a south Indian. According to some, he was the same as Vaidyānātha Pāyaguṇḍa.

Flourished probably between AD 1730 and 1820.

He wrote, *inter alia*, the *Bālambhaṭṭi* commentary on the *Mitākṣarā* of *Vijñāneśvara* (q.v.).

Ballālasena

Same as Vallālasena (q.v.).

Bāṇeśvara Vidyālaṃkāra

A renowned Bengal scholar who, at the instance of Warren Hastings, Governor-General (1774-85), compiled a voluminous *smṛti* digest, entitled *Vivādārṇava-setu*, in collaboration with ten other scholars.

Baudhāyana

To him is attributed a work on *Dhamasūtra* which is assigned, by P.V. Kane, to sometime between 500 and 200 BC.

Bhavadeva Bhaṭṭa

A famous pre-Raghunandana (q.v.) *smṛti* writer of Bengal. From his works we learn that, having the sobriquet *bālavalabhī-bhujaṅga*, he was minister for peace and war to king Harivarmadeva, and a native of village Siddhala in Rāḍha, now in West Bengal. Appears to have flourished sometime between AD 800 and 1100.

His *smṛti* digests are:

Karmānuṣṭhāna-paddhati (also called *Daśakarma-paddhati*, *Saṃskāra-paddhati* or *Chāndoga-paddhati*), *Prāyaścitta-prakaraṇa* (or *-nirūpaṇa*), *Sambandha-viveka*, *Śava-sūtakāśauca-prakaraṇa* and *Vyavahāra-tilaka* of which the *Dattaka-tilaka* is a part.

Bṛhaspati

One of the twenty traditional writers of original *smṛti*. The well-known *smṛti* digests and commentators on *smṛti* quote, *in extenso*, from his work which has not yet been found.

A *Dharmasūtra* appears to have been written by him. A short metrical *smṛti* of Bṛhaspati exists.

According to P.V. Kane, Bṛhaspati flourished sometime between AD 200 and 400.

Bṛhaspati Rāyamukuṭa

A well-known scholar at the time of Jalāluddīn, son of Rājā Gaṇeśa of Bengal. Rāyamukuṭa probably wrote his works in the first half of the fifteenth century.

His *smṛti* works are the *Smṛti-ratnahāra* and *Rāyamukuṭa-paddhati*.

His *Padacandrikā* commentary on the *Amarakośa* is noteworthy.

Caṇḍeśvara Thakkura (*c.* AD 1300-50)

One of the great *smṛti* writers of Mithilā. Son of minister Vīreśvara Ṭhakkura and grandson of Devāditya, minister of the Karnāṭaka king Harasiṃhadeva of Tirhut. He was minister for peace and war and Chief Judge under the king Harasiṃhadeva of Mithilā. He conquered Nepal, and weighed himself against gold on the bank of the Vegavatī in AD 1314.

The *Smṛti-ratnākara* or *Ratnākara*, his *magnum opus*, is divided into seven sections, viz. *Kṛtya*, *Dāna*, *Vyavahāra*, *Śuddhi*, *Pūjā*, *Vivāda* and *Gṛhastha*. His other works are: *Kṛtya-cintāmaṇi* *(Rāja)nīti-ratnākara*, *Dāna-vākyāvalī*, *Śiva-vākyāvalī* and *Śaivamānasollāsa*.

The following works are also attributed to him: *Ādhividhi*, *Kālanirṇaya*, *Dāsa-vimokṣa-vidhi*, *Svāmipāla-vivāda-taraṅga*.

For personal history of Caṇḍeśvara, see Introduction to K.P. Jayaswal's *Rājanīti-ratnākara*, Patna, 1924.

Candrakānta Tarkālaṃkāra (1836-1909)

Born at Town Serpur in the district of Mymensing (now in Bangladesh). Son of Rādhākānta Siddhāntavāgīśa and Brahmamayī, he was a Mahāmahopādhyāya and Professor of

Philosophy at Govt. Sanskrit College, Calcutta, during 1883-87.

He was versed in *Vyākaraṇa*, *Kāvya*, *Nāṭaka*, *Smṛti*, etc.

His digests on *smṛti* are *Udvāha-candrāloka*, *Śuddhi-candrāloka* and *Aurdhvadehikacandrāloka*.

The noteworthy characteristic of the author is that he has not blindly followed the earlier authors. He had the courage to differ even from the great Raghunandana by counter-arguments. His innovative spirit is reflected in the following prefatory remark in his *Udvāha-candrāloka*:

> *dharmaśāstraṃ ca mūlaṃ dharmādharmayor na nibandha-kartṛṇāṃ matam* । *tadyadi viparītaṃ śāstraṃ sphuṭamupalabhyate tadā nibandharṇāṃ matam anapekṣaṇīyameva bhavati śāstraikaśaraṇānām anusaraṇīyam ca śāstram* । .... *tad yena yāvanti śāstra-vākyānyupalabdhāni pakṣapātamutsṛjya dharma-rakṣārthaṃ tena tāvatām upanibandhanaṃ kartumucitam* । *tat sarvaṃ kilopalabhya sūkṣma-matayo dharma-tattvaṃ nirṇeṣyantīti* । *ata eva mamāyamudyamaḥ* ।

Dakṣa

One of the twenty traditional writers of original *smṛti*, mentioned by Yājñavalkya (I.4).

There is a *Dakṣa-smṛti*.

Dalādhīśa

Same as Dalapati (q.v.).

Dalapati (also called Dalapatirāja, Dalādhīśa)

Author of the *Nṛsiṃhaprasāda* (in 12 sections) which appears to have been written in the period AD 1490-1512.

From his autobiographical information, we learn that he

was son of Vallabha of the *Bharadvāja gotra* and of the *Yājñavalkīya-śākhā* (i.e., *Śukla-Yajurveda*). He was pupil of Sūryapaṇḍita. A great exponent of Vaiṣṇavism, he was Chief Minister and keeper of the records of Nijāmsāha, ruler of Devagiri. In some colophons, the author is styled *Mahārājādhirāja*. According to H.P. Sastri (*vide* Calcutta Asiatic Soc. MSS. Cat., vol. III, Preface), Dalapatirāya was Chief of Godhmandla, and held a commanding position in the Nizāmshāhi kingdom of Ahmednagar. Dalapati's wife was the renowned Durgāvatī who fought against the General of Akbar.

Devaṇabhaṭṭa

Also called Devaṇṇabhaṭṭa, Devānanda, Devendra, Devagaṇa or Devaṇācārya, he is described as son of Keśavāditya Bhaṭṭa. A south Indian, Devaṇa flourished probably in the second half of the twelfth century or the first half of the thirteenth.

His *Smṛti-candrikā*, composed before AD 1225, is a well-known *smṛti* digest.

The *Dattaka-candrikā* is probably a section of the above work.

Devaṇṇabhaṭṭa

Same as Devaṇabhaṭṭa (q.v.).

Devanātha Ṭhakkura Tarkapañcānana

Appears to have written two works on *smṛti*, called *Smṛti-kaumudī* and *Kālakaumudī*; the latter may be a part of the former. Also attributed to him are a *Divya-tantra* or *Tantra-kaumudī* (AD 1564-65) on *Tantra* and *Adhikaraṇa-kaumudī* on *Mīmāṃsā*.

A native of Mithilā, he was pupil of Somabhaṭṭa, and wrote on a variety of subjects, e.g. *Mīmāṃsā, Alaṃkāra, Tantra, Navya-nyāya*.

He was popularly known as *Sapta-kaumudīkāra* for his seven works, the titles of which end in *-kaumudī*. He appears to have had the title *Tarkapañcānana*.

In his *Mantrakaumudī*, he traces his descent from Ravikara who was the great grandfather of Devanātha's father, Govinda Ṭhakkura. Devanātha was the elder brother of the logician, Madhusūdana Ṭhakkura, and was born in AD 1490. His *Tantrakaumudī* is dated AD 1564. From the verses at the end of the same treatise, we learn that, after the downfall of the Oinavar dynasty in AD 1526, he left Mithilā, and went to the court of Malladeva Naranārāyaṇa (AD 1555-87), king of Kamatā or Coochbehar. In introductory verse 5 of his *Tantrakaumudī*, we are told that he enjoyed the patronage of another king, named Gajapati Govindadeva whose identity is still unknown.

[For MSS., see *NCC*, IX, pp. 110-11.]

Gautama

One of the twenty traditional writers of original *smṛti*. There is a *Gautama-dharmasūtra*. The work probably originated sometime between the fourth century and second century BC, and is regarded by some as the earliest work on *dharmasūtra*.

A *Pitṛmedha-sūtra* and a *Śrāddha-kalpa* are also attributed to Gautama.

Gopāla Nyāyapañcānana

The most prolific among the post-Raghunandana *smṛti* writers of Bengal. As many as eighteen digests, on different topics of *smṛti*, appear to have been penned by him. He frankly admits that he has followed Raghunandana (*Smārtasya vartmanā*); *Smārta* stands for Smārta-bhaṭṭācārya Raghunandana.

[S.C. Banerji, "Post-Raghunandana *smṛti* writers of Bengal", *NIA*, VII, Nos. 5, 6.]

Govindānanda

A well-known figure in the *smṛti* literature of Bengal. From his autobiographical account, we learn that he was son of Gaṇapatibhaṭṭa, a resident of Bāgḍi (= old Vyāghrataṭī) in Medinipur in West Bengal. Earned the sobriquet *Kavi-kaṅkaṇācārya*.

Appears to have flourished a little earlier than Raghunandana.

The titles of his works end in *-kaumudī*. The subjects, on which he wrote, are mainly *Dānakriyā, Śuddhi, Śrāddhakriyā, Varṣakriyā* and *Kriyā*.

He also wrote the following commentaries:

> *Tattvārtha-kaumudī* (on Śūlapāṇi's *Prāyaścittaviveka*), *Artha-kaumudī* (on Śrīnivāsa's *Śuddhi-dīpikā*, and a commentary on Śūlapāṇi's *Śrāddha-viveka*.

His date has been sought to be fixed as AD 1500-40.

[B. Bhattacharya, "The Bengal Nibandhakāra Govindānanda . . . . his date", *Pro. AIOC*, 1966, R.C. Hazra in *JOR*, Madras, XXIII, pp. 97-108, states all the works (eleven in all) of Govindānanda.]

Govindarāja

From his works we learn that son of Bhaṭṭa Mādhava and grandson of Nārāyaṇa, he lived in Uttararāḍhā on the Ganges.

Believed to have flourished during AD 1050-80.

His commentary on the *Manu-smṛti* is well-known. That his commentary had considerable impact on scholars can be inferred from references to him in Kullūka's commentary; Kullūka often makes a dig at Govindarāja.

Govindarāja, in his commentary on *Manu,* III.247, 248,

mentions his work, *Smṛtimañjarī*. In his commentary on *Manu*, IV. 212, Kullūka refers to Govindarāja's *Mañjarī*.

A *Saha-gamana-vidhi* is also ascribed to Govindarāja.

Govindarāja's commentary on the *Manusmṛti* was published by V.N. Mandlik. A portion of this commentary was published by Jolly in his *Manu-ṭīkā-saṃgraha*.

Halāyudha

From his personal account he appears to have been son of Dhanañjaya and Dharmādhyakṣa (Chief Justice). From Halāyudha's mention of Lakṣmaṇasena, he seems to have been a contemporary of that king (*c*. AD 1185-1205).

Author of the *Brāhmaṇasarvasva* or *Karmopadeśinī*.

The works, *Dvija-nayana* and *Śrāddha-paddhati-ṭīkā* are ascribed to a Halāyudha whose identity with our Halāyudha is not beyond doubt. For detailed information, see D.M. Bhattacharya, "A Pre-Sāyaṇa Vedic Commentator of Bengal", *Our Heritage*, I, pt. ii; papers of D.C. Bhattacharya and R.C. Hazra in *IHQ*, XXI. The above Halāyudha is to be distinguished from Halāyudha, author of the *Kavirahasya* and the lexicon, *Abhidhāna-ratnamālā*, who appears to have flourished in the tenth century.

Haridāsa Siddhāntavāgīśa

Born in B.S. 1283 in village Unasiyā in Koṭālipāḍā in Faridpur district of East Bengal (now Bangladesh). One of his paternal ancestors was the renowned philosopher, Madhusūdana Sarasvatī. Son of Gaṅgādhara and Vidhumukhī, he was a Mahāmahopādhyāya. He was at home in *Kāvya*, *Vyākaraṇa*, *Smṛti*, etc.

His *smṛti* work is the *Smṛti-cintāmaṇi*.

Haridāsa achieved wide recognition and popularity by his original Sanskrit commentary on and Bengali translation of the Sanskrit *Mahābhārata*.

Hārīta

One of the twenty traditional writers of original *smṛti*. There appear to have been two authoritative writers of this name. One was the author of a *Dharmasūtra* and the other of a metrical *smṛti* on legal matters. Verses of Hārīta appear to have been widely known long before the sixth century AD. Hārīta, the jurist, appears to have flourished sometime between AD 400 and 700. Some works refer to or quote from a *Vṛddha-hārītā* also.

[R.C. Hazra, "Did Hārīta know Tantras", *IHQ*, June and Sept., 1960.]

Hemādri

A renowned *smṛti* writer of south India. From his autobiographical account, we learn that he was son of Kāmadeva and grandson of Vāsudeva. He was in charge of the Imperial records of Mahādeva (1260-71) the Yādava king of Devagiri (modern Daulatābād) and also his minister.

His huge *Caturvarga-cintāmaṇi* is, as stated by the author himself, divided into five sections (*khaṇḍas*) called *Vrata, Dāna, Tīrtha, Mokṣa* and *Pariśeṣa*. A *Śrāddhakalpa* is also attributed to him; it is distinct from his *Śrāddha-khaṇḍa*.

Jagannātha Tarkapañcānana

Son of Rudra Tarkavāgīśa of Triveṇī in the Hughli district of West Bengal and teacher of Rāmacandra Vidyālaṃkāra, he compiled, at the instance of William Jones, the voluminous *smṛti* digest, entitled *Vivādabhaṅgārṇava* (AD 1773). He is to be distinguished from Jagannātha, author of the *Rasagaṅgādhara*.

[*Modern Review*, Nov., 1926, pp. 493-96 and Sep., 1929, pp. 261-62.]

Jīmūtavāhana

A noted pre-Raghunandana *smṛti* writer of Bengal. In his works, he is described as *Pāribhadrīya* which, perhaps, refers to a section of the Rāḍhīya Brāhmaṇas of Bengal. Date uncertain. His literary activity appears to have covered the period AD 1090-1120.

His works are *Kālaviveka*, *Vyavahāra-mātṛkā* or *Nyāya-mātṛkā* and *Dāyabhāga*, appear to have been parts of the larger treatise, called *Dharmaratna* which is mentioned in the above three works.

[*Calcutta Law Journal* 26, pp. 17 ff. (journal portion); R.C. Majumdar, *History of Bengal*, I, pp. 323-25.]

Kamalākarabhaṭṭa

Of several scholars of this name, the most famous was the author of the celebrated *smṛti* work, *Nirṇaya-sindhu*. Second son of Umā and Rāmakṛṣṇa Bhaṭṭa, and grandson of Nārāyaṇabhaṭṭa (b. AD1513) of Vārāṇasī and younger brother of Dinakara *alias* Divākara Bhaṭṭa and father of Ananta Bhaṭṭa. He is supposed, by P.V. Kane, to have written his works between AD 1610 and 1640. The *Nirṇaya-sindhu* was completed on February 20, AD 1612.

The different works, the titles of which end in *kamalākara*, e.g. *Dāna-kamalākara*, *Śūdra-kamalākara*, etc., appear to have been sections of his large work, called *Dharmatattva*, in ten sections. His other *smṛti* works are *Gotra-pravara-darpaṇa* or *Pravaradarpaṇa*, *Sarva-śāstrārtha-nirṇaya*, etc. Besides, several tracts on procedure of some rites, called *paddhati* or *prayoga*, are also attributed to him. At the end of his *Śānti-kamalākara*, it is stated that he wrote twenty-two works (*BBRAS*, 728).

Kāśīcandra Vidyāratna (1854-1917)

Born to a Brāhmaṇa family of Vikrampur in East Bengal (now Bangladesh).

He wrote commentaries on the works of the twenty traditional writers of original *smṛti*. Only his commentary only on Manu has been published. His *smṛti* digest is the *Uddhāra-candrikā*.

Kāśīnātha Upādhyāya

Also called Bābā Pādhye, he is the author of the extensive digest, entitled *Dharmasindhusāra*, popularly called *Dharmasindhu* (AD 1790-91) which was highly authoritative in Deccan; it was also called *Dharmābdhisāra*.

He belonged to a family which hailed from Golavali, a village in Ratnagiri district, and was a devotee of God Viṭṭhala at Paṇḍharpur. From his personal account, it is learnt that his ancestors migrated to Paṇḍharpur. He was son of Ananta and Annapūrṇā (who became a *satī*) and was related to the Marāṭhī poet, Moropant. He became a *saṃnyāsī*.

He wrote several other works, e.g. the *Prāyaścittendu-śekhara*, *Śrāddha-saṃgraha*.

He died in Śaka 1727 = AD 1805-6.

Kāśīrāma Vācaspati Bhaṭṭācārya

Well-known as the earliest commentator on many of the *smṛti* digests of Raghunandana, particularly on his works on *Malamāsa*, *Tithi*, *Udvāha*, *Śuddhi*, *Śrāddha*, *Prāyaścitta*, *Dāya*, *Ekādaśī*, *Janmāṣṭamī* and *Durgotsava*.

A native of Viṣṇupur in Bankurā district of West Bengal, he was son of Rādhāvallabha and grandson of Rāmakṛṣṇa. A *pāścātya* Vaidika Brāhmaṇa, he flourished about the beginning of the eighteenth century and enjoyed the patronage of king Gopālasiṃha of Malla (in Bānkurā). He commented also on the philosophical works of Ṇandarāma.

[See Sastri, *Notices*, I, Preface, pp. xx-xxi.]

Kātyāyana

One of the twenty traditional writers of original *smṛti*. There is a *Kātyāyana-smṛti* in verse. It is not definitely known whether or not the author is the same as the great traditional author of this name.

A Kātyāyana is supposed, by P.V. Kane, to have flourished sometime between the fourth century and the sixth century AD.

Appears to have been different from Kātyāyana (sometime between *c*. 500 and 350 BC), the author of the *Vārtika-sūtras* of Pāṇini.

The aforesaid *Kātyāyana-smṛti* is also called *Karma-pradīpa*, and known as *Chandoga-pariśiṣṭa*, *Gobhila-gṛhya-sūtra-pariśiṣṭa*, *Gobhila-smṛti*.

Kubera (Upādhyāya, Paṇḍita)

A Paṇḍita of Colebrooke (*c*. AD 1800).

Author of the *Dattaka-candrikā*, according to some. A *Smṛticandrikā* is ascribed to him.

He is, perhaps, the same as Kuberaśarman Paṇḍita *Kāñjivallīya*, quoted by Raghunandana in his *Śuddhi-tattva* (*vide Smṛti-tattva*, p. 258).

[*Poonā Orientalist*, XXI, p. 64.]

Kullūkabhaṭṭa

Author of the *Manvartha-muktāvalī*, a celebrated commentary on the *Manusmṛti*. From his own account we learn that he was son of Divākara Bhaṭṭa and was born in Vārendra family residing at Nandana in Bengal, and that he wrote the above commentary in collaboration with other scholars in Kāśī (Vārāṇasī).

According to some, he also wrote a *smṛti* digest, called *Smṛtisāgara*. The *Śrāddhasāgara* refers to itself as part of a larger treatise, called *Smṛti-sāgara*, and mentions two other sections, called *Aśauca-* and *Vivāda-sāgara*. The *Śrāddha-sāgara* (Cs. 446) is regarded as spurious, a fraudulent rehash of Śūlpāṇi's *Śrāddhaviveka*, with a number of citations of fictitious authors.

Generally believed to have flourished earlier than the

fifteenth century. According to P.V. Kane, the lower terminus of his date is AD 1100. He is later than Govindarāja and Medhātithi, renowned commentators of *Manusmṛti*, both of whom have been quoted by him.

[D.C. Bhattacharya in *IHQ*, XXVI, i, pp. 109-18. Also see *Śrāddhasāgara,* under chapter 4 WORKS.]

Lakṣmīdhara

There are several authors of this name. Most famous among them is Lakṣmīdhara, author of the *Kṛtya-kalpataru*, a celebrated *smṛti* digest.

He informs us that, son of Bhaṭṭa Hṛdayadhara, he wrote his work at the behest of Govindacandra, the Gāhaḍavāla or Rāṭhor emperor of Kannauj (AD 1114-56) under whom he was *Mahā-Sāndhī Vigrahika* and *Dharmādhikārin.*

Perhaps different from Lakṣmīdhara, author of the Vedāntic work, *Advaitamakaranda*.

Another Lakṣmīdhara, son of Malladeva and Śrīdevī, was author of the *Viruddha-vidhi-vidhvaṃsa*. He flourished earlier than AD 1525.

Likhita

One of the twenty traditional writers of original *smṛti*, mentioned by *Yājñavalkya* (I.4). A *Likhita-smṛti* in about 93 verses is included in Jīvānanda's collection of *smṛtis*, part II, pp. 372-82. The same text is contained also in the Ānandāśrama collection of *smṛtis* (pp. 182-86).

The latter contains also a *Śaṃkha-Likhita-Smṛti* in 32 verses. The Deccan College MS. 44 of 1866-68 contains a *Likhita-smṛti*, in six chapters; therein Vaśiṣṭha and other sages appear as asking Likhita about the duties of the four castes and *prāyaścitta*s.

A *dharmaśāstra* work is ascribed to Śaṃkha-Likhita. P.V.

Kane attempted a reconstruction of the *Śaṃkha-Likhita Dharmaśāstras* in *ABORI*, vols. VII, VIII.

Madanapāla

To him are ascribed the *Madanapārijāta*, *Smṛti-kaumudī*, *Mahārṇava-karmavipāka*, *Tithi-nirṇaya-sāra*, besides works on other subjects like *Āyurveda,* astronomy, etc.

Madana appears to have been a king, and a great patron of learning, and is supposed to have flourished about the middle of the fourteenth century.

The *Madanapārijāta* was compiled by Viśveśvarabhaṭṭa, a great authority on the Vārāṇasī school of Hindu Law.

Mādhavācārya

Son of Māyaṇa and Śrīmatī, and elder brother of the famous Vedic commentator, Sāyaṇa. Minister of King Bukka of Vijayanagar (fourteenth century). May or may not be identical with Mādhava, the supposed author of the *Sarva-darśana-saṃgraha*. Some take our Mādhava to be identical with Sāyaṇa. Mādhavācārya is said to have become an ascetic in later life under the name of Vidyāraṇya.

Mādhavācārya is credited with the authorship of the *smṛti* works, *Kāla-nirṇaya* and *Parāśara-mādhavīya* (commentary on the *Parāśara-smṛti*).

Some other works, including the philosophical treatise, *Pañcadaśī*, are also attributed to him.

[On relationship between Mādhava and Sāyaṇa, see R. Narasimhacharin *IA*, Vol. 45; L. Sarup in *B.C. Law Volume* II, Poona, 1946. Also see T. Shivamurthy, unknown works of Mādhava-mantrin, *ABORI*, 1976.]

Manu

Stands at the head of the list of twenty traditional writers of original *smṛti*. Traditionally regarded as the author of the *Manu-smṛti*. Regarded as most authoritative among the *smṛti* writers as the following time-honoured remarks prove:

> *manurvai yat kiṃ cāha tadbheṣajam* (whatever has been said by Manu is medicine); *manvartha-viparītā yā sā smṛtīrna-praśasyate* (that *smṛti*, which is opposed to the *Manu-smṛti*, is not commended).

A treatise on *Dharmasūtra*, called *Mānava-dharmasūtra*, is supposed by scholars to have existed at one time.

Date not known.

Medhātithi

Author of the *Manu-bhāṣya*, the oldest extant commentary on the *Manu-smṛti*.

Supposed to have flourished in the ninth century. Son of Vīrasvāmin, he is believed by some scholars to have hailed from south India.

A *Smṛti-viveka* is supposed, by P.V. Kane, to have been written by Medhātithi.

Misaru(u)Miśra

Author of the *Vivāda-candra*.

He says that he wrote the digest under orders from Lachimādevī, wife of prince Candrasiṃha of the Kāmeśvara dynasty of Mithilā.

Probably flourished in the earlier half of the fifteenth century.

Mitramiśra

A celebrated *smṛti* writer who exercised profound influence on the Vārāṇasī school of Hindu Law.

Son of Paraśurāma-paṇḍita and grandson of Haṃsapaṇḍita,

Mitramiśra states that he wrote his voluminous work, *Vīramitrodaya* at the behest of Vīrasiṃha, King of Orccha (AD 1605-27).

He also wrote a commentary, bearing the same title, on the *Yājñavalkya-smṛti.*

Nāgeśa

Same as Nāgojibhaṭṭa (q.v.).

Nāgojībhaṭṭa or Nāgeśabhaṭṭa

Same as Nāgeśa, author of the grammatical works, *Paribhāṣendu-śekhara*, *Vaiyākaraṇa-siddhānta-mañjūṣā*, etc. A Mahārāṣṭra Dīkṣita, he was son of Śivabhaṭṭa and Satī. He was a resident of Vārāṇasī, and a protegé of Rāmavarman or Rāmasiṃha (eighteenth century), a local prince of Śṛṅgaverapura (modern Singarour), a few miles north of Allāhabād. Nāgojī was a pupil of Hari Dīkṣita, grandson of Bhaṭṭoji Dīkṣita and author of commentary *Śabdaratna* or *Prauḍha-manoramā*. He was preceptor of Gaṅgārāma, Vaidyānātha Pāyaguṇḍa and his son Bālaśarman.

A prolific writer, he wrote works on *Dharma*, *Yoga*, *Alaṃkāra*, and about a dozen works on *Vyākaraṇa*, besides commentaries on the *Vālmīki-rāmāyaṇa*, *Gītagovinda*, etc.

His works on *dharmaśāstra* are 13 in number. Some of these are *Ācārenduśekhara*, *Tithi-nirṇaya-tattva*, *Prāyaścitta-sāra-saṃgraha*, *Saṃskāra-ratnamālā*, etc. None of his works appears to have been published. His literary activity is believed to have extended from AD 1670 to 1750.

Nandapaṇḍita

Also named Vināyaka Paṇḍita, he was son of Rāmapaṇḍita of Vārāṇasī, who was styled *dharmādhikārin*. Probably composed his works in the period between AD 1580 and 1630.

He was patronised by Paramānanda of Sahajila family of Sādhāraṇapura, Harivaṃsavarman of Mahendra family and Keśavạ Nāyaka of Vijayapura in Karnāṭaka.

Appears to have written thirteen works most of which are *smṛti* digests or commentaries on well-known *smṛti* works. Of his works the most notable is the *Dattaka-mīmāṃsā*. Noteworthy among his commentaries are the *Vidvanmanoharā* on *Parāśara-smṛti*, (Keśava) *Vaijayantī* on *Viṣṇu-smṛti*. He wrote also the *Pramitākṣarā* commentary on the *Mitākṣarā* on the *Yājñavalkya-smṛti*.

Nārada

An authoritative *smṛti* writer who is supposed to have flourished sometime between AD 100 and 300.

There is a *Nārada-smṛti* or *Nārada* (*Nāradīya*) *Dharmaśāstra*.

Nārāyaṇabhaṭṭa (Jagadguru)

Son of Rāmeśvara Bhaṭṭa and Umā, he was born in AD 1513, and wrote at Vārāṇasī. He was father of Śaṃkara Bhaṭṭa, Rāmakṛṣṇa Bhaṭṭa and Govinda, and grandfather of Kamalākara Bhaṭṭa (q.v.) and Lakṣmaṇabhaṭṭa. The period of his literary activity was between AD 1540 and 1570.

His *Tristhalī-setu* is well-known. His other *smṛti* works are *Antyeṣṭi-paddhati* and *Prayoga-ratna*.

He commented on the *Kālamādhava*, and wrote several tracts on *prayoga* and *paddhati*. He commented also on the Prākṛt passages of the *Abhijñānaśākuntalam* and on the *Vṛttaratnākara* of Kedārabhaṭṭa.

He is different from Nārāyaṇa, author of the *Dharmapravṛtti*.

[*IA*, 41, pp. 9-11.]

Nīlakaṇṭha Bhaṭṭa

One of the foremost digest writers, he was great grandson of Rāmeśvara Bhaṭṭa of Pratiṣṭhān, grandson of Nārāyaṇa Bhaṭṭa and son of Śaṃkara Bhaṭṭa; father of Śaṅkara Bhaṭṭa (author of *Karmavipākārka*) and Bhānu Bhaṭṭa; ancestor of Gaṅgārāma Jadin. Appears to have flourished in the seventeenth century.

Of the several scholars of this name, we are concerned with the author of the following *smṛti* digests: *Vyavahāra-mayūkha*, *Ācāramayūkha*, *Saṃskāra-mayūkha*, *Prāyścitta-mayūkha* and *Pratiṣṭhā-mayūkha*.

These digests formed parts of his encyclopaedic work on religious and civil law, entitled *Bhagavanta-bhāskara* or *Smṛti-bhāskara*, composed in honour of his patron, Bhagavantadeva, a Bundela Chieftain of the Seṅgara clan that ruled at Bhareha near the confluence of the Yamunā and the Cambal.

He was a great *mīmāṃsaka* too and wrote works on *Mīmāṃsā*.

Parāśara

One of the twenty traditional writers of original *smṛti*. There is a *Parāśara-smṛti*. To be distinguished from Parāśara, author of the *Jāti-viveka* and Parāśara, referred to as an author on politics.

Earlier than *Yājñavalkya-smṛti* which refers (I.4) to him.

The *Bṛhat-parāśara* appears to be a later recast of the *Parāśara-smṛti*. A *Vṛddha-Parāśara* is known from references by later writers.

Pratāparudradeva

A king of the Gajapati Dynasty which ruled at Cuttack in Orissa. Pratāpa reigned from AD 1497 to 1539.

His celebrated *smṛti* work is the *Sarasvatī-vilāsa*. His other works on the subject are: *Pratāpa-mārtaṇḍa*, or (*Prauḍha*)*pratāpa-mārtaṇḍa* and *Nirṇaya-saṃgraha*.

The works seem to have been composed by scholars enjoying his patronage.

Raghunandana

The foremost writer of *smṛti* digests in Bengal, sometimes referred to as Smārta Bhaṭṭācārya or simply Smārta. Born at Navadvīpa in West Bengal, he was son of Harihara Bhaṭṭācārya, and pupil of Śrīnātha Ācāryacūḍāmaṇi.

Appears to have flourished sometime between AD1500 and 1600.

Author of 28 *smṛti* digests, the titles of which end in *-tattva*. The subjects, with which these works deal, are stated by the author himself in the beginning of his *Malamāsa-tattva* (*vide* J. Vidyāsāgara's *Smṛti-tattva*, I, p. 736).

Besides the 28 tracts (enumerated under *Smṛti-tattva* in the part on Works), some minor works on *smṛti* are also ascribed to him.

He was an adept in the application of *Mīmāṃsā-sūtra*s and *Nyāya*s.

Rāyamukuṭa

See Bṛhaspati Rāyamukuṭa.

Rudradhara

Two writers of this name flourished in Mithilā. Rudradhara I, son of Lakṣmīdhara (not the author of the *Kṛtyakalpataru*), and younger brother of Haladhara, perhaps lived in the earlier half of the fifteenth century. His works are: *Śrāddha-viveka*, *Śuddhi-viveka*, *Varṣakṛtya* and *Vrata-paddhati*.

Rudradhara II, pupil of Caṇḍeśvara, who may or may not have been identical with Caṇḍeśvara Mantrin, probably flourished in the sixteenth century. His works are: *Śrāddha-candrikā*, *Kṛtyacandrikā* and *Vivāda-candrikā*.

Śaṃkha

One of the twenty traditional writers on original Smṛti. Author of a *Śaṃkha-smṛti* and a *Śaṃkha-dharmaśāstra* which is known only from quotations in later works. The *Śaṃkha-Likhita-smṛti* seems to be a joint work of Śaṃkha and Likhita. A *Laghu-śaṃkha-smṛti* exists. A *Śaṃkha-Likhita-dhamasūtra* is known from citations in later treatises.

The *Dharmasūtra* of *Śaṃkha* is assigned, by P.V. Kane, to the conjectural period between 300 BC and AD 100.

According to the *Mahābhārata* (*Śānti*, Chap. 23), Śaṃkha and Likhita were brothers.

[See under Likhita.]

Saṃvarta

One of the twenty traditional writers of original *smṛti*. A metrical *Saṃvarta-smṛti* is available. Saṃvarta's date is uncertain.

Sarvoruśarmā Trivedin

He compiled (1789) the work entitled *Vivāda-sārārṇava*.

Śātātapa

One of the twenty traditional writers of original *smṛti*. Several *smṛti* works, including the *Karmavipāka*, are ascribed to him. Of these, one is in mixed prose and verse.

There are references to Vṛddha-Śātātapa and Bṛhat-Śātātapa; a *Vṛddha-śātātapa-smṛti* is ascribed to the former.

Date uncertain.

Śrīdatta

One of the earliest among the medieval Maithila writers of *smṛti* digests. Styled as Upādhyāya, he is credited with the authorship of the following *smṛti* digests: *Ācārādarśa*, *Chandogāhnika*,

Pitṛbhakti (also *Kṛtyācāra*), *Samaya-pradīpa*, *Śrāddhakalpa*, *Vratasāra* (or *Vrata-paddhati*).

Supposed to have flourished in the latter half of the thirteenth century. He is to be distinguished from Śrīdatta, son of Nāgeśvara Miśra and author of the *Puraścaraṇa-paddhati*.

Śrīdhara

Author of the *Smṛtyarthasāra*.

From the colophon, we learn that he was son of Nāgabhartṛ Viṣṇubhaṭṭa of Viśvāmitra *gotra*.

In the opinion of P.V. Kane, his work appears to have been composed between AD 1150 and 1200.

Śrīkṛṣṇa Tarkālaṃkāra

A post-Raghunandana writer of about the middle of the eighteenth century.

Author of *Dāya-krama-saṃgraha*, *Śrāddha-viveka-vivṛti* (commentary on Śūlapāṇi's *Śrāddha-viveka*) and *Saṃskāra-paddhati-rahasya* (commentary on Bhavadeva Bhaṭṭa's *Karmānuṣṭhāna-paddhati*).

Śrīkṛṣṇa's *Dāyabhāga-prabodhinī* is a well-known and, perhaps, the most authoritative commentary on Jīmūtavāhana's *Dāyabhāga*.

Śrīnātha Ācārya-Cūḍāmaṇi

Teacher of Raghunanandana (q.v.) who respectfully refers to him as *gurucaraṇāḥ*, *gurupādāḥ*, etc.

He wrote a number of digests which may be divided into four groups:

(1) Titles of which end in *-arṇava*,

(2) Ending in *-dīpikā*,

(3) Ending in *-candrikā*,

(4) Ending in *-viveka*.

Of the *viveka* group, only the *Durgotsava-viveka* has been published. He also wrote commentaries on the *Chandoga-pariśiṣṭa-prakāśa* of Nārāyaṇa, *Tithiviveka* and *Śrāddha-viveka* of Śūlapāṇi and Jīmūtavāhana's *Dāyabhāga*.

Śūlapāṇi

A great pre-Raghunandana writer of *smṛti* digests. He describes himself as a Sāhuḍiyān which, perhaps, refers to a brand of Bengal Brāhmaṇas of Rāḍhī Śreṇī.

Supposed to have flourished sometime between the eleventh and the fifteenth century.

There are several authors of this name. The genuine *smṛti* digests of our Śūlapāṇi appear to be: *Dattaka-viveka*, *Ḍolayātrā-viveka*, *Durgotsava-viveka*, *Ekādaśī-viveka*, *Prāyaścitta-viveka*, *Rāsayātrā-viveka*, *Sambandha-viveka*, *Saṃkrānti-viveka*, *Śrāddha-viveka*, *Tithi-viveka*, *Vrata-kāla-viveka*.

Śūlapāṇi's *Dīpakalikā* is a commentary on the *Yājñavalkya-smṛti*.

Several other works, including a *Caturaṅgadīpikā* (on the game of chess), are ascribed to a Śūlapāṇi whose identity has not yet been established with certainty.

[S.C. Banerji, "Śūlapāṇi, the Sāhuḍiyān", *NIA*, Oct.-Nov., 1942.]

Sumantu

From quotations in later *smṛti* works and commentaries, he appears to have been an authoritative writer on original *smṛti*. These quotations are partly in prose, partly in verse. It is not known whether or not he wrote a prose *dharmasūtra* or a metrical *smṛti* work separately.

Date unknown.

Ṭoḍarmal

Rājā Ṭoḍaramalla, the renowned finance minister of Akbar. From the introductory verse 19 of the *Ṭoḍarānanda*, it is learnt that Ṭoḍarmal engaged some learned men of Vārāṇasī to compile their work which was designed to contain the quintessence of several Purāṇas and *smṛtis*. It was prepared under the general editorship of Nārāyaṇa Bhaṭṭa during AD 1572-89.

Uśanas

One of the twenty traditional writers of original *smṛti*. Author of an *Auśanasa-dharmaśāstra*, also called *Auśanasa-smṛti*, *Uśanas-smṛti*.

It exists in three forms:

(1) in prose and verse, in seven chapters,

(2) metrical; two versions — one short version in 51 verses and the other long in 9 chapters.

Some verses in the prose text occur also in the metrical texts.

Of the many quotations from Uśanas, in *smṛits* and *nibandhas*, some occur in the above three texts, while others do not.

Vācaspati Miśra

A great writer of Mithilā on *Navya-nyāya* and *Navya-smṛti*. To be distinguished from the philosopher Vācaspati (*c*. middle of ninth century), author of the *Bhāmatī*, *Sāṃkhya-tattva-kaumudī* and other philosophical works.

Our Vācaspati is also different from (Candraśekhara) Vācaspati, author of the *Smṛti-sāra-saṃgraha*.

Vācaspati Miśra, author of the *smṛti* works, appears to have flourished in the middle of the fifteenth century. His works may be divided broadly into two classes, viz., (1) those the titles of which end in *-cintāmaṇi* and (2) the titles of which end in *-nirṇaya*.

To the former class belong the works on *Tīrtha*, *Vyavahāra*, *Vivāda*, *Kṛtya*, etc. To the latter belong the works on *Tithi*, *Vivāda*, etc.

He wrote also some other digests which do not fall within the above groups.

According to the author's own statement, at the end of his *Śrāddha-kalpa*, he appears to have composed as many as 31 works on *smṛti*.

[For Vācaspati, the *smṛti* writer, see S.C. Banerji, *Contribution of Bihar to Sanskrit Literature*, p. 69. For a complete list of his *smṛti* works, see *Ibid.*, pp. 29-31.]

Vaidyanātha Pāyaguṇḍa

Perhaps same as Bālambhaṭṭa (q.v.).

Vallālasena

Son of Vijayasena and grandson of Hemantasena, he ruled over Bengal in the twelfth century.

Author of the works, *Dānasāgara*, *Adbhutasāgara*, *Pratiṣṭhā-sāgara* and *Ācāra-sāgara*. His *Vrata-sāgara* is mentioned in his *Dānasāgara*.

He is to be distinguished from Vallāla (end of sixteenth century) to whom the *Bhoja-prabandha* is ascribed.

Varadarāja

Author of the *Vyavahāra-nirṇaya*.

According to P.V. Kane, he should be assigned to a period between *c.* AD 1450 and 1493.

Vardhamāna

(1) Son and disciple of Gaṅgeśopādhyāya, the most eminent logician of Mithilā. Styled as Mahāmahopādhyāya, he is supposed to have flourished towards the end of the fourteenth century.

Besides works on *Nyāya*, he is credited with the authorship of the *Smṛti-paribhāṣā*.

(2) Another person of the same name was son of Bhaveśa and Gaurīdevī. His elder brother was Gaṇḍakamiśra. Śaṃkara Miśra and Vācaspati were his *gurus*. He flourished in the fifteenth century. Author of several *smṛti* works, viz., *Daṇḍaviveka* (part of the *Smṛti-tattva-viveka* or *Smṛti-tattvāmṛta*), *Gaṅgā-kṛtya-viveka*, *Gayā-vidhi-viveka*, *Gayāpaddhati*, *Śrāddha-pradīpa*, *Śāntikapauṣṭika*, *Kṛtya-nirṇaya*, *Pratihasta-paddhati*.

To be distinguished from Vardhamāna, author of the grammatical work, *Gaṇa-ratna-mahodadhi* (AD 1140).

Vaś(s)iṣṭha

One of the twenty traditional writers of original *smṛti*. P.V. Kane tentatively assigns Vaśiṣṭha to a period between 300 and 100 BC.

Author of the *Vāśiṣṭha-dharmasūtra*.

To be distinguished from Vaśiṣṭha to whom is ascribed the astronomical work, *Vaśiṣṭha-siddhānta* (*c.* third century AD).

Vidyāpati

Grandson of Jayadatta and son of Gaṇapati and a court-poet of the Maithilā monarchs Kīrtisiṃha, Devasiṃha (*d.* AD 1413), Śivasiṃha, and Viśvāsadevī, queen of Padmasiṃha. He is famous for his Vaiṣṇava *Padāvalī*s in Maithili language.

His *smṛti* works are: *Gaṅgā-vākyāvalī*, *Gayāpattalaka*, *Dāna-vākyāvalī*, *Durgā-bhakti-taraṅgiṇī*, *Varṣa-kṛtya*, *Vibhāga-sāra*, *Śaiva-sarvasvasāra* or *Śambhu-vākyāvalī*.

He wrote also poetical works, besides works on geography, moral tales, *Āyurveda*, letter-writing, etc.

[For details about his life and works, see *Puruṣa-parīkṣā*, ed. by R. Jha (Intro.), 1960; R.K. Choudhary, *Mithilā in the Age of*

Vidyāpati; S.C. Banerji, *Contribution of Bihar to Sanskrit Literature*, Patna, 1973.]

Vijñāneśvara

Author of the *Mitākṣarā* commentary on the *Yājñavalkya-smṛti*, he styles himself as *Vijñāna-yogin*. A *Paramahaṃsa* and pupil of Uttama, he was son of Padmanābhabhaṭṭa. He states that he worte his work when king Vikramārka or Vikramādityadeva had been reigning in the city of Kalyāṇa; the King was, most probably, Vikramāditya VI (reign *c*. AD 1076-1127).

Viṣṇu

One of the twenty traditional writers of original *smṛti*. There is a *Viṣṇu-dharmasūtra* the older portion of which is assigned by P.V. Kane approximately to a period between 300 and 100 BC.

Viśvarūpa

Supposed to have flourished in the first half of the ninth century AD. Identified with Sureśvara, a pupil of the great Śaṃkarācārya, and author of the *Naiṣkarmya-siddhi* and some other works.

Author of the *Bālakrīḍā* commentary on the *Yājñavalkya-smṛti*.

[K. Rönnow, Viśvarūpa, *E.J. Rapson Pres. Vol., BSOS*, IV, London, 1931; P.P.S. Sastri, "Viśvarūpa.... *alias* Sureśvarācārya — problems of identity", *P.V. Kane Pres. Vol.*, p. 8.]

Vyāsa

One of the twenty traditional authors of original *smṛti*, and is to be distinguished from Vyāsa, the legendary author of the *Mahābhārata*.

A *Vyāsa-smṛti* exists; references are found to Vṛddha-Vyāsa and Laghu-Vyāsa.

To Vyāsa is ascribed the work called *Vyāsa-siddhānta* which appears to be a part of the *Vyāsa-smṛti.*

According to P.V. Kane, he flourished sometime between the second and the fifth century.

Yājñavalkya

One of the twenty traditional writers of original *smṛti.* Date uncertain. The extant *Yājñavalkya-smṛti* is supposed to have been composed during the first two centuries of the Christian era or even earlier.

Vṛddha-Yājñavalkya, Yoga-yājñavalkya, Yogī-Yājñavalkya, and *Bṛhad-yogī-Yājñavalkya* appear to be different from one another and also from the *Yājñavalkya-smṛti.*

Yama

One of the twenty traditional writers of original *smṛti.* A *Yama-smṛti* exists in different versions. Date uncertain. *Bṛhad-yama, Laghu-yama* and *Svalpa-yama* are cited in later digests and commentaries.

4

Works

Ācārādarśa

A *smṛti* digest by Śrīdatta Upādhyāya of Mithilā. It is a manual of the daily duties of the followers of the *Śukla-Yajurveda*. The topics discussed are:

> *Ācamana*, *Dantadhāvana*, *Snāna*, *Sandhyā*, *Japa*, *Brahma-yajña*, *Tarpaṇa*, daily worship of deities, *Vaiśvadeva*, *Atithi-satkāra*, etc.

Besides an anonymous commentary, there are two commentaries, one named *Bodhinī* by Gaurīpati and the other *Ācāra-dīpikā* by Harilāla.

[Published by Veṅkaṭeśvara Press, Bombay, 1961. For MSS. of commentaries, see *NCC*, II, p. 33.]

Aṅgiras-Smṛti

Attributed to Aṅgiras, one of the traditional twenty writers of *dharmaśāstra*. It has a commentary by K. Śukla.

[Ptd. in *Smṛtīnāṃ Samuccayaḥ*, Ānandāśrama, I., and in *Adyar Library Bulletin,* vols. 15-17.]

Anukramaṇī or Nirṇaya-Sindhu-Anukramaṇikā

Index of topics discussed in the *Nirṇaya-sindhu* of Kamalākara.

[Ptd. at Benares, 1875.]

Aparārka

It is a learned commentary by Aparāditya on the *Yājñavalkya-smṛti*. Full title — *Aparārka-Yājñavalkya-dharmaśāstra-nibandha*. It is a sort of *Smṛti-nibandha*, because it cites numerous passages from different *smṛti* works, and discusses different views finally giving the author's own conclusions.

[Published in two vols. from Ānandāśrama Press, Poona, 1903-04.]

Āpastamba-Dharmasūtra

The contents are divided into two main chapters called *Praśnas*, each of which is divided into eleven *paṭalas*.

This work deals with the usual topics of *smṛti*, but does not discuss *Rājadharma*.

P.V. Kane assigns it to a period between 600 and 300 BC.

Haradatta's *Ujjvalā* is the only extant commentary on it. A *bhāṣya*, referred to in some later *smṛti* digests and commentaries, may have been by one Dhūrtasvāmin.

[Ed. by A.C. Sastri and A.R. Sastri with Haradatta's commentary, Banaras, 1932, Eng. tr. by Bühler, *SBE*, Vol. II.]

Aṣṭāviṃśati-Tattva

Same as *Smṛti-tattva* (q.v.).

Atri-Smṛti (Atri Saṃhitā or Ātreya Smṛti or Ātreya Dharmaśāstra)

Available in different versions. From quotations in later works, Atri appears to have written also a *Dharmasūtra*.

[Ptd. Ānandāśrama 48; 3rd in the *Smṛtīnāṃ Samuccayaḥ*. For a collection of prose passages of Atri, see S.C. Banerji, *Dharmasūtras*, pp. 244ff.]

Auśanasa-Dharmaśāstra

(1) Mainly in prose with some verses.

(2) In 51 verses.

No. 1 above is available in two MSS. of Deccan College (a) No. 644 of Viśrāmbāg and (b) No. 191 of A 1881-82.

No.2 is printed in Jīvānanda's Collection of Smṛtis (pt.I) and Ānandāśrama Collection.

Both prose passages and verses, attributed to Uśanas, are quoted in some later digests and commentaries.

Bālakrīḍā

By Viśvarūpa. It is the earliest extant commentary on the *Yājñavalkya-smṛti*. It is lucid and free from prolixity.

[Ed., in two parts, by T.G. Sastri, TSS.]

Bālambhaṭṭi

A commentary by Bālambhaṭṭa on the *Mitākṣarā* (q.v.).

[Book I (*Ācāra*), Book II (*Vyavahāra*), Book III (*Prāyaścitta*) — all ed. by J.R. Gharpure; the three Books were published from Bombay (1917), Bombay (1914) and Poona (1924) respectively.]

Baudhāyana-Dharmasūtra

It consists of four chapters, called *Praśnas*. While dealing with *Ācāra* and *Prāyaścitta*, it contains very little about *Rājadharma* and *Vyavahāra*.

The age of the author cannot be determined even approximately.

It has a well-known commentary, called *Vivaraṇa*, by Govindasvāmin. According to Burnell, the oldest commentator was Bhavasvāmin.

[Ed. L. Srinivasacarya, with *Vivaraṇa*, Mysore, 1907; A.C.

Sastri, with same commentary, Benares, 1934. Eng. tr. by Bühler, *SBE*, XIV.]

Brāhmaṇa-Sarvasva

Also called *Karmopadeśinī*, it is by Halāyudha. It deals with various sacraments (*saṃskāra*). The main object of the author is to explain the *mantras* used in the sacraments as well as those which are recited by Brāhmaṇas in daily observances from the cleansing of teeth to going to bed.

[Ed. by D. Bhattacharya, Calcutta, 1958.]

Bṛhaspati-Smṛti

In the 80-verse text, Bṛhaspati is represented as instructing Indra about gift.

Führer made a collection of 84 verses attributed to Bṛhaspati in the legal works of Aparārka and others with German translation and notes (Leipzig 1897). Jolly collected 711 verses of Bṛhaspati on law and translated them into English in *SBE*, vol. 33.

[Ptd. in Jīvānanda's Collection of Smṛtis (pt.I, pp. 644-51) and in Ānandāśrama collection in 80 verses.]

Bṛhaspati was, perhaps, the first writer to make a clear distinction between civil and criminal justice. He divided the eighteen titles of disputes (*vivādapada*) into two groups, those arising from wealth (14) and those from injury (4). *Vide* Jīmūtavāhana's *Vyavahāra-mātṛkā*, p. 277 — *tadāha bṛhaspatiḥ* etc., and *Smṛti-candrākā* (*vyavahāra*, p. 9) — *pāruṣye dve. . . . . bṛhaspatiḥ*.

Like Nārada, Bṛhaspati lays down the principle that a legal decision should not be taken only on the basis of *Śāstra*; when a decision is devoid of rationality, it causes dereliction of *dharma* (vide *Aparārka* on *Yājñavalkya-smṛti*, II.1).

[A *Bṛhaspati-smṛti* was published by K.V. Rangasvami Aiyangar in *GOS*, 1941. It is a collection of verses on *Vyavahāra, Saṃskāra, Ācāra, Śrāddha, Aśauca, Āpaddharma, and Prayaścitta.*

L. Renou contributed to vol. VI, 1962, of the *Indo-Iranian Journal* (published by Moulton and Co., the Hague), pp. 81-102 a paper, in French, on the above collection by Aiyangar.]

Caturvarga-Cintāmaṇi

A huge *smṛti* digest by Hemādri. He states that his intention is to deal with *dharmaśāstra* in five sections, called *Vrata*, *Dāna*, *Tīrtha*, *Mokṣa* and *Pariśeṣa*. The last section was divided into four parts, viz., *Devatā*, *Kāla-nirṇaya*, *Karmavipāka* and *Lakṣaṇa-samuccaya*.

In the introductory portion of the *Vratakhaṇḍa*, he gives a detailed genealogy of the Yādavas of Devagiri. *Vyavahāra-khaṇḍa* is also ascribed to him.

Of the four volumes of the work, published hitherto, the fourth, dealing with *Prāyaścitta*, does not appear to be the work of Hemādri.

The third and fourth sections, mentioned above are not available; some information is available also in the part on *Kāla* (vol. III, pt. 2).

[Pub. in *Bib. Ind.* Series, vol. I (*Dāna-khaṇḍa*); vol. II (*Vrata*), pts. i, ii, 1878-79; vol. III (*Pariśeṣa*), pts. i, ii, 1895; vol. IV (*Prāyaścitta*), 1911. Also published in four vols. (*Dāna, Vrata, Praiśeṣa, Prāyaścitta*), Varanasi, 1985 (rpt.).]

Chandoga-Paddhati

Same as *Karmānuṣṭhāna-paddhati* (q.v.).

Dakṣa-Smṛti

The highlights of its contents are: Four *āśramas*, various sub-divisions of actions, nine things not to be gifted, praise of a good housewife, *yoga* and its six *aṅgas* viz. *prāṇāyāma*, *dhyāna*, *pratyāhāra*, *dhāraṇā*, *tarka* and *samādhi*, etc.

It has two commentaries, one by Kṛṣṇanātha and the other by Takanalāla.

[Ptd. in Jīvānanda's Collection of Smṛtis (Calcutta, pt. II, pp. 383-402, in seven chapters and 20 verses); Ānandāśrama collection, pp. 72-84; N.N. Datta's collection, vol. I, pp. 291-309.]

Dāna-Kriyā-Kaumudī

A *smṛti* digest, by Govindānanda, dealing with various gifts.

[*Bib. Ind.*, 1903.]

Dāna-Ratnākara

A part of Caṇḍeśvara's *Smṛtiratnākara*. Consisting of 29 chapters (*taraṅgas*), it deals with various gifts and matters connected with them.

[Composed in AD 1314 . For MSS., see *NCC*, IX, p. 9.]

Dāna-Sāgara

A voluminous *smṛti* digest, attributed to Vallālasena. It deals with gifts, including 16 *mahādānas*. The author states that he has described 1375 kinds of gifts.

[*Bib. Ind.*, 1953. See R.C. Hazra, "Critical Examination of some Readings of the *Dānasāgara*", *Our Heritage*, VIII, 1960.]

Daṇḍaviveka

A part of the *Smṛti-tattvaviveka* by Vardhamāna. In seven chapters, it deals with penal offences, the propriety of inflicting punishments, and the different forms of punishment.

[Ed. by K.K. Smṛtitīrtha, *GOS*, 1931, Eng. tr. by B. Bhattacharya, Calcutta, 1973.]

Daśa-Karmapaddhati

Same as *Karmānuṣṭhāna-paddhati* (q.v.).

Dattaka-Candrikā

A work, in seven *prakaraṇas*, on adoption, generally ascribed to Kubera, but really perhaps written or compiled by Raghumaṇi, spiritual preceptor of the king of Nadīyā, West Bengal.

It had been regarded, in Bengal, as the most authoritative work on the subject.

It has a commentary by Rāmeśvara Śukla.

[Published Lahore, 1882 (with Hindī tr.); Calcutta, 1896 with Bengāli tr.; *ASS*, 1942. Eng. tr. (1) by J.C.C. Sutherland, Calcutta, 1881; (2) S.S. Setlur, *A Complete Collection of Hindu Law Books on Inheritance*, work No. 7, Madras, 1911. French tr. by C. Orianne, Paris, 1844.]

Dattaka-Mīmāṃsā (also called *Datta-putra-nirṇaya-mīmāṃsā* or *Putrīkaraṇa-mīmāṃsā*)

By Nandapaṇḍita, it deals with all aspects of adoption, and the ceremonies connected with it. In British Indian courts, it was regarded as the most authoritative work on adoption, particularly in Mithilā and Banaras.

Besides the commentators mentioned below, Vṛndāvana Śukla also commented on it.

[Ed. by B. Siromani, with his own commentary, Calcutta, 1885; R.P. Pandeya, with commentary of Madhusūdana and notes of V.V. Deshpandeya, Varanasi, 1980. Eng. tr. by J. Sutherland (comprised in Stoke's *Hindu Law Books*); by Setlur, *A Complete Collection of Hindu Law Books on Inheritance*, Madras, 1911.]

Dāyabhāga

By Jīmūtavāhana. Probably part of a bigger treatise, called *Dharmaratna*. It deals with the inheritance and succession in respect of properties in general and *Strīdhana* in particular, partition, etc. It was of paramount authority in British Courts of Bengal.

To be distinguished from the works of the same title by Kamalākara and Gopāla Nyāyapañcānana.

Jīmūtavāhana's *Dāyabhāga* has over a dozen commentaries for which see *NCC*, IX, pp. 26-28.

[Of various editions, the most noteworthy is the one with seven commentaries by B. Śiromaṇi, Calcutta, 1863-66. *Dāyabhāga of Jīmūtavāhana*, vol. I, ed. by H.N. Chatterji, Howrah, West Bengal. Eng. tr., with *Mitākṣarā*, by Colebrooke, Calcutta, 1810. See I.S. Pawate, *Dāyabhāga*, Dharwar, 1975; H.N. Chatterji, *Dāyabhāga, the Institutes of Jīmūtavāhana*, Calcutta.]

Dāyabhāga-Prabodhinī

Well-known commentary, by Śrīkṛṣṇa Tarkālaṃkāra, on Jīmūtavāhana's *Dāyabhāga*.

[Included among seven commentaries on *Dāyabhāga*, ed. by B. Śiromaṇi, Calcutta, 1863-66.]

Dharma-Ratna

Referred to in Jīmūtavāhana's *Kālaviveka*, *Dāyabhāga* and *Vyavahāra-mātṛkā*, each of which appears to have formed parts of the *Dharma-ratna*.

[See *HDH*, vol. I, pt. 2, p. 699.]

Dharma-Ratna

Appears to have been a large work of Jīmūtavāhana in whose *Dāyabhāga*, *Kālaviveka* and *Vyavahāra-mātṛkā* it is mentioned. It is different from the work of the same title, also called *Sujana-dharma-ratna* by Kṛṣṇabhaṭṭa, named after his patron, Sujānasiṃha, a Bundela Chief. This latter work is divided into ten sections called *Dīdhitis*.

Dharma-Sindhu-Sāra or Dharmābdhi-Sāra

By Kāśīnātha Upādhyāya.

It is in three *Paricchedas*, the third being in two parts.

[Often printed, Bombay, 1850, Poona, 1925.]

Dharma-Tattva

See under Kamalākarabhaṭṭa (Authors).

Dīpakalikā

A commentary, by Śūlapāṇi, on the *Yājñavalkya-smṛti*. It is brief but lucid.

[Ed. by J.R. Gharpure, Bombay, 1939. Eng. tr. by same scholar, with Eng. tr. of *Yājñavalkya-smṛti* and two other commentaries on it, by J.R. Gharpure, 4 pts., Bombay, 1936-39.

See S.C. Banerji, *The Dīpakalikā of Śūlapāṇi* with special reference to the *Vyavahāra* section, *NIA*, V, 1942.]

Ḍolayātrā-Viveka

By Śūlapāṇi.

[Ed. with Intro. by S.C. Banerji, *Kane Festschrift*, Poona, 1941.]

Durgā-Bhakti-Taraṅgiṇī

By Vidyāpati. Written under the patronage of King Dhīrasiṃha of Mithilā, it is a metrical work, in 1000 verses, on the ceremony of the autumnal worship of Durgā.

[Ptd., Calcutta, 1909.]

Durgotsava-Viveka

By Śūlapāṇi. It deals, in some details, with various matters relating to *Durgā-pūjā*.

There is also a work of the same title by Śrīnātha Ācāryacūḍāmaṇi.

[Both works published by Saṃskṛta Sāhitya Pariṣad, Calcutta, 1331 B.S.]

Gaṅgā-Vākyāvalī

By Vidyāpati. It deals with the advantages of visiting and worshipping the Ganges and bathing in it, the efficacy of meditation on it and of its sight, etc.

[Ed. by J.B. Chaudhuri, Calcutta.]

Gautama-Dharmasūtra

Perhaps the oldest of the extant *dharmasūtras*. Consisting of 28 chapters, it deals with both civil and criminal law. The contents, like those of *smṛti* works in general, can be broadly divided as *Ācāra*, *Vyavahāra*, *Prāyaścitta* and *Rājadharma*.

It has a commentary by Kulamaṇi Śukla besides the two mentioned below. The work perhaps originated a century or two earlier than second century BC.

[Ed. by L. Srinivasacarya, with *Maskari-bhāṣya*, Mysore, 1917; Ānandāśrama edn., with Haradatta's *Mitākṣarā*, Poona, 1931. Eng. tr. by Bühler, *SBE*, II.]

Gṛhastha-Ratnākara

By Caṇḍeśvara. In 68 chapters (*taraṅgas*), it deals with duties of householders. Forms part of the author's *Smṛti-ratnākara* (q.v.).

[*Bib. Ind.*, 1928.]

Hāralatā

By Aniruddha. It deals with impurity (*aśauca*) consequent on birth, and with practices allowed and forbidden during the period of impurity.

[*Bib. Ind.*, 1909.]

Hārīta-Smṛti

From the quotations from Hārīta in *Dharmasūtras* of Āpastamba, Baudhāyana, etc., Hārīta appears to have been a *dharama-sūtrakāra*. Numerous prose passages on different topics of *smṛti* have been quoted in later *smṛti* digests. Numerous verses on *smṛti* topics are also found in different *smṛti* digests like the *Smṛti-candrikā* (III, p. 344) and such well-known commentaries as the *Mitākṣarā* and *Aparārka* on *YS*, I.86.

In the *smṛti* collection of Jīvānanda, there is a *Laghu-Hārīta-smṛti* (I, pp. 177-93), and a *Vṛhda-Hārīta-smṛti* (I., pp. 194-409), the former comprising about 250 verses in seven *adhyāyas*, and the latter about 2600 verses in eight chapters. The Ānandāśrama Collection of *smṛtis* contains a *Laghu-Hārīta-smṛti* in 117 verses; it is different from the above version. The Ānandāśrama Collection contains also a *Vṛddha-Hārīta-smṛti*, divided into eleven chapters, the first two of Jīvānanda's text being split up into five chapters.

Some observations of Hārīta are non-conventional. For example, he mentions eight forms of marriage, but in place of the conventional *Ārṣa* and *Prājāpatya* he reads *Kṣātra* and *Mānuṣa*. [See Vīrami]

Again, Hārīta mentions two kinds of women, viz., *Brahmavādinīs* and *Sadyovadhūs*; the former are stated to have been entitled to *Upanayana*, maintaining the sacred fire and to Vedic study.

Hemādri mentions, in *Caturvarga-cintāmaṇi* (III, 1, p. 559), a commentator of Hārītā. There is a commentary by Takanalāla.

[For a collection of prose passages on *smṛti* attributed to Hārīta, see S.C. Banerji, *Dharmasūtras*, pp. 257-89. Jolly collected (1889) most of the prose and verse citations from Hārīta on *Vyavahāra*. P.V. Kane states (*History of Dharamaśāstra*, vol. I (rev. edn.), pt. 1, p. 128) that V.S. Islampurkar discovered, at Nasik, a MS. of *Hārīta-dharamasūtra*.]

Kāla-Sāra

By Gadādhara. It deals with the periods of time suitable for various rites and observances.

[*Bib. Ind.*, 1900-04.]

Kāla-Viveka (AD 1092)

By Jīmūtavāhana. It deals with various matters relating to the suitability of seasons, months, *tithi*s, etc., for various rites and festivals; among the festivals are *Durgā-pūjā*, *Kojāgara*, etc.

[*Bib. Ind.* ed., with commentary, New Series 136, 1905.]

Karmānuṣṭhāna-Paddhati

By Bhavadeva Bhaṭṭa. Also called *Daśa-karma-paddhati*, *Saṃskāra-paddhati* or *Chandoga-paddhati*, it deals with the procedure of performing the various sacraments of the followers of the *Sāmaveda*.

[Ed. by S. Kaviratna, Calcutta, 1384 B.S.]

Karmavipāka

See *Śātātapa-smṛti*.

Karmopadeśinī

Same as *Brāhmaṇa-sarvasva* (q.v.).

Karmopadeśinī-Paddhati

Another name of the *Pitṛdayitā* (q.v.).

Kātyāyana-Smṛti-Sāroddhāra

It is a collection of 973 Kātyāyana verses quoted in later works, edited with Eng. tr. by P.V. Kane, published in 1933. 121 additional verses of Kātyāyana, culled from Varadarāja's *Vyavahāra-nirṇaya*, were published by R. Aiyangar in *Kane Festschrift* (pp. 7-17).

Kriyā-Kaumudī

By Govindānanda. It is mentioned in the *Āhnikatattva* of Raghunandana. An incomplete MS. of this work is preserved in Asiatic Society, Calcutta (No. IB 57).

Kṛtya-Cintāmaṇi

(1) By Caṇḍeśvara. It deals with astronomical matters relating to the performance of various religious ceremonies and *Saṃskāras*, the movements of Saturn, the sun's passage from one zodiac to another, etc.

(2) By Vācaspati Miśra. It deals with the festivals that are performed on different days in the year.

[For MSS. of *Kṛtya-cintāmaṇi* of Caṇḍeśvara, see *I.O.* Cat., VI, No. 1621, Calcutta Skt. College MS. No. Smṛti 107; Sarasvatībhavana Cat. III. No. 13475.]

The *K.C.* is mentioned, by the author, as his own work (*vide Gṛhastha-ratnākara*, folio 113a of Deccan College MS. No. 44 of 1883-84). Curiously enough, the printed text of the *G.R.*, has *Kṛtyaratnākara* for *Kṛtyacintāmaṇi*, p. 551.

Vācaspati's work published at Banaras, Śaka 1814. Partly published from Skt. Sāhitya Pariṣat, Calcutta, 1924.]

Kṛtyakalpataru

By Lakṣmīdhara. The *kāṇḍa*s or chapters, discovered hitherto, are:

I. Brahmacārī

II. Gṛhastha

III. Naiyatakāla (Āhnika)

IV. Śrāddha

V. Dāna

VI. Pratiṣṭhā

VII. Pūjā
VIII. Tīrtha
IX. Vrata
X. Śuddhi
XI. Rājadharma
XII. Vyavahāra
XIII. Śānti
XIV. Mokṣa

[GOS edns. *Dāna-kāṇḍa*, 1941; *Tīrtha-vivecana*, 1942; *Rājadharma*, 1943; *Mokṣa*, 1945, *Brahmacārī*, 1948; *Śrāddha*, 1950; *Naiyata-kāla*, 1950, *Śuddhi*, 1950; *Vyavahāra*, 1953-58; *Vrata*, 1953; *Pratiṣṭhā*, 1979; *Gṛhastha*, 1944.]

Kṛtya-Ratnākara

By Caṇḍeśvara. In 22 chapters (*taraṅgas*), it forms part of his *Smṛti-ratnākara*.

The topics discussed are: *Dharma*, *Vrata*, observance in intercalary month, *Saṃkrānti*, eclipse, new moon day, etc.

[*Bib. Ind.*, 1921-25.]

Kṛtya-Tattvārṇava

By Śrīnātha Ācārya-Cūḍāmaṇi. The title indicates the contents.

[Partly ed. by R.C. Hazra and published by Asiatic Society, Calcutta.]

Likhita-Smṛti

See under Likhita (Authors).

Madana-Pārijāta

Attributed to Madanapāla; actually supposed to have been composed by Viśveśvarabhaṭṭa. Consists of nine chapters (*stavakas*) on *Brahmacarya*, *Gārhasthya*, daily duties, *Saṃskāras*, impurity caused by birth and death, *Dravya-śuddhi*, *Śrāddha*, *Dāyabhāga* and *Prāyaścitta*.

[*Bib. Ind.*, 1887-93.]

Mānava-Dharmaśāstra

Same as *Manu-smṛti* (q.v.).

Manu-Bhāṣya

The earliest and highly authoritative commentary, by Medhātithi, on the *Manu-smṛti*.

[For eds. see under *Manu-smṛti*.]

Manu-Smṛti

Earliest and most authoritative metrical *smṛti* ascribed to Manu or his followers. Consists of 2,694 verses, divided into 12 chapters.

According to Bühler, followed by Kane, the extant *Manu-smṛti* was probably composed in the period between the second century BC and second century AD.

The contents can be broadly divided into the following heads: *Ācāra*, *Prāyaścitta*, *Vyavahāra* and *Rājadharma*.

The authority of Manu spread far beyond India, both in the east and the west.

[Ed. by G. Jha, with *Medhātithi-bhāṣya*, Eng. tr., explanatory and comparative notes, indices, etc., Asiatic Soc., Calcutta, Vol. I, 1932; Vol. II, 1939; J.L. Sastri, with Eng. Intro. by S.C. Banerji, Kullūka's commentary, Collection of verses attributed to Manu but missing in the present edn., index of verses, Delhi, 1975.

See *Manu-ṭīkā-saṃgraha*, ed. by Jolly, *Bib. Ind.*, 1885.

Derrett, J.D.M. (ed. and tr.): *Bhāruci's commentary on the Manusmṛti*, Wiesbaden, 1975.

Text with commentaries and Bengali tr.

Text, with intro., Bengali tr., notes, glossary, bibliography and *pāda-index* of verses (all in Bengali characters), by Sureśa Vandyopādhyāya, Calcutta.

Eng. tr. by Bühler, SBE, Vol. 25; by A.C. Burnell (ed. by Hopkins, London, 1884) and also by Strehly, Paris, 1893.

For various matters and problems, relating to Manu and the *Manu-smṛti*, see:

Agrawala, S. : *India as Described by Manu*, 1969.

Banerjee, N.N. : *Manu and Modern Times*, New Delhi, 1983.

Bhargava, D. : *Manu-smṛti, A Sociological Analysis.*

Bhattacharya, Parnasabari: *Conceptualisations in the Manu-smṛti.*

Das, B. : *The Science of Social Organisation or Laws of Manu*, Adyar, Madras, 1932-33.

Das, R.M. : *Women in Manu and his Seven Commentators.*

———: *Crime and Punishment in Ancient India with particular reference to Manusmṛti.*

Donigar, W. Smith, Briant : *The Laws of Manu*, Penguin Books, 1991.

Haughton, G.C. : *Mānava-dharmaśāstra or the Institutes of Hindu Laws of Manu*, Vols. I-IV.

Hopkins, E.W. : *Mutual Relations of the four castes according to Mānava-dharmaśāstra.*

Kane, P.V. : *History of Dharmaśāstra*, I, Poona, 1968.

Ketkar, S.V. : *History of Caste in India*, evidence of Laws of Manu during third century AD, New Delhi, 1988 (rpt.).

Laine, J.W. : On Creation Account, *ABORI*, LXII, 1951, p. 157.

Laszlo, F. : *Die parallel version der Manusmṛti in Bhaviṣya*

Purāṇa, Wiesbaden, 1971.

Paradkar, M.D. : *Similes in Manu-smṛti*.

Patwardhan, M.V. : *Manu-smṛti or the Ideal Democratic Republic of Manu*, 1968.

Sharma, R.N. : *Ancient India according to Manu*, Delhi, 1980.

Sternbach, L. : *Mānava Dharmaśāstra* (i-iii) and *Bhaviṣya Purāṇa*, Varanasi, 1974.

Tewari, C. : *Śūdras in Manu*, 1963.

Verma, P. : *Social Philosophy of the Mahābhārata and the Manu-smṛti*.

For influence of Manu abroad, see K. Motwani, *Manu Dharmaśāstra*, Madras, 1958; S.C. Banerji, *Sanskrit Beyond India*, pp. 15, 17, 21, 23, 26, 33, 34, 38, 40, 49, 51, 55, 71, 72, 85, 95, 112, 123, Calcutta, 1978.]

Manu-Ṭīkā

By Govindarāja.

[Ptd. by V.N. Mandlik and partly ed. by Jolly in *Manu-ṭīkā-saṃgraha*.]

Manvartha-Muktāvalī

Title of Kullūka's commentary on the *Manu-smṛti*. It combines the qualities of lucidity and brevity, and is very popular.

[Ed., with text of *Manu-smṛti*, by J.L. Sastri, Delhi, 1975. Published with *Manu-smṛti* several times. Also see Jolly, *Manu-ṭīkā-saṃgraha* under *Manu-smṛti* above.]

Mitākṣarā

(1) Title of Vijñāneśvara's commentary on the *Yājñavalkya-smṛti*. It is a sort of *smṛti* digest as it cites and discusses the views of different writers on *smṛti*. It was of paramount importance in

matters relating to adoption, inheritance and succession all over India excepting Bengal where Jīmūtavāhana's *Dāyabhāga* prevailed.

It recognises the birth-right of a son to the father's ancestral property.

There are many sub-commentaries on it, e.g., those of Viśveśvara and Bālambhaṭṭa.

[Ed., with *Yājñavalkya-smṛti*, by V.L.S. Pansikar, NSP, 1926 (3rd. edn.); S.S. Setlur, with sub-commentaries *Subodhinī* and *Bālambhaṭṭī*, Madras, 1912; Eng. tr. with *Dāyabhāga*, by H.T. Colebrooke, Calcutta, 1810; with the Eng. tr. of *Yājñavalkya-smṛti*, by J.R. Gharpure, 4 pts., Bombay, 1936-39.]

(2) It is the title also of Haradatta's commentary on *Gautama-dharmasūtra*.

(3) S.S. Svāmin's commentary, on Gauḍapāda's *Māṇḍūkya-kārikā*, has also this title.

Nārada-Smṛti

A highly authoritative work on ancient Indian law (*vyavahāra*).

According to Lariviere, it is "the juridical text par excellence, the best single summary of . . . Hindu legal system". He speaks of three extant recensions — the version called Vulgate by J. Jolly, a longer version and a third version, both shorter and older of which the other two are explanatory.

The third recension, presented by Lariviere, is divided into sections:

(1) *Mātṛkā* (prolegomena)

(2) *Vyavahāra-padāni* (titles of law — 18) and *Pariśiṣṭa* (Addenda — one chapter each on ordeals).

Most noteworthy features — while Manu is ambiguous about *Niyoga* (levirate marriage), Nārada clearly provides for it

(12/79-87). Manu condemns widow-remarriage; Nārada allows it (12/87-102), and also supports remarriage of women whose husbands turn out to be impotent (12/16/18) on the ground that a field should be given to one who has seed; one without seed is not entitled to a field (12/19).

Several classifications are unique:

(1) Three kinds of remarried women (*punarbhū*)—12/45-48.

(2) Four kinds of loose women (*svairiṇī*) — 12/49-52.

(3) Fourteen types of impotent men (*paṇḍaka*) — 12/11-18.

The work contains two remarkable rulings:

(1) Younger son may take over the father's position as the head of the household if the elder is deemed incompetent; it is competence that matters, but not the accident of birth (13/5).

(2) If a man has no son, his daughters may inherit, as they are just as much parts of his lineage, and should, therefore, take precedence over other close relatives (13/47-48).

The work is important for the social, cultural and legal history of India.

Besides the commentary by Asahāya, there is one by Ramānātha.

[Third recension ed. and tr. into Eng. by R.W. Lariviere; pt. 1 — text; pt. 2 — translation. Asahāya's commentary presented for the first time, Philadelphia, 1989. Vulgate version tr. by Jolly, 1876. Longer version ed. and tr. by Jolly, 1889. For details about different versions, see *HDS*, I, pt. 1, p. 467 ff and T.R. Chintāmaṇi, C.K. Raja Pres. Vol. pp. 154-96.]

Nirṇaya-Kamalākara

Same as *Nirṇaya-sindhu* (q.v.).

Nirṇaya-Sindhu (AD 1612)

Also called *Nirṇaya-kamalākara*, it is by Kamalākara.

Divided into three chapters (*paricchedas*). The main topics discussed are: proper time for various religious observances, *vratas*, *saṃskāras*, *sapiṇḍa* relationship, consecration of images, auspicious time for sowing operations, buying horses and cattle, etc., *śrāddha*, impurities caused by birth and death, rites after death, rites for *satī* and *saṃnyāsa*. It has at least four commentaries including the one by Kṛṣṇa Bhaṭṭa, which appears to have been most popular.

[NSP edn., Bombay, 1905, with Mārāṭhī tr. with commentary *Ratnamālā* of Kṛṣṇa Bhaṭṭa, Benares, 1919-20; with Hindī commentary, Lucknow, 1894; Eng. tr. *Complete Collection of Hīndu Law Books on Inheritance*, 1911. See *Anukramaṇikā*.]

Nirṇaya-Sindhu-Anukramaṇikā

See *Anukramaṇikā*.

Nṛsiṃha-Prasāda (AD 1490-1512)

By Dalapati. Divided into twelve sections, called *sāra* on *Saṃskāra*, *Āhnika*, *Śrāddha*, *Kāla*, *Vyavahāra*, *Prāyaścitta*, *Karmavipāka*, *Vrata*, *Dāna*, *Śānti*, *Tīrtha*, *Pratiṣṭhā*.

[The following parts have been published in Princess of Wales Sarasvatī Bhavana Texts Series, Varanasi; *Vyavahāra*, ed. by V. Tillu, 1934; *Prāyaścitta*, ed. by Sharma and Sharma, 1934. *Śrāddha*, ed. by V. Misra, 1934; *Tīrtha*, ed. by S. Sukla, 1936. A complete MS. of the work is in Benares Sanskrit College.]

Nyāya-Mātṛkā

Same as *Vyavahāra-mātṛkā* (q.v.).

Parāśara-Smṛti

Regarded as highly authoritative in *kali* Age. It is noteworthy that, on the authority of this work, Īśvar Candra Vidyāsāgar justified widow-remarriage. The verse concerned is —

naṣṭe mṛte pravrajite klīve'tha patite patau ।
pañcasvāpatsu nārīṇāṃ patiranyo vidhīyate ॥

It has the following well-known commentaries : by (1) Mādhavācārya (2) Govindabhaṭṭa, (3) Nandapaṇḍita (commentary called *Vidvanmanoharā*), (4) Vaidyanātha Pāyaguṇḍa, (5) Kāmeśvara Somayājin (commentaries called *Laghu-hitadharma* and *Guru-hitadharma*).

Parāśara-Mādhava

It is a noted commentary, by Mādhavācārya, on the *Parāśara-smṛti.* Besides these commentaries, there are some anonymous commentaries.

[See *NCC*, XI, pp. 212-14.]

Parāśara-Smṛti

The *Parāśara-smṛti* deals in 12 chapters, only with *ācāra* and *prāyaścitta*. The extant text is a recast. The text is summarised in the *Garuḍa Purāṇa*, chap. 107. The *Bṛhat* (or *Vṛddha*) *Parāśara-saṃhitā* (in Jīvānanda's Collection of smṛtis, pt. II, pp. 53-309, in 12 chapters is, perhaps, a recast by Suvrata, of *Parāśara-smṛti*.

Mādhavācārya's *Parāśara-mādhava* is a renowned commentary on it. Mādhava adds a discussion on *vyavahāra*, which forms about one-fourth of his exhaustive commentary; he has codified the few references to *vyavahāra* in the *Parāśara-smṛti*.

[*Bib. Ind.*, ed. with Mādhava's commentary, 1883-99; with same commentary, by V.S. Islampurkar, vols. I, II, *BSS*, 1893-1911. Eng. tr. *Bib. Ind.*, 1887. Translations in Bengali, Gujarātī, Hindī, Kannaḍa, Oriyā, Tāmil and Telugu have also been published.]

Pitṛdayitā

By Aniruddha, it is for the followers of the *Sāmaveda*. It deals with daily duties, gifts, *śrāddhas*, and rites to be performed at the time of death and during the period of mourning. Also called *Karmopadeśinī-paddhati*.

[Pub. in Calcutta Skt. Sāhitya Pariṣad Series, No. 6, Calcutta.]

Prāyaścitta-Prakaraṇa (or -Nirūpaṇa)

By Bhavadeva Bhaṭṭa. It deals with various sins and the modes of expiation.

[Published from Varendra Res. Soc., Rajshahi (now in Bangladesh), 1927.]

Prāyaścitta-viveka

By Śūlapāṇi. In it, the author defines *prāyaścitta*, defines and prescribes different modes of atonement.

[Ed. by J. Vidyasagara, Calcutta, 1893.]

Pūjā-Ratnākara

Forming a part of Caṇḍeśvara's *Smṛti-ratnākara* (q.v.), it deals with the worship of various gods and goddesses according to Tāntric rules.

[Mitra, *Notices*, VII, no. 2398].

Rājanīti-Ratnākara

By Caṇḍeśvara. In 16 chapters (*taraṅgas*), written at the command of King Bhaveśa of Mithilā, it deals with the usual topics of *Arthaśāstra* and the *Rājadharma* of *dharmaśāstra*.

[Ed. by K.P. Jayaswal, Patna, 1924.]

Rāsayātrā-viveka

By Śūlapāṇi.

[Ed., with intro., by S.C. Banerji, *Saṃskṛta Sāhitya Pariṣat Patrikā*, Calcutta, 1941.]

Sambandha-Cintāmaṇi

By Vācaspati Miśra. It deals with persons eligible for marriage.

[Ed., with Intro. and index, *IHQ*, XXXII, 1956.]

Sambandha-Viveka

(1) By Bhavadeva. It discusses the persons eligible for marriage.

[Ed. by S.C. Banerji, with Intro., Eng. tr. and Index of verses, *NIA*, VI, Aug.-Sept., 1943 and Jan.-Feb., 1944.]

(2) By Śūlapāni.

[Ed. by J.B. Chaudhuri, Calcutta, 1942.]

Śaṃkha-Likhita-Dharmasūtra

See under Likhita (Authors).

Śaṃkha-Smṛti

A *Śaṃkha-smṛti* in 18 chapters and about 330 verses contained in Jīvānanda's Collection of Smṛtis, pt. II, pp. 343-74. The same text is contained also in the Ānandāśrama collection of Smṛtis. The latter also contain a *Laghu-Śaṃkha-smṛti* in 71 verses and a *Śaṃkha-Likhita-Smṛti* in 32 verses.

Saṃskāra-Paddhati

Same as *Karmānuṣṭhāna-paddhati* (q.v.).

Saṃvarta-Smṛti

There is a work of this title in Jīvānanda's Collection of Smṛtis (I) as well as in the Ānandāśrama Collection; the former containing 227 and the latter 230 verses. It deals with the usual topics of *smṛti*.

It is noteworthy that, according to Saṃvarta, the king

should start a case *suo motu* against persons committing the following offences: restraint of the defendant (before judgment), obstruction of a public road, conception of a woman resulting from adultery, accumulation of wealth without any ostensible means, destruction of meeting hall and of trees and crops, abduction of a maiden, commission of sin by a Brāhmaṇa, champerty, destruction of roads where tolls are to be paid, apprehension of robbery, rape, injury to cow or Brāhmaṇa.

A *Bṛhat-Saṃvarta* and a *Svalpa-saṃvarta* are known from quotations.

Sarasvatī-Vilāsa

By Pratāparudradeva. It consists of two parts, the *Vyavahārakāṇḍa* and the *Ācārakāṇḍa*. The former is regarded as highly authoritative in south India on matters of Hindu Law; the *Mitākṣarā* of Vijñāneśvara is, however, of paramount authority.

[*Dāyabhāga* portion of *Vyavahārakāṇḍa* pub., with Eng. tr., by Rev. T. Foulkes in 1881. Entire *Vyavahāra-kāṇḍa* pub. in Mysore Govt. Pub. Ser. On authorship of *Sarasvatī-vilāsa*, see P.K. Gode, *Studies in Indian Literary History*, I, p. 423 ff.]

Śātātapa-Smṛti

In Jīvānanda's Collection of Smṛtis, a *smṛti* of Śātātapa is entitled *Karma-vipāka*. It is in six chapters and about 231 verses. There is nothing striking about its contents. According to Kane, it is a late work.

The Ānandāśrama Collection of Smṛtis contains a *Vṛddha-Śātātapa-smṛti* in 68 verses; two prose passages also occur.

For collection of prose passages attributed to Śātātapa, see S.C. Banerji, *Dharmasūtras*, p. 325 ff.

Smṛti-Candrikā

By Devaṇabhaṭṭa. It deals with *Saṃskāra*, *Āhnika*, *Vyavahāra*, *Śrāddha* and *Aśauca*.

According to judicial decisions, it was of great authority in south India.

[Ed. by J.R. Gharpure (up to *Śrāddha*), Bombay; Mysore Govt. Oriental Ser. (up to *Aśauca*), 1914-21 (5 vols.) *Dāyabhāga* portion tr. into Eng. by T.K. Iyer, Madras, 1867. For authority in south India, see, for example, 11 Moo. 1.A. p. 487, 2 Mad. H.C.R., p. 206, at p. 209 I.L.R. 3 Mad. 290 (P.C.) at p. 302, etc.].

Smṛti-Cintāmaṇi

A digest by Haridāsa Siddhāntavāgīśa. It deals with the religious observances as well as the daily duties of the Hindus from birth to death. The Sanskrit text has also been translated into Bengali.

[First published at Nakipur (in Khulna district of Bengal), 1319 B.S. It ran into the fourth edition.]

Smṛti-Kaumudī

(1) By Devanātha Ṭhakkura. It is a digest on *Cāturvarṇya*, *Ācāra*, *Āhnika*, *Saṃskāra*, *Śrāddha*, *Āśauca*, *Dāyabhāga*, *Vrata*, *Dāna* and *Utsarga*.

[For MS., see *NCC*, IX, p. 111.]

(2) By Madanapāla. It is also called *Śūdra-dharmotpala-dyotinī*; this title indicates the contents of the work. It is divided into four chapters, called *Kalollāsa*s, each *Kalollāsa* being sub-divided into *kiraṇas*. The work has 17 introductory verses of which 13 give the genealogy of Madanapāla. Verse 14 sets forth the titles of the works of Madanapāla including the *Pārijāta*; verse 15 clearly states that he got the work composed by the learned.

[For MSS., see Aufrecht's *Oxford Cat.*, p. 275 b, *I.O. Cat.*, p. 524, No. 1649 and Deccan College MS. No. 51 of 1872-73.]

Smṛti-Kaustubha

By Anantadeva II. It is divided into several parts, called *Kaustubhas* dealing with *Saṃskāra, Ācāra, Rājadjarma, Dāna, Utsarga, Pratiṣṭhā, Tithi* and *Saṃvatsara*; each *Kaustubha* is sub-divided into sections, called *Dīdhitis*. The *Saṃskāra-kaustubha* was recognised as authoritative all over India by the then Privy Council and High Court of Bombay. It deals with *Saṃskāras* from *Garbhādhāna* to *Vivāha*.

[NS Press edn., 1909. *Saṃskāra-kaustubha*, NSP edn., 1913; also published at Baroda (1914) Mārāṭhī tr. *vide Collector of Madura* vs. *Mootooramalinga* 12 Moo. 1A 397, p. 438; *Sukharam* vs. *Sitabai*, ILR 3 Bom. 353, p. 361.]

Smṛtimañjarī

By Govindarāja. For references to it, see under Govindarāja.

H.P. Sastri gives, in *Des. Cat. of MSS. in Asiatic Society*, Calcutta, Vol. III, pp. 51-54, No. 1924, a description of the *Smṛti-mañjarī* on *Ācāra* and *Prāyaścitta*.

[There is a MS. of this work also in India Office.]

Smṛti-Ratna-Hāra

By Bṛhaspati Rāyamukuṭa. The main topics of discussion are : Determination of time appropriate for different *vratas* and *pūjās* (including *Jagaddhātrī-pūjā*, *Aśauca* caused by birth and death, *Śrāddha*, etc.

[See *Des. Cat. of MSS. of Asiatic Soc.*, Calcutta, Vol. III, No. 2138 incomplete.]

Smṛti-Ratnākara

By Caṇḍeśvara. Consists of seven sections: *Kṛtya* (dealing with *vratas* and other observances in different periods), *Dāna, Vyavahāra* (judicial proceeding), *Śuddhi* (*aśauca* and means of purification), *Pūjā*, *Vivāda* (dealing with subjects of dispute and civil and criminal law), *Gṛhastha* (proper conduct of householders).

[For eds. and MSS., see under respective parts.]

Smṛti-Sāra

Also called *Smṛti-sāra-samuccaya*. By Harinātha. It covers the entire field of *smṛti*, including *vyavahāra*.

[For MSS., see *10 Cat.*, pp. 448, 1488 and 449, No. 1489; Mitra, *Notices*, V, p. 232, No. 1913.]

Smṛti-Sāra-Samuccaya

Same as *Smṛti-sāra* (q.v.).

Smṛti-Tattva

By Raghunandana. It comprises the following 28 tracts the titles of which end in *-tattva*: *Āhnika*, *Chandoga-vṛṣotsarga*, *Dāya*, *Deva-pratiṣṭhā*, *Dīkṣā*, *Divya*, *Durgotsava*, *Ekādaśī*, *Janmāṣṭamī*, *Jyotiṣa*, *Kṛtya*, *Malimluca*, *Maṭhapratiṣṭhā*, *Puruṣottama-kṣetra*, *Prāyaścitta*, *Ṛgvṛṣotsarga*, *Saṃskāra*, *Sāma-śrāddha*, *Śūdra-kṛtya*, *Śuddhi*, *Taḍāga-bhavanotsarga*, *Tithi*, *Udvāha*, *Vāstuyāga*, *Vrata*, *Vyavahāra*, *Yajur-vṛṣotsarga*, *Yajus-śrāddha*.

[Ed. by J. Vidyasagar, Calcutta, in two vols. 1347. B.S. (new edn.); S. Vidyabhusan (in Bengali characters), Calcutta, 1347 B.S. (new edn.). *Divyatattva*, ed. by R.W. Lariviere, New Delhi. See B. Bhattacharya, *Raghunandana's Indebtedness to his Predecessors*, Calcutta, 1995.]

The following papers are useful:

R. C. Hazra, "Works and Time of Raghunandana", *Bhāratīya Vidyā*, XI, pt. 2. 1950, pp. 178-82.

B. Bhattacharya, "Devotional Element in Raghunandana's Works", *Siddhabhāratī*, pt. 1, pp. 225-29, Hoshiarpur, 1950.

Kāśīrāma Vācaspati Bhattacharya is the best known commentator of Raghunandana's *Tattvas*. See Kāśīrāma under Authors.]

Śrāddha Kriyā-Kaumudī

By Govindānanda,

[*Bib. Ind.*, 1904.]

Śrāddha-Sāgara

Attributed to Kullūkabhaṭṭa.

[See S.G. Moghe, *Śrāddha-sāgara of Kullūkabhaṭṭa*, with a critical exposition and intro., New Delhi, 1994. Also see our observations on Kullūkabhaṭṭa under Authors.]

Śrāddha-Viveka

(1) By Śūlapāṇi.

[Ed. by C. Smṛtibhūṣaṇa, Calcutta, 1314 B.S.]

(2) By Rudradhara.

[Ṗtd. at Benares, 1936-37.]

Śuddhi-Kaumudī

By Govindānanda. It deals with the means of purification from *aśauca*, caused by birth and death.

[*Bib. Ind.*, 1905.]

Śuddhi-Ratnākara

By Caṇḍeśvara. Consisting of 34 chapters (*taraṅgas*), it forms a part of the author's *Smṛti-ratnākara*, and deals with various means of purification.

[For MSS., see *10 Cat.*, III. No. 1389; Mitra, *Notices*, VII, No. 2384; *Des. Cat. of MSS. in Asiatic Soc.*, Sastri, III, No. G 3826; *Mithilā MSS. Cat.* I, No. 331 A.]

Tīrtha-Cintāmaṇi

By Vācaspati Miśra. Divided into five chapters (*prakāśas*), viz., *Prayāga, Puruṣottama, Gaṅgā, Gayā, Vārāṇasī.*

It deals with such topics as purpose of pilgrimage, preliminaries of pilgrimage, rites to be performed at various *tīrthas*, etc.

[*Bib. Ind.*, 1910-12.]

Tithi-Nirṇaya

By Vācaspati Miśra. It discusses the different *tithis*, both *śuddhā* (pure) and *viddhā* (mixed), and the various rites to be performed in them.

Some doubt the authorship of Vācaspati.

[See Mitra, *Notices*, V, No. 1839.]

Tithi-Viveka

By Śūlapāṇi.

[Ed., with Intro., by S.C. Banerji, *P.O.*, Oct., 1941 and Jan. 1942.]

Tristhalīsetu (Śaka 1540 = AD 1618)

Composed at Agastyapurī by Nārāyaṇabhaṭṭa. In three *prakaraṇas*, it deals with pilgrimage at Prayāga, Kāśī and Gayā which together are called *Tristhalī*.

[Published by Ānadāśrama 78.]

Uddhāra-Candrikā

A *smṛti* digest by Kāśīcandra Vidyāratna.

[Ptd. at Calcutta, 1321 B.S. See *ABORI*, XI, p. 256.]

Udvāha-Candrāloka

By Candrakānta Tarkālaṃkāra. It deals with matters connected with marriage.

Regarding the author's originality, see remarks under the name of the author.

[Published, Calcutta, 1897.]

Varṣa-Kriyā-Kaumudī

By Govindānanda. It deals with rites to be performed in the course of a year.

[*Bib. Ind.*, 1902.]

Vasiṣṭha-Dharmasūtra (or -Dharmaśāstra)

Consisting of 30 chapters, it discusses the usual *smṛti* topics, but not *Rājadharma*.

It has a commentary called *Vidvanmodinī* by Kṛṣṇa-paṇḍita Dharmādhikārin.

Probably originated in the first century of the Christian era.

[Ed. by K. Dharmadhikarin, with *Vidvanmodinī* commentary, Benares, Śaka 1781. Eng. tr. by Bühler, *SBE*, XIV.]

A *Vasiṣṭha-Smṛti,* in 10 *adhyāyas* and about 1100 verses appearing to be meant for *Vaiṣṇavas*, is available in two MSS. —(i) *I.O.Cat.* III, p. 392, No. 1339; (ii) Baroda O.I. MS. No. 1885 (*Śaka* 1564).

Vīramitrodaya

By Mitra Miśra. An authoritative and extensive commentary on the *Yājñavalkya-smṛti*.

It is also the title of the author's *smṛti* digest. The latter is divided into the following *prakāśas* (chapters): *Paribhāṣā*, *Saṃskāra*, *Āhnika*, *Pūjā*, *Lakṣaṇa*, *Rājanīti*, *Tīrtha*, *Vyavahāra*, *Śrāddha*, *Samaya*, *Bhakti* and *Śuddhi*.

[Comm., with original and *Mitākṣarā*, ed. by N. Sastri, CSS, 1930. Eng. tr. with tr. of *Yājñavalkya-smṛti* and two other commentaries on it, by J.R. Gharpure, 4 pts., Bombay, 1936-39.

The *smṛti* has been published in *CSS*.]

Viruddha-Vidhi-Vidhvaṃsa

By Lakṣmīdhara. It deals with the disputed points of secular law, such as the persons entitled to perform *śrāddha* to the deceased, *Śūdra-prāyaścitta*, etc.

[For MS., see *I.O.Cat.*, p. 489, No. 1577; MS. dated Saṃvat 1582 = AD 1526.]

Viṣṇu-Dharmasūtra (or -Smṛti)

It discusses the usual *smṛti* topics including *vyavahāra* and *Rājadharma*.

Nandapaṇḍita's *Vaijayantī* is the only commentary on it. Perhaps, one Bhāruci also commented on it.

It is a very late work, perhaps the latest among the works of this class.

[Ed. with *Vaijayantī* commentary by V. Krishnamacharya, Adyar, 1964. Eng. tr. by Jolly, *SBE*, VII.]

A *Laghu-Viṣṇusmṛti*, in five chapters and 114 verses, occurs in the Ānandāśrama Collection of Smṛtis. Verses from *Laghu-Viṣṇu* and *Vṛddha-Viṣṇu* are quoted in some well-known commentaries like the *Mitākṣarā*, *Aparārka*, *Parāśara-mādhavīya*.

Vivāda-Bhaṅgārṇava

Compiled in 1792, at the instance of William Jones, by Jagannātha Tarkapañcānana who is different from Jagannātha, author of the *Rasa-gaṅgādhara*. Compiled in nine sections, it was designed to facilitate the perception of Hindu Law by British Judges. The portions of the work, on succession and contract, were translated into English by H.T. Colebrooke in AD 1796; the translation is known as *Colebrooke*'s *Digest*.

[Eng. tr., in four vols., by H.T. Colebrooke, Calcutta, 1797-98.]

Vivāda-Candra

By Misaru Miśra.

[MS. Deccan College No. 57 of 1883-84.].

Vivāda-Ratnākara

By Caṇḍeśvara Ṭhakkura. The title indicates the contents. It is in hundred sections, called *taraṅgas*.

[Ptd. in *Bib. Ind.*, 103.]

Vivādārṇava-Setu

Compiled by Bāṇeśvara Vidyālaṃkāra, along with ten other scholars, at the instance of Warren Hastings, for the settlement, by British Judges, of disputes arising in connexion with Hindu Law.

Divided into 21 chapters (*ūrmīs*); the total number of verses is 1632.

[Published by Veṅkaṭeśvara Press, Bombay. First tr. into Persian and thence to English by Halhed under the title: *A Code of Gentoo Law*, London, 1776.]

Vivāda-Sārārṇava

Compiled by Sarvaru-Śarmā Trivedin. It deals with disputes and their settlement. It is in nine sections, called *taraṅgas*.

[See *Cat. of Madras Govt. MSS.*, vol. VI, p. 2467, No. 3203.]

Vivāha-Tattvārṇava

By Śrīnātha Ācārya-Cūḍāmaṇi.

[Ed. with Intro., verse-index etc., by S.C. Banerji, *ABORI*, Poona, 1951.]

Vrata-Kāla-Viveka

By Śūlapāṇi.

[Ed. with Intro., by S.C. Banerji, *IHQ*, XVII, 1941.]

Vyāsa-Smṛti

It occurs in the collection of *smṛtis*, both in Jīvānanda (Pt. II) and in the Ānandāśrama edn. Excepting a few variations, the two texts are the same. It contains four chapters and about 250 verses. The main contents are rules about mixed castes, sixteen *saṃskāras*, duties of a *brahmacārin*, marriage, duties of householder, eulogy of *gārhasthya* and gifts. It has a commentary by Kṛṣṇanātha.

[See the Collection of 268 verses of Vyāsa on judicial procedure and substantive Law, by B.K. Ghosh, in *Indian Culture*, vol. IX, pp. 65-98.]

Vyavahāra-Cintāmaṇi

By Vācaspati Miśra. It deals with judicial procedure.

[Ed. with Eng. tr., annotations, intro., etc. by L. Rocher, Gent, 1956.]

Vyavahāra-Mātṛkā or Nyāya-Mātṛkā

By Jīmūtavāhana. It is on judicial proceeding which consists of four parts (*pādas*), viz.

Bhāṣā — plaint,

Kriyā — proof, evidence,

Uttara — reply,

Nirṇaya — decision, judgment.

[Ed. by Asutosh Mukherji, Asiatic Society, Calcutta.]

Vyavahāra-Mayūkha

By Nīlakaṇṭha. It is of paramount authority on matters of Hindu Law according to decisions of Bombay High Court, in Gujarat, Bombay and northern Koṅkaṇa.

[Published by BORI, Poona, 1926. Eng. tr. with notes and refs. to decided cases, by P.V. Kane.]

Vyavahāra-Ratnākara

By Caṇḍeśvara. It forms a part of the author's *Smṛti-ratnākara*, and deals with civil and criminal law.

[See Mitra, *Notices*, VI, No. 2036.]

Yājñavalkya-Smṛti

Consisting of a little over 1000 verses, it is divided into three chapters, *Ācāra*, *Vyavahāra* and *Prāyaścitta*. Each chapter is sub-divided into several sections, called *prakaraṇas*. Curiously enough, *Rājadharma-prakaraṇa* is the thirteenth and the last section of *Ācārādhyāya*.

[Ed. with *Mitākṣarā* commentary, NSP, 1926 (3rd edn.); with *Bālakrīḍā* commentary, TSS, with *Aparārka* commentary, *ASS*, with *Mitākṣarā* and *Vīramitrodaya*., CSS, with *Dīpakalikā* commentary by J.R. Gharpure, Bombay, 1939. Eng. tr. of *Mitākṣarā*, *Vīramitrodaya* and *Dīpakalikā* commentaries by J.R. Gharpure, in 4 pts., Bombay, 1936-39. See R.C. Hazra : Yājñavalkya's attitude to Arthaśāstra as an authority in judicial administration", *Our Heritage*, XII, pp. 19-31; Manjushree : *The Position of Women in the Y.S.*, Delhi, 1990; S.C. Banerji: *Principles of Hindu Jurisprudence*, in 2 pts., Delhi, 1992.]

Yama-Smṛti

In Jīvānanda's Collection of Smṛtis (pt.1), there is a *Yama-smṛti* in 78 verses on *prāyaścitta* and *śuddhi*. The work of the same title in the Ānandāśrama Collection contains 99 verses on *prāyaścitta*, *śrāddha* and *śuddhi*. There is considerable divergence in the two versions. The latter collections contains also a *Bṛhad-Yama-smṛti* which is divided into five chapters and 182 verses. It deals with *prāyaścitta, śuddhi*, *śrāddha*, partition of property and some matters relating to medical procedure. Verses from Yama and Bṛhad-Yama have been quoted in several *smṛti* digests and commentaries.

5

Aspects of Society in Ancient and Medieval India

Reflected in Smṛti-Śāstra

As we have stated, in the Preface, the *smṛti* works are indispensable for the study of the society in ancient and medieval India. The present is the child of the past. The thoughtful people of India, who are neither obscurantist nor iconoclastic, but try to follow the Buddhist ideal of *madhyama panthā* (middle course), are intent on social reforms. Radhakrishnan rightly said — India is wailing for a new *smṛti*.

Reform does not necessarily mean rejection. It means such changes as are called for in a progressive society in consonance with the needs of the hour. So, a conscientious reformer has to consider the genesis of a particular custom not only as it prevails at present, but as it was ordained by the old scriptures. The prospective reformer has to know the ethos of the people of ancient times as well as the ambience in which customs and practices originated. Some important social practices, obtaining now, have lost their original significance and forms, sometimes influenced by superstitions and covetousness of the sacerdotal class. For example, let us consider *upanayana*. It has become a mockery of the original institution. It means the taking of a boy of a certain age to *guru-gṛha*. There he has to undergo a rigorous training in study and habits in a manner that he may become a complete man capable of facing life. The duration of residence in *guru-gṛha* was usually twelve long years. This has been reduced, in many cases, to three nights or one night. Sometimes, no such practice is observed. The ceremony is brief, and the boy concerned expects and gets presents. The ceremony being over, the boy has no connexion with the so-called *ācārya*, and casts to the four winds all that has been sought to be inculcated into him through Sanskrit *mantras* which are Greek to him.

Take the case of *srāddha*. On such an occasion, the priest grenerally gives a long list of articles required for the rites. If objection is raised, the common argument of the priest is that *vitta-sāṭhya* (deceitful economy) is sinful so that the performer must spend as much as he can. In some cases, it is pleaded that the degree of *puṇya* and satisfaction of the manes depend on the number of Brāhmaṇas sumptuously fed. But, *Manu* (III.125) provides for the feeding of only three Brāhmanas in *pitṛ-kārya*, and clearly prohibits the feeding of many Brāhmaṇas even if the performer of the *śrāddha* is very rich (*susamṛddho'pi na prasajjeta vistare*). We have seen that, in some rural areas, the performer of a *srāddha* has to sell off a portion of his property to mitigate the intransigence of the priest.

Here we shall have a brief look at some of the social customs as they are preached in the *smṛti-śāstra* and not as they prevail in the modern society. We shall dwell on the following subjects only: Position of Women, Polygamy, Widow-remarriage, Divorce, *Satīdāha*, Prostitution, Sūdra and other So-called Low-class People, Slavery, Untouchability, Euthanasia, Democratic and Socialistic Trends in *Manu-smṛti*, Basic Juridical Principles, *Rājadharma*.

Position of Women

One of the iconoclastic tendencies in the present times is to categorically brand *smrti-sāstra* as misogynic. We shall try to make an assessment of the position of women in the light of mainly the works of Manu and Yājñavalkya.

Manu declares (IX.3) that a woman is protected by her father in girlhood, by her husband in youth, and by her son in old age; a woman does not deserve independence (in any stage of life). The same idea is expressed in V.148. Again, he ordains (V.155) that no separate sacrifice, no *vrata* nor fast is prescribed for a woman; by her service to the husband she is honoured in heaven. Kullūka explains that a woman can participate in a sacrifice with her husband; she can perform *vrata*s and fast only with the permission of her husband. From IX.18, it is learnt that a woman has no *saṃskāra* (viz. *upanayana*, etc.), with the recital of Vedic *mantras*; women are *anṛta* or falsehood incarnate (*anṛtavad asubhāḥ*—Kullūka). II.67 lays down that the marriage of a woman is her Vedic sacrament; for her the service of the husband is equivalent to residence in *guru-gṛha,* and domestic duties correspond to the tending of fire. IX.17 holds that Manu (at the time of creation) provided bed, seat, ornament, passion, crookedness, animosity and ugly conduct for women. It is observed (IV.15) that women, even though carefully guarded, habitually and, for lack of affection and fickleness of nature, betray their husbands (IX.15). A woman should serve her husband when alive, and should not disregard him when dead (i.e., by non-performance of obsequial rites). The climax of a woman's servitude is found in V.154 in which a chaste woman is required always to serve her husband like God even if he is *viśīla* (of evil conduct), *kāmavṛtta* (attached to some other woman — Kullūka), *guṇaih parivarjita* (devoid of learning and other good qualities).

The discrimination against women is discernible even in law, civil and criminal. According to *Yājñavalkya* (II.70), Nārada (*Ṛṇādāna*, 178, 190, 191), a woman is unfit to be a witness in a court of law. But, *Manu,* VIII.68, 70, *Yājñavalkya* II.72 and Nārada, *Rnādāna* 155, allow women to be witnesses in disputes between women and in cases where no other witness is available or in the cases of theft, adultery and other offences in which there is an element of force. According to *Yājñavalkya*, II.31, a transaction with women is not valid.

A woman does not inherit the property either of her husband or of her father. Yājñavalkya provides that when a man divides the property equally among his sons, then his wives also shall share euqally with them. But, if a wife has exclusive property (*strīdhana*) obtained from her husband or father-in-law, she will get a half share only. The same rule applies when the sons make a partition after the death of their father. Of a man, dying childless, the property devolves upon his wife; her claim has the priority. It should be noted that ordinarily a daughter has no claim to paternal property.

As regards succession to *strīdhana*, however, the daughter has preference over all others.

In the matter of adoption, a woman has no right to adopt except with the permission of her husband.

In some cases, a woman even of a higher caste is equated with a śūdra. For example, a woman should get *homa* in *vrata* performed through a Brāhmaṇa (*vide Nirṇayasindhu*, III, *Pūrvārdha*, p. 249). Like Śūdras, women, irrespective of caste, were debarred from reciting Vedic *mantras*. The same penance is prescribed for a killer of Śūdra and that of a woman (*Baudhāyana-dharmasūtra*, II.1.11-12; *Parāśara* VI.16.)

According to Atri (136-37), the following practices of a woman make her a sinner:

> *japa*, *tapas* (austerity), *pravrajyā* (asceticism), pilgrimage, attempt at acquisition of miraculous power by reciting spells, sole devotion to the worship of a goddess.

In this respect, she stands on an equal footing with a Śūdra who is also debarred from these practices.

In *Manu*, II. 213-14, women, as a class, have been condemned as leading even wise people astray.

The picture of women, depicted in *smṛti*, is not wholly sordid. It has also many good words to say about them.

Manu declares (II.145) that, in point of honour, mother exceeds a thousand fathers. He holds (III.56) — gods are pleased at a place where women are honoured; where women are not honoured, all rites (*Yāgādikriyāḥ* — Kullūka) become futile. The family, in which ladies become sorrowful, soon perishes; that, in which they are not so, always prospers (III.57). So, one, desiring welfare, should always honour them with ornaments, clothes and feast in festivals (III.59).

Even in some serious cases, a liberal attitude to women is noticeable in some works. For example, if a woman is raped, she is not to be forsaken; she will remain impure till her next menstruation (Atri, 197-98). Devala (48-49) perscribes means of purification for a woman conceiving as a result of raping by a *mleccha*.

Āpastamba (I.10.28.19) condemns the abandonment of a faultless wife; the husband who abandons such a wife should be put on ass-skin with hairs outside and beg for alms at seven houses for six months. Nārada (*Strīpuṃsa,* V.95) provides for punishment to be inflicted on the husband who abandons the wife who does not deserve such treatment.

According to the *MS*, II.138, one (of any caste) should leave the road for a woman (to whichever class she may belong).

SATĪ-DĀHA (BURNING OF WIDOWS)

Smṛti-śāstra is rooted in the Vedic literature. So, we shall see what the predecessors of *smṛti* writers have to say on this subject.

The *Taittirīya Saṃhitā* (*Aukhya śākhā*), as quoted in the *Nārāyaṇopaniṣad* (*Anuvāka* 84) (*vide* H.H. Wilson's Works, II, pp. 293-305; P.V. Kane, *History of Dharmaśāstra*, II, pt. 1, p. 625, fn.) says —

agne . . . . patnyānugama-vratam̄ cariṣyāmi . . . .

naya mā patyuragre ।

P.V. Kane, however, doubts the authenticity of the above text (*vide History of Dharmaśāstra*, II, p. 625, fn. 1462).

No *Gṛhyasūtra* refers to this practice.

Among the *dharmasūtras*, only the *Viṣṇu-dharmasūtra* (25.14) declares — *mṛte bhartari brahmacaryam̄ tadanvārohaṇam̄ vā*; the husband being dead, the wife will either lead a life of continence or mount the funeral pyre of the husband.

The *Manu-smrti*, which is the most authoritative among the *dharmaśāstras*, and is believed, by P.V. Kane, to have originated and evolved between 200 BC and AD 200, is absolutely silent about *satī-dāha*.

From quotations from such ancient *smṛtikāras* as Paiṭhīnasi, Aṅgiras, etc., contained in the *Aparārka* commentary (*c*. twelfth century) on the *Yājñavalkya-smrti* (*c*. first two centuries AD or sometime earlier), we learn that this custom was prohibited for Brāhmaṇas. For example, Aṅgiras holds —

mṛtānugamanam̄ nāsti brāhmaṇyāḥ . . . . itareṣām̄ strīdharmo'yam̄ paraḥ smṛtaḥ ।

Thus, he clearly forbids the practice for Brāhmana women, but regards it as the best religious act for other women. Aṅgiras emphatically asserts that widows (obviously of non-Brāhmana castes) have no other *dharma* than *agni-prapatana* (falling into the fire of their husband's funeral pyres).

The later writers of *smrti* digests explain such injunctions in this way. A Brāhmana woman must not embrace death except in the funeral pyre of her husband; she cannot do so anywhere else. Thus, if she learns of her husband's death in another country, she is not allowed to consign her body to fire. Uśanas also clearly declares that a Brāhmana widow shall not take recourse to the practice anywhere except in the funeral pyre of her husband.

According to the *Vedavyāsa-smṛti* (11.53), the said widow will court death by embracing the corpse of her husband. But, if she chooses to live as a widow, she will have to abjure hair-dressing, etc.; she shall practise physical mortification by austerities.

Among the ancient *smṛti* writers, Śamkha and Aṅgiras praise *satī-dāha* as conducive to infinite *puṇya*. According to Hārīta, a woman, who follows her husband to death, sanctifies the families of her father, mother and husband.

Some old commentators of *Smṛti-śāstra* oppose this custom. Medhātithi (*c.* ninth century), in commenting on the *Manusmṛti*, compares this practice with the much maligned *Syena-yāga*, a kind of sacrifice designed to cause harm to others. On *Manu,* V.156, he says that, though Aṅgiras has approved this practice, yet it is, in reality, suicide and is forbidden. This practice has been contemptuously characterised as *adhama* (worst) and *aśāstrīya* (unapproved by scriptures). He further holds that this practice runs counter to the Vedic injunction *tasmāduha na purāyusah preyāt* — one should not go to the other world before the longevity (fixed for him).

Vijñāneśvara (*c.* eleventh-twelfth centuries), in his commentary on the *Yājñavalkya-smṛti*, I.86, has supported *satī-dāha* after refuting the arguments of the opponents. In his opinion, the widows of men of all classes, from Brāhmanas to Cāndālas, should court death. He says that the comparison of this practice with *Śyena-yāga* is not proper. While the latter is intended to cause mischief to others, the result of the former is access to heaven.

In some important later *smrti* digests, e.g. *Madana-pārijāta* (p. 199), *Parāsara-mādhavīya* (II, pt. 1, pp. 55-56), etc., this practice has been supported.

The famous *smṛti* digest-writer, Devaṇabhaṭṭa (*c*. twelfth-thirteenth centuries) does not agree with the supporters of *satī-dāha*. He avers, in the *Vyavahāra* portion of his renowned *Smṛti-candrikā*, that, for a widow to lead a life of continence is far more beneficial and conducive to *puṇya* than burning herself in the aforesaid manner.

According to a quotation from the *Nāradīya Purāṇa* in the *Parāśara-mādhavīya* (II.1, p. 58), for a widow, who is *bālāpatya* (having infants) or is in the family way, *satī-dāha* is prohibited.

About this practice the views of Raghunandana (sixteenth century), the master-writer of Bengal on *smṛti,* are as follows. Subject to the above proviso of the *Nāradīya Purāṇa*, he lays down the procedure of the *satī-dāha* in his *Śuddhi-tattva*. There is no *dharma* other than *agniprapatana* for a widow — about this remark of Aṅgiras, he holds that this word is used simply to boost the glory of *satī-dāha*, and should not be taken literally. According to an observation of Āpastamba, quoted in the *Śuddhi-tattva* (Jīvānanda's edn., p. 243) and the above-mentioned Aparārka commentary (p. 1193), there is a stentorian provision that if a widow, after resolving to resort to *sahamaraṇa*, backs out at the last moment, then she will have to undergo the hard penance, called *Prājāpatya*.

It is interesting to note that widow-burning did not prevail in India alone. This reprehensible practice prevailed also among the Greeks, Germans, Slavs and some other races too.

POLYGAMY

A study of the *smṛti* literature, right from the *dharmasūtra*s down to the period of *nibandha*s, appears to indicate that, though monogamy was the ideal, polygamy was not banned. The possession of several wives was not only the prerogative of the kings and nobles, but the right of all who could afford.

The *Āpastamba-dharmasūtra* (II.5.12-13) lays down that a man, having a wife, endowed with *dharma* and issues, shall not marry another woman. If the wife lacks any of the above two, the husband may marry another woman.

From the *YS* (II.125), it is clear that a Brāhmaṇa could marry women of all castes. It is implied that a member of any caste may marry women of his own caste as well as of castes inferior to his. No limit, however, appears to be set to the number of women that can be married by a man. It is interesting to note that, according to an authority, quoted in Raghunandana's *Smṛti-tattva*, II, p. 115, one who has married three women, must marry a fourth one. The injunction may be based on the superstition that the number three is ominous. Whatever the reason underlying this rule, it clearly testifies to the vogue of polygamy. This custom is vouchsafed by ancient legends too. King Daśaratha of the *Rāmāyaṇa* had three wives. King Hariścandra is said to have been the husband of a hundred wives (*Aitareya Brāhmaṇa*, 33.1). The sage-philosopher, Yājñavalkya had two wives, Maitreyī and Kātyāyanī (*Bṛhadāraṇyaka Upaniṣad*, IV.5.1-2 and II.4.1).

In the period of the Vedic *Saṃhitā*s, there are many references to polygamy. Co-wives appear to have been a source of great trouble, so much so that a deity, named *sapatnī-dhāvana* (who drives away co-wives) was conceived in the *Ṛgveda* (X.145).

DIVORCE

Unlike registered marriages of today, which is a contract, marriage according to *smṛti-śāstra* was a sacrament. A contract is voidable under certain circumstances. So, in modern times, there are divorce cases galore. In ancient times, it was believed that once the sacrament before fire is solemnly performed, there could be no dissolution or complete severance of the marriage-tie. We shall briefly state the views of different *smṛti* writers on the separation of the husband and the wife. *Manu,* IX.101 states that mutual fidelity of the husband and wife till death is the greatest *dharma*. In IX.46, it is held that neither sale nor desertion of the wife can break her tie with the husband. The force of sacrament is so strong that, as Viśvarūpa comments on *Yājñavalkya,* III.254, even *pātitya* (apostasy) on the part of the husband or wife cannot obliterate their marital relation. Even if a wife is tainted by adultery, she still remains a wife. If she performs the proper penance, there will be no necessity of a fresh sacrament of marriage.

According to both *Manu* (V.80) and *Yājñavalkya* (I.80), a man is allowed to supersede his wife (and marry another woman) if she drinks wine, suffers from a protracted disease, is deceitful, extravagant, harsh-tongued, and gives birth to female children only. Supersession, however, does not mean divorce.

In connexion with remarriage of women, there is provision, according to some *smṛti* writers, that a married woman can marry another man under certain circumstances even when her husband is alive. But, it is not clear whether or not, in such cases, the marriage-tie is broken.

According to an anonymous verse, quoted in the *Baudhāyana-dharmasūtra* which, in all probability, preceded the *Manu-smṛti*, a wife of the following descriptions may be abandoned after the lapse of the specified periods:

Barren — in the tenth year of marriage,
Giving birth only to female issues — in the twelfth year,
All of whose children die — in the fifteenth year,
Uttering harsh words — immediately.

It is not clear whether or not divorce was allowed in these cases. According to the commentator, Govindasvāmin, in these cases, only supersession (*adhivedana*) and not divorce is meant.

REMARRIAGE OF WOMEN

It is said that Īśvaracandra Vidyāsāgara's (1820-91) mother, a kind-hearted lady, was moved to pity at the plight of the young Hindu widows. In those days, girls had to be married before they menstruated. Widows in general, and young widows in particular, were subjected to draconian rules and regulations. They were objects of contempt and regarded as unholy creatures. Eating vegetarian food once a day only, abjuring all kinds of dress and decoration, observing complete fast on occasions like *ekādaśī* (eleventh lunar mansion in each fortnight) in which even drinking of water was forbidden, they used to live a life of seclusion. Those among them, who embraced death in the funeral pyres of their husbands, were adored posthumously. Some of them, quite unwilling to do so, were forced, by designing relatives, to burn themselves in the above manner.

The above lady, in great anguish and agony, asked her son, versed in scriptures, to find out a śāstric rule allowing widows to remarry. To Vidyāsāgara the mother's request was a sacred and binding order. He started ransacking the *smrti-sāstra*. After some days, he came across a verse allowing remarriage of widows; with ecstasy he reported it to his mother. In course of time, mainly at his instance, the remarriage of Hindu widows was legalised by the British Government, by an Act in 1856.

The verse, referred to above, runs thus:

naste mṛte pravrajite klīve' tha patitepatau ।
pancasvāpatsu nārīṇāṃ patira-nyo vidhīyate ॥
— *Parāśara,* V.30; *Nārada* (*Strīpuṃsa,* 97);
Agni Purāṇa, 154.5-6.

Women are allowed to have other husbands if their husbands are missing, dead, take to mendicancy, are impotent or become degraded as apostates.

The contemporaneous orthodox Brāhmana scholars of Bengal rejected Vidyāsāgara's interpretation of the above verse. They pointed out that the word *patau*, in the text, is ungrammatical; the correct form should be *patyau*. *Patau*, however, can be justified only if this portion is read as *apatau* (in *nañ samāsa*). Here *nañ* can be justified in the sense of *īsat* or *alpa* (slight). In that case, marriage of a woman under the circumstances, stated in the above verse, would be permissible if she was betrothed (not married).

Some (notably *Parāśara-mādhava*, II, Pt. 1, p. 53) giving a simplistic interpretation of the above verse hold that this rule is meant for another age excepting the *kali* age. Medhātithi (on *MS*, V.157) and some other interpreters would take *pati* to denote *pālaka* (fosterer), not husband. The *Smṛtyarthasāra* of Śrīdhara (*c.* AD 1150-1200) refers to the following views on the subject:

(1) If the bridegroom dies before the ritual of *Saptapadī* while the marriage ceremony is going on. In this connection, it may be noted that, according to *MS*, VIII.227, a marriage is concluded with the performance of *Saptapadī*. Kullūka adds — *saptapadī-dānāt prāg bhāryātvā-nispatteḥ satyanuśaye jahyān-nordhvam.* This means — as wifehood does not arise before *Saptapadī*, in the event of repentance, one may forsake, but not after *Saptapadī*; it is not clear as to who, the bridegroom or the bride or any one of them, can exercise this right.

(2) The married girl may be remarried if the husband dies before consummation of the marriage.

(3) If the husband dies before the wife's monthly course starts.

(4) Remarriage of a girl is allowed before conception. In the fourth case, the ground for remarriage is not stated; does it imply the death of the husband before the wife's conception?

From the foregoing facts about the remarriage of a girl, it is clear that various attempts have been made to circumvent the clear provision of the remarriage of women in the *Parāsara-smṛti*; it is odd to explain *pati* as *pālaka*.

The *MS* is opposed to the remarriage of a widow as the verses V.162, IX.65, VIII.226, etc., indicate. This work declares unequivocably — *sakṛt kanyā pradīyate*; a girl is given (in marriage) only once (IX.47). The *YS*, I.65 also speaks in the same vein. Here, a subtle point may be noted. *Kanyā* or an unmarried girl is given by her father or any other person entitled to do so, only once. But, after her marriage, the father, etc., cease to have guardianship over her. Moreover, after marriage, she no longer remains a *kanyā*, but becomes a *vadhū* under new guardians. So, according to the above rule of Manu, there cannot be a bar to the remarriage of a widow if it is arranged by her new guardians.

YS, I.52 ordains that one of the qualifications of a girl, to be married, is that she must be *ananya-pūrvikā*, i.e., she must be such as had no husband before. From *YS*, I.67, we learn that *anyapūrvā* (having a husband before) was of two kinds, viz. *punarbhū* and *svairinī*. The former was of two types — (i) one who had sexual intercourse with a man even before marriage; (ii) one whose marriage was not consummated, and was remarried. *Svairiṇī* was one who, before puberty, deserted her husband and, out of lust, used to live with another man of the same caste. *Ananyapūrvikā*, as an essential qualification of a bride, clearly hints at the vogue of remarriage of a woman in the society.

PROSTITUTION

Prostitution is known to be the oldest profession in the world. It is no wonder, therefore, that we find references to this institution in ancient Indian literature right from the Vedas. Here, we are concerned with the works on *smṛti-sāstra* only.

According to the *Gautama-dharmasūtra* (22.27), a Brāhmaṇa woman, taking to prostitution, is to be killed; the murderer of such a woman does not become liable either for atonement or for punishment. *Manu* (IX.259-60), as explained by Kullūka, holds that the prostitutes are expert in bringing others under control; they are openly *loka-kaṇṭaka*s (like thorns to the people). Similar is the opinion also of *Nārada* (*Pariśiṣṭa*, 2.3). According to *Manu* (IV.209) and *Yājñavalkya* (I.161), the eating of food from a strumpet has been prohibited presumably for a Brāhmaṇa. *Nārada* (*Strīpuṃsa*, 78-79) declares that the enjoyment of a prostitute of a higher caste is prohibited; but one, having sex-relation with such a woman of the lowest caste, is not blamed. The *Mitākṣarā* on *Yājñavalkya*, II.290 lays down that the prostitutes, being descended from a nymph, named Pañcacūḍā, belong to the fifth caste. Sexual intercourse of a prostitute with a man of the same or of a higher caste does not result in fault on either side. According to *Parāśara* (12.12), sexual intercourse with a prostitute is tantamount to homosexuality. *Atri* (5.271) ordains *Prājāpatya-vrata* as expiation of the sin arising from sexual union with a prostitute. *Vasiṣṭha* (14.10) and *Viṣṇu* (5.17) condemn sexual relation with prostitutes; it is not clear for which caste this prohibition is intended.

In IV.84, Manu forbids a Brāhmaṇa to receive gifts from a Veśajīvin, i.e., one who earns livelihood by *veśa* which, according to Kullūka, means maintenance of prostitutes.

According to *Yājñavalkya* (2.266), a characteristic trait of offenders, especially thieves, is *aśuddha-vāsaka* or living in prostitutes' quarters. *Nārada*, *Parāśara* (12.12) and *Manu* (X.256 ff) connect offenders with prostitutes in several ways, and speak of prostitutes' quarters as a rendezvous of criminals.

That the State allowed prostitution or acquiesced in it is obvious from the provision by *Nārada* (18.10) that, under no circumstances, the ornaments of a prostitute should be confiscated; because, these are indispensable for her profession.

A prostitute, refusing to yield her body after receiving payment, was to pay a fine equivalent to three times the amount received (*Yājñavalkya*, II.292). Likewise, a man, who does not pay the dues of a prostitute after enjoying her, is also liable to punishment. *Manu* (IX.289) provides punishment for a deceitful prostitute. Manu and some other *smrti* writers consider a prostitute to be of the same status as the thief and a criminal who extorts money by coercion. In the same works, the warning given against the trickery of prostitutes reminds one of the *Book of Proverbs of the Jews*.

According to *Nārada* (9.18-19), for offences, on the part of prostitutes, there will be eight times the penalty prescribed in the *Matsya Purāṇa* (227.147). The Purānic text in question ordains that, if a strumpet, after accepting money from a man, refuses to be enjoyed by him or approaches another man, then she must pay to the former twice the amount given by him and an equivalent amount of fine to the king.

On Nārada's authority, the *Smṛticandrikā* (II, p. 206) suggests that prostitutes, and those, who live with them, should settle disputes relating to these women.

According to the *Dāyabhāga*, an unchaste woman is debarred from inheriting the property of her parents. But, according to the *Mitāksarā*, as interpreted in modern courts of law, a woman, in the keeping of a man or taking to the profession of prostitutes, has right to her parents' property, but only after having virgin daughters or married daughters, as the case may be. In their absence or if they do not claim, an unchaste woman shall have the right (*Vide Tara* vs. *Krishna* 31 Bom. 495; *Govind* vs. *Bhiku*· 45 Bom. L.R. 699).

It has been decided, in law courts, that though according to ancient Hindu Law, prostitution causes apostasy, yet it does not sever blood-connexion. So, a married woman, taking to the profession of *naikin* (*nartakī* or *gaṇikā*), can be heir to *strīdhana* (a woman's exclusive property).

(*Vide Hiralal* vs. *Tripura* 40 Cal 650 F.R.; *Narayan* vs. *Laxman* 51 Bom. 784; *Narayandas* vs. *Tirlok* 29 A1.4. *Subbaraya* vs. *Ramasami* 23 Mad. 171.)

It is interesting to note that some Vedic works, e.g., *Atharvaveda,* III.29.7; *Taittirīya Brāhmana,* II.2.5.5-6;

Āpastamba-śrautasūtra, V.13; *Matsya Purāṇa,* 70 (= *Padma Purāṇa,* V. 23.74-146), followed by some *smṛti* digests, e.g., *KKV,* 27-31; *CCV,* II. 544-48; *KR* 605-8, prescribe a peculiar *vrata* for prostitutes; it is called *Anaṅga-dāna-vrata* (*Veśyādityāṅgadāna-vrata* in *KKV*). In it, which is to be performed on Sunday with any of the *nakṣatras*, Hastā, Puṣyā or Punarvasu, a prostitute has to offer herself to a Brāhmaṇa who recites the *mantra* — *ka idaṃ kasmā adāt kāmaḥ*, etc. *CCV* — *Caturvarga-cintāmaṇi, Vrata; KVV* — *Kṛtyakalpataru, Vrata; KR* — *Kṛtyaratnākara.*

Levirate (Niyoga)

In ancient times, the birth of a son was very much coveted for various reasons, religious and secular. It was believed that only a son could prevent one from falling into hell, called *put*. The following verse occurs in the *Padma Purāṇa* (*Svarga-khaṇḍa,* chapter 3):

> *puṃnāmno narakād yasmāt pitaraṃ trāyate sutaḥ* ।
> *tasmāt putra iti proktah* . . . . . . ॥

As the son rescues the father from hell, named *put,* he is called *putra* (or *puttra*); it is derived from root *trai* (to save), preceded by *put*. The property of a person devolves, after his death, on his son in the absence of whom it goes to others. Another reason, which is common almost among all people even nowadays, is that, in one's old age, his son will be the financial prop of the family, and will look after his decrepit parents. The urge for having a son gave rise to the system of adoption of sons by sonless persons.

There was another way of getting a son by one's own wife. This was called *niyoga*; the word denotes appointment. *Niyoga* meant the appointment of a man to beget a son on the wife or widow of a sonless man. This did not mean licence to the woman to indulge in sexual enjoyment with a man other than the husband. There were restrictive rules for the purpose. *Niyoga* has been included among *kalivarjyas* or practices to be shunned in the *kali* age.

That this practice dates back to pre-Christian times is proved by the provision of it in the *Guatama-dharmasūtra,* 18.4-14, 28.32, etc. We shall confine our discussion only to the *MS.* The son, begotten by a man on the wife of another, is called *kṣetraja*; the woman being termed *kṣetra*, her husband *kṣetrin* or *kṣetrika* and the begetter *bījin*. In such a case, the son belongs to the *kṣetrin*.

Manu, IX.59, as interpreted by Kullūka, provides that a woman, having no issue (*santāna*), with the permission of her superiors like the husband, should approach her *devara* or a *sapiṇḍa* of the husband. In Sanskrit, *devara* may mean the husband's elder or younger brother; it is not clear which kind of brother is intended by the authorities. Manu's text reads *santānasya parikṣaye* as a prerequisite of *niyoga*. Kullūka interprets it as *santānābhāve* (in the absence of progeny). If the woman concerned has a daughter who is a *santāna*, will she be debarred from *niyoga*? Are we to understand that the practice is admissible only for a childless woman? *Manu,* IX.60 ordains that a widow, by means of *niyoga*, can get only one son, never a second. Manu, however, refers (IX.61) to the practice of getting a second son according to the opinion of some (*eke*). Manu declares (IX.62) that, after the birth of such a son, the begetter and the woman should regard themselves as father and daughter-in-law respectively. From *MS*, IX.58, 63, 143, 144, it appears that if the practice is resorted to in violation of the rules, the man will be guilty of incest, and the son will be regarded as illegitimate.

One question that naturally arises is — what will happen if the woman concerned gives birth to a daughter as a result of *niyoga*? Will she try again for a son? One feels also inclined to ask — if the second issue too be a daughter, then what will happen?

Śūdras and other So-called Low-class People

The *R̥gveda* (X.90.12) states that Brāhmaṇa, *rājanya* (i.e. Kṣatriya), Vaiśya and Śūdra were born respectively out of the mouth, arms, thighs and feet of the great *puruṣa*. From this it is obvious that Śūdras were looked upon as belonging to the lowest rung of the social ladder. Kṣīravāmin (*c*. eighth century, according to some, *c*. eleventh century, according to others), the renowned commentator of the *Nāmaliṅgānuśāsana* or *Amarakośa*, gives the derivative meaning of the word, *Śūdra* thus —

su pūjitaṃ kṛtvo-ndanti sūrīn kledayanti śūdrāḥ ।

Śūdras are so-called as they, after worshipping (honouring ?) the learned men (perhaps referring to Brāhmaṇas whose occupation was the study and teaching of the Vedas), bathe (or wash the feet of) them. Some think that the word *śūdra* comes from *kṣudra*, the initial *k* being elided owing to the phonetic tendency not tolerating an initial conjunct in Prākṛit. But, had *śūdra* been a Prākṛit vocable, we would expect the form *sudda*.

From the *Ṛgveda*, the existence of the four castes in those times is clear. We learn from this Veda that the Vedic deity Indra vanquished the *dāsa*s or *dasyu*s. In one verse of the above Veda (II.12.4), he is stated to have pushed the *dāsa-varṇa* to the caves. It seems, among non-Aryans, some submitted to Aryans, while others were recalcitrant. Those of the former class came to be designated Śūdra, and were engaged as servants or slaves, and those of the latter fled away to their mountainous abodes. From some Vedic texts, e.g. *Taittirīya Saṃhitā,* VII.1.6, it is clear that Śūdras were debarred from Vedic sacrifice, and were presumably employed to carry people in palanquins and the like.

Coming to the Brāhmaṇa period, we find, for example, in the *Tāṇḍya-mahābrāhmaṇa* (VI.1.11), that the Śūdras, having been created from the feet, had to wash the feet of the people of the three upper castes. An attitude of contempt towards Śūdras is revealed in some *Brāhmaṇas*. For instance, according to the *Śatapatha* (*SBE*, vol. 44, p. 446), Śūdra is untruth; he is to toil (*Ibid.*, p. 410). The same *Brāhmaṇa* ordains (*SBE*, vol. 26, p. 4) that one, initiated for Vedic sacrifice, shall not speak to a Śūdra.

Pāṇini's rule *Śūdrāṇāmaniravasitānām* (II.4.10) and Patañjali's comments thereon mention the class of Śūdras, called *a-niravasita* or not excommunicated. From this the existence of a class, called *niravasita* (excommunicated) can be inferred. From the illustrations we learn at least the following professions belonged to the *a-nirvasita* class:

> Gopa, Nāpita, Karmāra (blacksmith), Kumbhakāra, Takṣan (carpenter), *Ayaskāra* (metal-worker), Rajaka, Tantuvāya (weaver), Bhilla (a tribe) and Dhīvara.

Aniravasita means *a-bahiskṛta*. These people were allowed to live in the society. *Niravasita* means *bahiṣkrta*. Such people had to live outside the society, and the vessels, used by them at the time of eating in the house of a person in the society, could not be purified except by making them anew. To this class belonged the Haḍḍipa (Bengali Hāḍi), Malegrahī, Caṇḍāla, Mṛtapa, etc.

From the above, we learn that the word *Śūdra* stood for quite a number of groups of people; even the Caṇḍāla, regarded as the most abominable, were included in the Śūdra caste. *Manu,* X.41 says that all *pratiloma* castes (i.e., those born in the reverse order) are similar to Śūdras in their *dharma*.

It is interesting to note that a division of Śūdras as *sat* and *asat* is found, for example, in *Bhaviṣya Purāṇa*, Brahmā section, chapter 44.32. To the former class belonged those who used to adopt good occupations or trades, serve *dvija*s, and abjured meat-eating, drinking and sale of wine.

Against this background, we shall briefly deal with the position of Śūdras and other so-called low-class people, as reflected in *Smṛti-śāstra*, i.e., in the prominent works on *dharmasūtra*, metrical *dharma-śāstra* and *smṛti-nibandha*s as well as in the renowned commentaries on *smṛti* works.

Manu, VIII.413 declares that God created Śūdras for the service of Brāhmaṇas; a Śudra, purchased (i.e., a slave) or not, should be made to serve. In *Manu,* XI.123, the service of Brāhmaṇas, alone is held to be the Śūdra's best work. In the absence of Brāhmaṇas, a Śūdra may serve a Kṣatriya, in his absence a Vaiśya.

According to *Manu* (X.129), a Śūdra, despite his ability to amass wealth, should refrain from doing so. Otherwise, out of vanity and ignorance, he may cause obstruction and troubles to Brāhmaṇas; he may also slight them. *Gautama* (X.64-65) allows a Śūdra to accumulate wealth, but provides that it should be spent for the benefit of the higher castes.

All the prominent authorities, e.g. *dharmasūtras* like those of *Āpastamba* (1.1.1.7-8), *Gautama* (X.57-59), *Dharmaśāstras of Manu* (X.121-23), *Yājñavalkya* (I.120), etc., are unanimous in holding that the duty of a Śūdra is to serve the members of the upper castes. According to some authorities, e.g. *Gautama* (X.60-61), *Manu* (X.124-25), a Śūdra is to put on the worn-out or thrown away clothes of his master, use his umbrella, sandals, mattress, etc., of a similar condition, and eat the remnants (*ucchiṣṭa*) of his food.

The *Gṛhastharatnākara* (p. 479), on the authority of the *Kālikā Purāṇa*, allows a Śūdra to sell everything excepting honey, skin, lac, wine and flesh.

In some works, Śūdras are clearly branded as *anāryas* or non-Aryans. For example, *Āpastamba* (I.1.3.40-41) holds that if a *brahmacārin* is unable to eat all the food, collected by begging, then he may keep the surplus with an *ārya* or give it to a Śūdra who is a *dāsa* (of his teacher). *Gautama,* X.69 uses the word *anārya* to denote Śūdra.

It was ordained that a Śudra could not be an ascetic. So, in the *Viṣṇu-dharmasūtra*, V.115 and *YS*, II.241 (as read by Viśvarūpa), a fine of one hundred *paṇas* is prescribed for one feeding Śūdra ascetics in the rites for gods and *manes*. According to *Atri*, 136-37, the following practices make a Śūdra sinful:

> *Japa*, *tapas* (austerity), *pravrajyā* (asceticism), pilgrimage, attempt to acquire miraculous power by reciting *mantras*, sole devotion to the worship of a goddess.

Manu, IV.80 ordains that one (a *dvija*?) should not give advice to a Śūdra in mundane matters nor any religious instruction; one should not directly prescribe an expiatory *vrata* for him; Kullūka adds that the last can be done through the medium of a Brāhmaṇa. The *YS*, III.262, as interpreted by the *Mitākṣarā*, states that a Śūdra, though devoid of the privilege of *japa*, etc., can be purified from sin by the performance of *vratas* through twelve years, etc. Instead of *Gāyatrī,* etc., the Śūdra will recite *namaskāra-mantra*. Aparārka, on the above verse of Manu, says that a Śūdra can perform *vratas* through the medium of a Brāhmaṇa.

Śūdras were reduced to a despicable condition in certain cases. *Gautama* (XII.4) makes the following inhuman pronouncement:

> If a Śūdra listens to the study of the Veda with the intention of memorising it, then his ears should be filled with (molten) lead and lac; if he recites the Veda, his tongue will be cut off; if he masters the Veda, his body should be hacked.

The *Śūdra-kamalākara* (pp. 13-14) cites Purāṇic authority to the effect that a Śūdra cannot study the *smṛtis* and Purāṇas by himself; he can gather knowledge about these works through a Brāhmaṇa (p. 17). *Manu,* II.16 appears to suggest that only *dvijas* have the privilege of listening to (and reading) the *Manu-smṛti*. *Manu*, X.127 enjoins that all religious rites for Śūdras are to be performed without (Vedic) *mantras*.

As regards *vaivāhika* fire or the fire kindled at the time of marriage, opinions differ. According to *Manu,* III.67 and *YS*, I.97, the Śūdra can have this special fire. But *Medhātithi* on this verse of Manu, the *Mitākṣarā* on *YS*, I.121, *Madana-pārijāta* (p. 231), etc. hold that a Śūdra should offer oblations in the ordinary fire.

Regarding a Śūdra's right to adopt a son, authorities differ. According to Rudradhara and Vācaspati, since a Śūdra is debarred from *homa* with Vedic *mantras*, he is not entitled to adopt a son. But, Parāśara (VI.63-64) allows a Śūdra to perform the aforesaid *homa* through a Brāhmaṇa. So, stalwarts like Raghunandana, Nīlakaṇṭha and Harinātha allow adoption by a Śūdra (*vide* Nīlakaṇṭha's *Vyavahāra-mayūkha*, p. 112).

The *Āpastamba-dharmasūtra*, I.9.27.11, which is the same as *Baudhāyana dharmasūtra*, II.1.59, characterises Śudras as *Kṛṣṇa-varṇa*. The *Vaśiṣṭha-dharmasūtra*, 18,11-12 holds that a Śudra is *śmaśāna* (funeral place), so one should not study the Veda near a Śūdra.

It appears that, in course of time, the status of Śūdras was raised to a considerable extent. According to Devala, quoted in the *Mitākṣarā on YS*, I.120, they were allowed to take to the following occupations also:

> agriculture, cattle-rearing, carrying loads, sale of various commodities (excepting wine and flesh according to the *Bṛhat-parāśara*, p. 101), dancing, painting, singing and playing certain muscial instruments.

It is a historical fact that some Śūdras became kings. Candragupta Maurya (reign *c*. 322-298 BC) is an instance in point. *Manu* (IV.6) forbids Brāhmaṇas to live in the kingdom of a Śūdra. This injunction does not seem to have been universally followed. We find the Brāhmaṇa Kauṭilya as minister of the *vṛṣala* (Śūdra) Candragupta.

Manu severely condemns a Brāhmaṇa who acts as a priest in the sacrifice, etc., performed by Śūdras (III.178) and accepts gifts from them (III.170).

The *smṛti* literature is not entirely devoid of some good

words for and humane considerations with respect to Śūdras. *Gautama* (X.63) provides that when a Śūdra, engaged in the service of any one of the three higher castes, becomes too old to work, he is to be fed by his master. We have already seen that, besides the service of the higher castes, Śūdras were allowed to pursue various vocations. The *Śaṃkha-smṛti* (I.5) provides *sarva-śilpāni* (all crafts) for a Śūdra besides *dvija-śuśrūṣā*. While some texts appear to allow a Śūdra to take to various means of livelihood as alternatives to the service of *dvija*s, *Manu* (X.99) allows him to resort to other crafts when he is unable to perform his primary duty of service. *Manu* (X.100) adds that he should take to such arts and crafts as are helpful to the *dvija*s.

The *Kṛtyakalpataru* and some other works allow the Śūdra to read and recite Purāṇic *mantras*. The *Śūdra-kamalākara* (pp. 30, 31) cites Purāṇic authority which entitles Śūdras to learn and recite *Viṣṇu-mantra*s from *Pañcarātra* texts.

The *YS* divides Śūdras into two classes, viz., *abhojyānna* (from whom food cannot be eaten by Brāhmaṇas?) and *bhojyānna* (from whom food can be eaten by a Brāhmaṇa?). In the *YS*, I.160, among the persons, from whom food has been prohibited, Śūdra is not expressly mentioned; he is indicated by the word *agnihīna*, i.e., one not entitled to perform *Śrauta* or *Smārta* rites in fire. It should be noted that this prohibition is meant for normal times only (*anāpadi*), but not for emergency. The *YS*, I.166 mentions the following Śūdras as *bhojyānna*:

> *dāsa* (*garbhadāsa* etc. — *Mit.*), *gopāla* (cowherd), *kulamitra* (hereditary), *ardhasīrin* (share-cropper), *nāpita*, one who dedicates himself to another saying 'I am yours'.

To this list, the *Mit.* adds *kumbhakāra*. The following Śūdras are mentioned, in the *MS* (IV.253), among the Śūdras of the *bhojyānna* class:

> *ārdhika* (share-cropper), *kulamitra* (hereditary friend), *gopāla* (cowherd), *dāsa* (servant or slave), *nāpita* (barber) and one who surrenders oneself by saying like this — I am in a wretched condition, I shall live with you and serve you.

The above kinds of Śūdras are *bhojyānna* to one with whom they are connected as *ārdhika*, etc.

Āpastamba-dharmasūtra, II.2.3.4 lays down that a Śūdra can cook food for a Brāhmaṇa only under the supervision of a member of any of the three upper castes, provided he (Śūdra) observes the hygienic rules of cutting nails and hairs, etc.

In course of time, the prohibition relating to taking food from Śūdras became stricter. For instance, *Śaṃkha*, 13.4 observes that a Brāhmaṇa, fattened by the food given by Śūdras, is *Paṃkti-dūṣaka* (defiler of company). *Parāśara,* XI.13 declares that a Brāhmaṇa may take from a Śūdra ghee, oil, milk, molasses and food fried in oil or ghee, but should eat the same at a place excepting the Śūdra's house. *Parāśara-mādhava* (II.1, pp. 411-12) comments that this permission holds good only when a Brāhmaṇa is tired by travel, and no food is available from any member of the other castes.

We have already mentioned the two-fold division of Śūdras as *sat* and *asat*. The *Śūdra-kamalākara* (p. 60) declares that an *asat* Śūdra does not incur any sin even as a result of eating meat and drinking wine provided he abjures forbidden meat.

Manu's following remarks about Śūdras in X.126 appear to be ambiguous: there is no sin in a Śūdra, he is not entitled to *saṃskāra* nor to the practice of *dharma* nor is there any prohibition for him with respect to *dharma*. Kullūka elucidates Manu's above remarks as follows. A Śūdra does not incur sin by eating garlic, etc., but he is not exempted from the grave sin of killing a Brāhmaṇa, etc. He has no right to sacraments like *upanayana*, performance of *agnihotra*, etc. But, there is no prohibition of *pāka-yajña* and the like. In the next verse, Manu ordains that a Śūdra, who is pious and of good conduct, performing rites without (Vedic) *mantras*, is not blamed: he is rather praised. According to Kullūka, this confers on Śūdras the right to perform *Pañca-yajñas* using the word *namas* (and not *oṃ*). The *YS*, I.121 has been quoted by Kullūka in support of his view; Yājñavalkya emphatically asks a Śūdra not to abstain from *pañca-yajñas* (*pañca-yajñānna hāpayet*).

The *Śūdra-kamalākara* (p. 38) allows Śūdras to perform *vrata*, *upavāsa*, *mahādāna* and *prāyaścitta*, but without *homa* and *japa*. Śaṃkha, as quoted by Viśvarūpa in his commentary on the *YS*, I.13, allows *saṃskāras* for Śūdras, but without Vedic *mantras*. Similar are the opinions of *Yama*, quoted in the *Smṛti-candrikā*, I, p. 14, *Vedavyāsa*, I.17, Haradatta on *Gautama* X.51.

The *MS*, II.123 advises one (to whichever caste he may belong) to imitate a good deed done by a Śūdra. Manu subordinates casteism to pragmatism. The *MS* provides (II.238) that one (obviously of any caste) should respectfully learn *śubhā vidyā* even from an *avara*. Kullūka explains *śubhā vidyā* as *dṛṣṭa-śakti gāruḍādi-vidyā*, i.e., such a charm as *garuḍa*, etc., the power of which has been seen. *Gāruḍa-vidyā* is a charm against (snake) poison. *Avara* is Śudra. The same verse ordains that one should acquire *para dharma* even from an *antya*, i.e., Caṇḍāla. *Para dharma*, according to Kullūka, means self-knowledge as the means to the attainment of salvation (*mokṣopāya*). Medhātithi, however, takes the word to mean *laukika dharma* which is *para* (superior to *śruti* and *smṛti*). Thus, one (irrespective of caste) should follow the advice even of a Cāṇḍāla who says — do not remain here for long or do not bathe in this water. Some other instances also of the humane treatment towards Śūdras and other so-called low-class people are found in the *Manu-smṛti*. The *MS* (II.137) laying down that even a Śūdra, who has crossed the ninetieth year of age, deserves honour by the *dvijas*. The next verse provides that, irrespective of one's caste, one should leave the road for the following to whichever caste they may belong:

cakrin (riding a wheeled vehicle like a chariot), *daśamīstha* (one who is in the tenth stage of life, i.e. crossed the age of ninety, considering one hundred years as the life-span), *rogin* (patient), *bhārin* (carrying a load), *strī* (woman), *snātaka* (one who has just completed studenthood), *rājan* (king), *vara* (bridegroom).

An extremely liberal attitude to women, Śūdras and other so-called low-class people is noticed in connexion with *Durgā-pūjā*. Hemādri (on *Vrata* I, p. 910), Raghunandana (in *Tithi-tattva*, p. 68), Kamalākara (in *Nirṇaya-sindhu*, p. 164) and Madanapāla (in *Smṛti-kaumudī*, p. 201) quote the following from the *Bhaviṣya Purāṇa*, apparently with approval:

> *pūjanīyā janair-devī .... śūdrair-bhakti-yuktair-*
> *melcchair-anyaiśca mānavaiḥ* । *strībhiśca ....* ॥

Kamalākara (in *Nirṇaya-sindhu*, p. 114), Raghunandana (in *Tithi-tattva*, p. 68), Lakṣmīdhara (in *Kṛtyakalpataru*, *Naiyatakālika*, p. 410) quote, without any adverse comment, the following from the *Bhaviṣyottara Purāṇa*:

> *evaṃ nānā-mlecchagaṇaiḥ pūjyate sarva-dasyubhiḥ* ।
> *aṅga-vaṅga-kaliṅgaiśca kinnarair-barbaraiḥ śakaiḥ* ॥

Thus, it is clear that women and all so-called low-class people, including the tribals and robbers, were entitled to worship goddess Durgā. The question is whether these people could directly worship Durgā or through the medium of Brāhmaṇas, as in the cases referred to earlier. None of the *nibandhakāras*, excepting Madanapāla (in *Smṛti-kaumudī*, p. 291), raises this question. So, it can, perhaps, be asserted that they accepted Purāṇic authority in this matter. Madanapāla's conclusion (*Smṛti-kumudī*, p. 291) is that *mlecchas*, etc., are neither eligible for worship as Śūdras are through the medium of Brāhmaṇas in *japa, homa*, nor entitled to worship with *mantras*; they can only mentally offer to goddess the articles for worship and the animals for sacrifice.

Let us now examine the position of Śūdras in law, civil and criminal. First of all, it may be noted that a Śūdra can never be a judge. When the king is unable to supervise the litigation of the people, he can appoint a Brāhmaṇa, with requisite qualifications, to represent him (*Manu*, VIII.9 and *YS*, I.3). According to the *Mit.* on *YS*, I.3, when a Brāhmaṇa is not available, a duly-qualified Kṣatriya or even a Vaiśya can be appointed for the purpose, but never a Śūdra. The anti-śūdra feeling, in this respect, finds blatant expression in the provision that a *dvija*, even if *duḥśīla* (of evil conduct), should be engaged, but not a Śūdra even if he is *vijitendriya* (with senses controlled). Raghunandana, in his *Smṛti-tattva*, II, p. 198, quotes an authority in support of his view.

According to *Gautama*, XII.1-2, for adultery with a woman of any of the three upper castes, a Śūdra is to have his penis cut off and property confiscated. If he was engaged for her protection, he is to suffer death in addition. *Vaśiṣṭha-dharmas* (21.1) and *Manu* (VIII.366) prescribe death for a Śūdra having sexual intercourse with a Brāhmaṇa woman, whether willing or not. For *vākpāruṣya* (slander or libel) towards a Brāhmaṇa, a Śūdra has to suffer painful corporal punishment or has to get his tongue cut off (*Manu*, VIII.270).

The life of a Śūdra was considered to be insignificant. Both *Manu* (XI.66) and *YS* (III.236) hold that the killing of a Śūdra is an *upapātaka* (minor sin). The *Āpastamba-dharmasūtra*. (I.9.25.14, I.9.26.1) states that the *prāyaścitta* for killing a Śūdra is the same as that for killing a crow, dog, cow, etc. According to *Manu* (XI.131), the *prāyaścitta* for killing a Śūdra is the same as that for killing a cat, frog, owl, etc.

For abusing a person of any of the three upper castes, leading a religious life, a Śūdra's tongue should be cut off (*Āpastamba*, II.10.27.14). According to *Gautama*, XII.1, *Manu*, VIII.279, *YS*, II.215, etc., the limb, with which a Śūdra strikes a person of a higher caste, is to be cut off. *Manu*, VIII.280 ordains the same punishment for a Śūdra who merely raises his hand or a club to strike the aforesaid person. A Śūdra defiantly spitting on the body of a Brāhmaṇa will have his lip cut off. His hands will be cut off if he seizes a Brāhmaṇa by the hair, feet, beard, neck or testicles (*Vide Manu,* VIII.281-83 = *Nārada,* XVIII.26-28).

SLAVERY

The Greek ambassador, Megasthenes (visit to India in *c.* 302 BC) wrote (McCrindle, p. 71) that no Indian used to keep slaves. Perhaps, following him, Arrian and Strabo also made similar statements. As a matter of fact, however, slavery existed in India ever since the Vedic times. It might be that slavery was not in vogue in the regions visited by Megasthenes or no slave was seen by him. It might be the case that the Greek ambassador was accustomed to seeing the brutal treatment meted out to slaves in his own country. In India, the attitude of the masters to their slaves was so humane that Megasthenes could not conceive that slavery prevailed in this country.

Here, we are concerned with the information about slavery, contained in *dharmasūtras*, *dharmaśāstras* and later *smṛti* digests and commentaries. The word *dāsa* occurs at several places in the *Manu-smṛti*, e.g., VIII.415, 416. The term *dāsya* is found in VIII.410, 412-16. Seven kinds of *dāsa* are mentioned in VIII.415. These, as explained by Kullūka, are:

Dhvajāhṛta (acquired from a defeated adversary),

Bhakta-dāsa (one who voluntarily becomes a slave for food),

Gṛhaja (son of a female slave),

Krīta (purchased),

Dattrima (given by another person)

[It should be noted that, in verse IX.141, this word has been used to mean adopted son.]

Paitṛka (hereditary),

Daṇḍadāsa (one who, being unable to pay fines, becomes a slave of the person concerned).

According to Nārada, the various kinds of *dāsa* are as follows:

Gṛhajāta — born to one's female slave,

Krīta — purchased,

Labdha — acquired,

Dāyādupagata — inherited,

Annākālabhṛta — maintained at the time of scarcity of food, i.e., famine,

Āhita — mortgaged,

Mokṣita — one who has adopted slavery of the creditor to free himself from debt,

Yuddheprāpta — captured from a defeated enemy,

Paṇe jita — won in a wager,

Tavāhamityupāgata — one who accepts slavery after saying, 'I am yours',

Pravrajyāvasita — fallen from mendicancy,

Kṛta — one who makes a pledge by saying — I shall remain your slave for such and such period,

Bhaktadāsa — one who takes to slavery for food even when there is no famine,

Vaḍavāhṛta — who out of lust for a domestic female slave marries her and becomes so,

Ātma-vikrayī — one who sells himself.

A slave cannot own any money or property; whatever is earned by him must belong to his master (*Manu*, VIII.416). According to Kātyāyana, a slave is the owner of the money obtained by selling himself and of whatever the master gives him out of kindness. A Brāhmaṇa could engage a Śūdra, whether purchased or not, as his slave. Even if manumitted by the master, a Śūdra cannot be free from servitude; the servitude (*dāsa-jīvana* — *Manu,* X.32) of Brāhmaṇas is his natural occupation. Kullūka explains *dāsa-jīvana* as *aṅga-saṃvāhanādi-karma-jīvanam*, i.e., work like shampooing the body. In this context, *dāsa* may mean servant or slave.

In the *Yājñavalkya-smṛti*, I.166, a *dāsa* is called Śūdra; he is that kind of Śūdra the food cooked by whom can be eaten by a Brāhmaṇa. The Śūdras were divided into two classes, viz., *bhojyānna* (the food cooked by whom can be eaten by a Brāhmaṇa) and *abhojyānna* (the food cooked by whom cannot be eaten by a Brāhmaṇa). That *dāsa*, in this context, means slave is clear from the *Mitākṣarā* commentary (*dāsā garbha-dāsādayaḥ*).

The *Bṛhad-Yama-smṛti* (III.10) echoes the above verse of *Yājñavalkya*.

According to Yājñavalkya (*Vyavahāra*, 13), the son, born to a female slave by a Śūdra, will get a share of his father's property according to the desire of the latter. After the death of the father, his sons by his wife will give half of the property (that falls to the share of one son by a married woman?) to the *dāsī-putra*. [In such a case, the principle of apportionment is not clear.] The *Mitākṣarā* adds that, in case the father leaves no son or daughter (or son of such a daughter) by his wife, the entire paternal property will be inherited by the *dāsī-putra*. On the authority of Nārada, the *Mitākṣarā* provides that a slave, who rescues his master from a situation, jeopardising his life, will share the master's property equally with the latter's son.

Manu ordains (VIII.412) that even a Brāhmaṇa, engaging

an initiated (*upanīta*) *dvija* in *dāsya* (work like washing feet), out of greed, will be liable to punishment. In a passage, quoted from Kātyāyana in the *Aparārka* commentary (p. 789) and in the *Smṛti-candrikā*, the engaging of a Brāhmaṇa as a slave of a Brāhmaṇa, has been prohibited. It should be noted that in the place of *dvija*, used by Manu, Kātyāyana has used *vipra*. From this, it may be inferred that, if necessary, a Brāhmaṇa could have a Kṣatriya or Vaiśya as his slave. This difference, perhaps, indicates the gradual establishment of superiority of Brāhmaṇas over the other two kinds of *dvija*s, viz., Kṣatriya and Vaiśya. At least two centuries elapsed between the completion of the present *Manu-smṛti* and Kātyāyana's work.

According to Kātyāyana, a Brāhmaṇa, if he so desires, can work under another Brāhmaṇa of character and learning; but he cannot do any work which is *aśubha* or debasing. The same author provides that a Kṣatriya or Vaiśya, who is *patita* (apostate or degraded), can serve a king. According to Nārada, quoted in the *Mitākṣarā*, work is of two kinds — *śubha* and *aśubha*. The former is done by a servant, and the latter by a slave. *Aśubha* work is as follows: cleaning the gateway of a house, an impure place, road, stool and urine, touching the private parts (of the master's body), eating the remnants of food, etc.

Yājñavalkya's clear directive (*Vyavahāra*, 183) is that, among the four castes, a man of a lower caste can be *dāsa* of one of a higher caste. The *Mitākṣarā* adds that a renegade, who has taken to mendicancy, can serve as a *dāsa* of even a person of a lower caste.

One rule, formulated by Kātyāyana, is that the master should grant manumission to both his female slave and her son begotten by him.

Nārada (42-43) provides for the ceremonial manumission of a slave by his master at his pleasure.

According to the *Kālikā Purāṇa*, quoted in Nīlakaṇṭha's

Vyavahāra-mayūkha, the adopted boy, whose sacraments of *cūḍā* (tonsure) and *upanayana* (sacred thread ceremony) have been performed with the mention of the adopter's *gotra*, is really his son. Otherwise, the adopted boy will be regarded as a slave of the adopter. The same Purāṇic verse, with a little change, has been quoted in Nandapaṇḍita's *Dattaka-mīmāṃsā*. Nīlakaṇṭha considers this verse as spurious, because it does not occur in some of the manuscripts of the above Purāṇa. Among the fifteen kinds of *dāsa*, mentioned by Nārada, there is no mention of *dattaka-dāsa*. The verse concerned in the *Kālikā Purāṇa* may imply this: unless an adopted boy does not undergo sacraments with the mention of the adopter's *gotra*, he will acquire no right over the adopter's property; the boy, in such a case, will be entitled only to maintenance like a slave.

According to Nārada (*Ṛṇādāna*, 12) and Kātyāyana, the master will be responsible for the debt, incurred, for his family, by his slave.

According to *Manu* (VIII.66) a person, who is *adhyadhīna*, is unfit for being a witness. Kullūka explains the word as *atyanta-paratantra-garbhadāsa* (extremely dependent slave of the *garbhadāsa* type). In verse VIII.70, it has been ordained that even such a person can be a witness in the absence of qualified witnesses. Uśanas, quoted in the *Vyavahāra-mayūkha* (p. 37), is also of this opinion.

Cruel treatment of slaves is not approved by the *śāstra*. We have it, in the *Āpastamba-dharmasūtra* (2.4.9.11), that if a guest arrives at the house, the householder can feed him with the savings from the food of himself or of his wife and son, but not from that of the domestic slave.

In the matter of corporal punishment, *Manu* (VIII.299) places a slave on an equal footing with one's son, uterine brother and wife. If they commit a (minor) offence, they may be lightly struck with a piece of rope or *veṇudala* (*ati-laghu-veṇu-śalākā* —*Kullūka*; i.e., a very light bamboo-stick). The offender may be struck on the back, never on the head. One, who flouts this rule, becomes punishable like a thief (VIII.300).

We have seen earlier that, as a rule, a man of a lower caste might be the slave of one of a higher caste. The slavery of a man of a higher caste under a person of a lower one was a punishable offence. Thus, it is obvious that a Brāhmaṇa, being in the topmost echelon, could not be reduced to slavery.

According to Yājñavalkya (*Vyavahāra*, 182), one who has been forcibly enslaved or has been carried away by a thief who sold (or mortgaged — *Mitākṣarā*) him must be set free by his master or, on his failure, by the king.

A *bhakta-dāsa* or a slave, maintained with food at the time of famine, may be set free if he makes *bhakta-tyāga* (giving up food); this word has been interpreted as the return of the amount of money spent for his food since the beginning of his slavery. A slave, who has been mortgaged and a *ṛṇadāsa* i.e. one who, having failed to repay debt, has embraced slavery, may be released on payment of *niṣkraya*. In the former case, *niṣkraya* means the entire amount paid by the mortgagee. In the case of the latter, *niṣkraya* means the amount by paying which the master has secured his manumission from his creditor. The *Mitākṣarā* notes that, in *niṣkraya*, the principal amount, along with interest, is to be paid.

According to Nārada, quoted in the *Mitākṣarā*, a slave, maintained in famine, may be released on his giving two cows to the master. In such a case, the expense, incurred for feeding the slave, cannot be repaid by him by service. The slaves of the following classes may secure manumission by giving the master *tulyakarmā pratiśīrṣa*s, i.e., representatives doing the same kind of work. A man, enslaved for a fixed period, will be set free after the expiry of that period. A slave of the *vaḍavāhṛta* type may be released if the *vaḍavā* is maltreated (*nigraha*). *Vaḍavāhṛta* is one who, out of lust for a domestic female slave (*vaḍavā*), marries her and becomes a slave. *Nigraha* or maltreatment means the prohibition of sexual intercourse with the male slave.

According to Yājñavalkya (*Vyavahāra*, 183) a man, fallen from mendicancy (*pravrajyā-bhraṣṭa*), shall remain the king's slave till death; he cannot be released under any circumstances. The *Mitākṣarā* adds that the above rule will apply to one who has not performed expiatory rites.

UNTOUCHABILITY

Mahātmā Gandhi ruefully said that untouchability was a blot on Indian society. Even after half a century since Independence, and despite legal ban, this scourge still vitiates the society, and stands as an impediment to national integration. Way back in 1317 B.S., i.e., 86 years ago, Rabīndranātha, in his poem *Apamānita* (insulted), said to his countrymen: *mānuṣer paraśere pratidin ṭhekāiyā dūre ghṛṇā kariyācha tumi mānuṣer prāṇer ṭhākure .... apamāne hote have tāhāder savār samān*. The idea is: you will have to be equal, in disgrace, to those whom you insulted by not touching them. His prophecy proved true.

We shall briefly deal with the attitude of *smṛti* writers towards untouchability. In some cases, untouchability does not necessarily convey the idea of inferiority. The concept of untouchability appears to have originated from the idea of impurity for religious and ceremonial purposes. For example, even one's mother, wife or daughter is untouchable in her monthly periods. Such a woman is debarred from active participation in a religious rite or a festive occasion. For touching even a close relative, who is in mourning due to the death of a member of his family, one has to be purified by bath.

In course of time, some professions and crafts came to be looked upon as nasty, and the people pursuing those occupations were considered untouchable to the members of the four castes, especially to Brāhmaṇas who used to do the holy acts of Vedic study, worship, etc. Gradually, untouchability became hereditary.

Untouchability naturally breeds hate. This hatred sometimes reduced the so-called untouchables to the abject position of animals. For example, in some parts of south India, particularly in Malabar, a social outcast, called *pāriāh*, while using a public thoroughfare, had to tie a bell around the neck to indicate his presence so that people in general might not come into contact with him. Such people had to maintain a distance from high caste Hindus (*Vide* Wilson, *Indian Castes*, Vol. II, p. 74 fn.).

The Cāṇḍālas, included among *antyajas*, were the only class of people who were regarded, in most ancient *dharmaśāstra*, as untouchable by birth. According to several authorities, e.g. *Gautama*, IV.15-16; *MS*, X.12; *YS*, I.93, etc., a Cāṇḍāla is born out of the union of castes in the reverse order (*pratiloma*); he is the offspring of a Śūdra from a Brāhmaṇa woman. He is the lowest among men (*MS*, X.12). *Vedavyāsa-smṛti* (1.9-10) divides Cāṇḍālas into three classes, viz., (1) born to a Śūdra by a Brāhmaṇī, (2) child of an unmarried woman, (3) offspring of the union of a man and a woman of the same *gotra*.

Some authorities reveal a comparatively liberal attitude to the untouchables on certain occasions, and at certain places. For example, *Atri* (V.249) ordains that no taint attaches to a person touching an untouchable in a temple, religious procession, marriage and other festivals. According to *YS*, I.194, public roads, even used by Cāṇḍālas, become purified by sunshine, moonbeam and wind.

Besides the untouchables by birth, there were untouchables as a result of certain sinful acts. For example, according to *MS*, IX.235-39 the perpetrator of a *Mahāpātaka* is to be ostracised. By performing the prescribed *prāyaścitta*, however, such a man can be restored to his caste, and become touchable. Another cause of untouchability is affiliation to certain heretic communities. For instance, Aparārka (p. 923) and *Smṛti-candrikā* (I, p. 118) cite authorities providing that a person can be purified by bath with clothes on if he touches any one of the following:

> Buddhist, Jaina, Pāśupata, Lokāyatika, Kapila (follower of Sāṃkhya), Śaiva, Nāstika.

It is interesting to note that to the above list is added a Brāhmaṇa resorting to practices inconsistent with his caste.

According to Aparārka (p. 923), the following are untouchable, but after touching them one can be purified by bath with clothes on:

> Cāṇḍāla, Pukkasa, Mleccha, Bhilla, Pārasīka, one who has committed a *Mahāpātaka*.

Some people, though not ordinarily untouchable, are stated (e.g., *Mit.* on *YS*, III.30, Aparārka, p. 922) to become so as a result of some actions, e.g., by touching a Brāhmaṇa *devalaka* or one who acts as a priest for an entire village, or a seller of *soma* plant. Besides, the following actions also render a person untouchable:

> touching a sacrificial post (*yūpa*) or a funeral pyre or wood at such a place or a corpse.

As stated earlier, persons, following some occupations, are regarded as untouchable. For example, according to Saṃvarta, quoted by Aparārka, p. 1196, the fisherman, deer-hunter, hunter in general, butcher, bird-catcher and washerman are untouchable.

The hatred towards the untouchables took deep root in the minds of the *smṛti* writers. According to the *Viṣṇu-dharmasūtra*, V.104, an untouchable, willingly touching a man of any of the higher castes, must be beaten up as punishment. A *Cāṇḍāla*, for doing so, should be fined one hundred *paṇa*s.

Drinking from the wells or vessels of untouchables, eating their food (cooked or uncooked), staying with them, sexual union with untouchable women were supposed to give rise to sin which could be atoned for by penance.

The upshot of the foregoing discussion is that, excepting *Cāṇḍālas*, none is untouchable by birth. It is also clear that, by touching an untouchable, one does not become untouchable for life, and can be free from taint by purificatory bath and, in some cases, by performing some rites.

It should be noted that the *smṛti* writers are not totally devoid of humane considerations for the untouchables. For example, on Purāṇic authority, the *Nirṇayasindhu* (III, under Devapratiṣṭhā) allows an *antyaja* or *Cāṇḍāla* to establish a temple of Bhairava. This does not run counter to *Guatama,* 14.2, or *YS*, I.93 wherein a *pratiloma* (one born of the union of persons in the reverse order of castes; a *Cāṇḍāla* is born in this way) is stated to be *dharmahīna*. This means that a *pratiloma* is debarred from Vedic rites like *upanayana*.

Euthanasia

In many progressive countries of the world, there has been a clamour for the right to die with dignity. Suicide, rather attempt at suicide, is generally regarded as a criminal offence. Some raise the moral question as to whether a person can take away his life which is not his own creation.

In ancient India, the close relatives of a person, who committed suicide, were not required to observe the usual *aśauca* or the period of impurity (*Gautama,* 14.11). *Manu,* V.89 holds that no water is to be offered for the benefit of the soul of one who puts an end to his life. According to *Vaśiṣṭha-dharmaśāstra*, 23.14-16, there should be no death-rites for such a person. It is ordained that a *dvija* who, out of affection, performs the last rites of a person who has committed suicide, must undergo the penance of *Cāndrāyaṇa* with *Taptakṛcchra*. The same work provides (23.18) *prāyaścitta* even for merely resolving to kill oneself. A person, trying to commit suicide by hanging, etc., may either succeed or fail. If he succeeds, that is, he dies, his body should be besmeared with impure substances. If his attempt fails, he should be fined 200 *paṇas*; his son and those close to him should be fined one *paṇa* each, and should undergo penance (*Yama*, 20-21).

In the modern world, many thoughtful people feel that that a person, unwilling to protract a miserable life of pain caused by an incurable malady or physical infirmity, should be given the right to kill himself; it is far more dignified to die in such a manner than ignominous dependence on others. Of the Western countries, we know of at least Australia where such a right has been recognised by law. The Calcutta daily newspaper, *Telegraph* of 28 September 1996, records the first case of euthanasia in that country.

In *Smṛti-śāstra*, voluntary death was of two kinds, religious and secular. At very holy places, like Vārāṇasī and Prayāga, people were allowed to kill themselves by drowning in the holy waters; this was done for release from rebirth.

According to *Atri* (218-19), one can embrace death without incurring any sin by jumping down a precipice, throwing himself into fire or water or by fasting under any of the following circumstances: very old age (over 70), inability to observe rules of bodily purification, infirmity, terminal illness. To the prescribed modes of death, Aparārka (p. 536), on certain authorities, adds *mahāprasthāna* (like that undertaken by the Pāṇḍavas in the *Mahābhārata*) or a long journey ending in death. To the circumstances, justifying suicide, the same commentary adds lack of desire for the pleasures of any of the senses, completion of the duties of a householder. Such a death is not only not sinful, but, in fact, better than *tapas* or austerities involving pain. It is enjoined that one should not desire to live in vain (*vṛthā necchettu jīvitum*).

That euthanasia existed not only in the Śāstric precepts, but was practised in very early times is attested by some Greek writers. According to the account of Megasthenes (McCrindle, p. 106), who visited India in *c*. 302 BC, the Indian gymnosophist, Kalanos, at the age of 73, consigned himself to the flames before Alexander (327-326 BC). Strabo (XV.1.4) writes that an Indian gymnosophist, who accompanied the Indian ambassadors that came to Augustus Caesar, burnt himself in blazing fire like the aforesaid Kalanos.

Democratic and Socialistic Trends in Manu-smṛti

The *Manu-smṛti*, no doubt, prescribes the monarchical form of government. But, this monarchy is not absolute, but limited. There are curbs on the king's power.

The word 'democracy' contains two components, *demos* and *cracy*. *Demos* means people and *cracy* denotes rule. Thus, democracy stands for rule by the people. In democracy, each individual has the right and opportunity to grow according to his or her aptitude. In a true democracy, there should not be any class struggle and exploitation of one group by another.

As we have stated, Manu's form of government is monarchical. But, there are elements of democracy in the *Manu-smṛti*.

It is interesting to note that the *Mahābhārata* relates the democratic origin of kingship. The *Śānti Parva* has this to say in chapter 67. Even before Manu's time, the society was guided by the principles of *varṇa*. But, the people were not happy. They suffered from the evil effects of class-struggle in the form of *Mātsya-nyāya*, i.e., oppression of the weak by the powerful section of the society. In such a chaotic condition, the people approached God Brahmā with a request to give them a king. Brahmā directed Manu to be the king. He, however, refused. He accepted the royal status only when the people elected him as their king. There was a clear understanding between Manu and the people. The people would obey, respect and protect the king, and pay him taxes. Manu, in his turn, would protect the people, and create a society free from the bad effects of class-struggle.

The entire populace, comprising the Aryans and the Dravidians, approached Manu. So, Manu introduced a social structure for the mixed population of Aryans and Dravidians. In doing so, he took elements from the Vedas and other sources. He interpreted and used these elements in such a way as to make it possible for every member of the society to lead an honourable life without any hindrance caused by anybody.

The structure of the society, envisaged by Manu, ensured freedom from class-struggle, and generated a feeling among the people that the society was formed by them, for their benefit and was run by them.

According to the Brāhmaṇical ideal, the four ends of life are *dharma*, *artha*, *kāma* and *mokṣa*. The last of these was beyond the scope of the *Manu-smṛti*. It concentrates on the other three.

In the matter of taxation, Manu protects the subjects against arbitrary imposts by the king, as we have seen in our account of taxation. He sets definite limits to taxation in respect of various commodities.

There are marked democratic principles in the system of rural administration formulated in the *Manu-smṛti*; with this we have dealt separately. We notice, in it, decentralisation of power much of which is vested in the people. Ideas of local self-government are manifest.

In a democracy, a great desideratum is the protection of the people against the rapacity and corruption of the government officials. In this respect, Manu shows considerable regard for the interest of the people. He states the plain fact that the king's men are mostly wicked and in the habit of appropriating others' things. From them he should protect his subjects (VII.123). He provides for ruthless punishment for those royal employees who take bribe from those who approach them in connexion with some business. Those extorting such graft must be deprived of all their belongings and banished from the country (VII.124).

A careful study of the *Manu-smṛti* reveals certain salutary democratic principles which appear to excel even modern laws in certain respects. For instance, in the case of an unclaimed treasure-trove, found by king, he should take only half, the other half should be given to Brāhmaṇas (VIII.38). Though, in this rule, partiality towards Brāhmaṇas is evident, yet it cannot be denied that the king is not allowed to appropriate the entire thing to himself. This rule appears to be more liberal than the present rule by which the State takes the whole of the find.

The democratic spirit is noticeable in another provision made by Manu. He ordains that the king should allow people to follow the rules relating to their own caste, own family prevailing in their respective regions, as well as those pertaining to their *śreṇī* (a guild or association of traders dealing in the same articles); VIII.41. Kullūka adds the proviso that the above rules are permissible only if they do not militate against the Śāstric injunctions. Here, it should be added that the original verse of Manu does not contain any restriction as pointed out by Kullūka. It may be that Manu categorically allowed the above rules to be followed by the people concerned without any interference by the king. But, as time passed, the Śāstric injunctions were more rigidly enforced, and, therefore, Kullūka, who flourished perhaps over a thousand years after Manu, added the above proviso.

Manu speaks against all the accumulated wealth of a king to be the hereditary property of his family. He ordains that a king, whose death is imminent due to an incurable disease or otherwise, should distribute all his money, acquired by way of fines, among the Brāhmaṇas before getting ready for death (IX.323). Here also partiality of Manu towards his community is obvious. Nevertheless, the rule has a democratic colour inasmuch as it attempts to socialise a portion of the amassed wealth of the king.

A salutary democratic, rather socialistic principle, laid down by *Manu* (IV.7-8) relates to anti-hoarding. He divides *dvija* householders into four classes, viz. *kusūladhānyaka*, *kumbhīdhānyaka*, *tryahaihika* and *aśvastanika*. These mean respectively, according to Kullūka:

(1) One who has corns sufficient for three years;

(2) One who has a store of corns for one year;

(3) One who has provision for three days;

(4) One who has a store just enough for the day without leaving anything for the morrow.

Of these, each succeeding one in the list is stated to be better than the preceding one. That is to say, one who has no provision for the next day is the best. In IV.2 and 3, Manu clearly declares that a Brāhmaṇa should accumulate only as much money as is sufficient for bare subsistence and the discharge of normal duties; he should do so without causing trouble to others, and resorting to reprehensible activities (*agarhitaiḥ karmabhiḥ*). Thus, it is clear that Manu does not support the accumulation of wealth in the hands of a few people to the detriment of the interest of others.

In certain minor matters, a sort of socialistic outlook is noticeable in the *Manu-smṛti*. For example, according to the provisions of this work, the king must take stern steps against theft. But, one taking the following things, without the knowledge or consent of the owner, should not be regarded as a thief. The spirit of this rule is explained by Kullūka by quoting Gotama. This authority allows a person to collect, with impunity, the following things from others' unenclosed fields; these are as if the collector's own property. The things are:

> Flowers, fruits, roots of trees, wood for sacrifice and grass for cows. (VIII. 339)

A traveller of the regenerate class, whose provisions for the journey have been exhausted, is allowed, with impunity, to collect two sugarcanes and two radishes from another person's field; this does not constitute theft on his part (VIII.341). Thus, a socialistic tendency is evident: Manu is against the idea that all the natural resources should be under the absolute control of the owners; they must share them with others.

Despite a pro-Brāhmaṇa or pro-*dvija* bias, the *Manu-smṛti* reveals some measure of egalitarianism in certain respects. This is particularly noticeable in the ethical principles inculcated by Manu. He ordains the following as the common traits to be practised by all alike, the high and the low:

> non-violence, truthfulness, non-theft, restraint of the senses and purity. (X.63)

Thus, in the society of Manu, the upper and lower echelons stand on a common platform so far as ethical principles are concerned; these principles are a sort of *pañcaśīla* which has been adopted by some non-aligned countries of the modern Third World.

Manu provides that a person with a load, to whichever level of the society he may belong, must be given way even by persons of high castes (II.138). A person of a high caste must give way to a person of any caste, who has crossed ninety years of age. A person of high caste must respectfully acquire salutary knowledge from even a Śūdra, and learn supreme *dharma* (means of salvation) even from a *Cāṇḍāla*. A man of a high caste, though ordinarily debarred from marrying a girl of a low class, is allowed to do so if the girl concerned is the best of her class (*strīratna*), II.238. All this shows that, in the eyes of Manu, in certain matters affecting cultural life, all people, high and low, stand on an equal footing. This is distinctly an egalitarian feature.

We have already referred to the fact that the king was debarred from interfering with the customary rules prevailing among particular groups of people. Such customs or conventions existed in the *jātis* or castes, *janapadas* or people of certain regions, *kulas* or families and *śreṇīs* or associations of traders

(VIII.41). This provision clearly demonstrates a democratic tendency of Manu. It should be pointed out that this provision was not confined to any particular caste, but was equally applicable to all irrespective of caste or creed; even the untouchables were not excluded. It is, therefore, obvious that the people, belonging to all sections of the society, had full opportunity of enjoying their rights.

The foregoing account of the *Manu-smṛti* will make it clear that Manu laid the foundation of democracy which, through centuries, developed into a mighty edifice of social system.

Basic Juridical Principles

The outlook and culture of a society are reflected considerably in its legal system. It is not possible here to give a full account of the ancient Indian legal system which was extensive. We shall set forth, mainly on the basis of *MS* and *YS*, only the fundamental juristic principles prevailing in those times.

Unlike the present Indian system, in which there are separate Civil and Criminal Procedure Codes, ancient India had a common Code. There are differences in detail in matters, Civil and Criminal.

The term *vyavahāra* has been used to denote a judicial proceeding. It consists of the components *vi* in the sense of 'various' (*nānārthe*), *ava* denoting doubt and *hāra* meaning 'removal'. Thus, *vyavahāra* means the removal of doubts about various doubtful matters, i.e., legal transaction. A judge is called *prādvivāka*. He is one who at first asks questions (*prāṭ* root *pracch*) and then tries (*vivāka*, i.e., *vivecayati*).

Traditionally, there were generally eighteen *vyavahāra-padas* or titles of law or matters of dispute. These, according to the *MS*, VIII.4-7, are (1) *Ṛṇādāna* (recovery of debt), (2) *Nikṣepa* (deposit of property with another), (3) *Asvāmī-vikraya* (sale by a non-owner), (4) *Sambhūya-samutthāna* (partnership business),

(5) *Dattasyānapākarma*, (resumption of gift), (6) *Vetanādana* (non-payment of wages), (7) *Saṃvid-vyatikrama* (breach of contract), (8) *Kraya-vikrayānuśaya* (dispute arising from repentance for purchase or sale), (9) *Svāmīpāla-vivāda* (dispute between owner and keeper), (10) *Sīmāvivāda* (dispute about boundary), (11) *Vāk-pāruṣya* (abuse), (12) *Daṇḍa-pāruṣya* (assault, too severe punishment), (13) *Steya* (theft), (14) *Sāhasa* (act of violence), (15) *Strī-saṃgrahaṇa* (relation of a woman with a man other than her husband), (16) *Strīpuṃsadharma* (mutual duties of woman and man), (17) *Vibhāga* (partition of inherited property), (18) *Dyūta-samāhvaya* (gambling and animal-betting).

Judicial Procedure

At the outset, it should be noted that, unlike the present system there were no separate courts for trying civil and criminal cases.

The fundamental principle is that the king cannot initiate a law-suit *suo motu*. *YS*, II.5 says — a *vyavahāra-pada* or subject of a law-suit arises when a person, harassed by others in a manner contrary to *smṛti* and *ācāra* (usage, custom), reports to the king. Thus, unless there is a complaint, there is no litigation. A complaint may be of two kinds, viz., *śaṃkābhiyoga* (based on apprehension) and *tattvābhiyoga* (based on fact). Supposing a man, suspiciously moving about like a thief, is reported against. Such a complaint is of the former class. A thief is caught red-handed. A complaint against him is of the latter type. *Tattvābhiyoga* is of two kinds, negative and positive. For example, a man, after taking gold, etc., from the owner, does not return it; a man takes away the property, etc., from the owner.

A law-suit, according to the *YS*, II.8, has four stages (*catuṣpād vyavahāraḥ*):

(1) *Preparation of the plaint* (*bhāṣā, pratijñā* or *pakṣa*)

After the plaintiff (pf) lodges a complaint, it should be written in presence of the defendant (dft), stating the year, month, fortnight, date, names of pf and dft, their castes, etc.

(2) *Reply* (*uttara* or *pratipakṣa*)

The reply of the dft, who has already heard the complaint, is to be written in presence of the pf. The reply may generally be of four kinds, viz., *saṃpratipatti* (admission by the dft as true), *mithyā* (stated by dft as false), *pratyavaskandana* or *kāraṇa* (of special plea or demurrer; e.g., I really borrowed the money, but gave it back or I received it by way of *pratigraha*); *pūrva* (or, *prāṅ*)-*nyāya* (statement of the dft that the issue in question was already decided, in his favour, in a previous suit). This principle, called *res judicata*, holds good even today.

(3) *Evidence* (*kriyā*)

The second stage above being over, the pf shall, at once (*sadyaḥ*), get the evidence in support of his complaint, written.

It should be noted that this stage does not arise if the reply is of the first kind, stated above.

(4) *Sādhya-siddhi* (*establishment of what is to be established*)

Some would call it more appropriately *nirṇaya-pāda* (the stage of decision or judgment).

It should be noted that, if the reply is of the first kind, mentioned above, then there remains nothing to be decided. Thus, there are only two stages (*pādas*), viz., *bhāṣā-pāda* and *uttara-pāda* in such a case.

Guiding Principles for Administration of Justice

We shall deal with the prominent principles only according to the *YS*, II.9 ff.

A dft cannot be allowed to complain against the pf so long as the complaint lodged by the latter against the former is not disposed of. Exception, however, has been made in the case of disputes arising for *vāk-pāruṣya* and *daṇḍa-pāruṣya* as also in *sāhasa*; in such cases, the dft can file a complaint against the pf even during the pendency of a case against himself, started by the latter. One cannot file a plaint against a person against whom a plaint has already been filed by another person. The pf cannot change or distort what has been stated by him before.

A surety, who is capable, may be accepted from each of the pf and dft. Sureties may be of three kinds:

(1) *Darśane* — one who undertakes to produce the litigant before the court.

(2) *Pratyaye* for creating confidence, e.g., you may pay him the money if you believe me.

(3) *Dāne* — e.g., one who promises to repay money in case the borrower refuses to do so.

In case the dft denies all the several things (e.g., gold, silver, cloth, etc.) mentioned in the plaint against him, but even if one of them is proved to have been taken by him, then the king should make him give all the other things. But, anything, not mentioned in the plaint, cannot be recognised.

In case of conflict between two *smṛti* texts, equity (*nyāya*) is to be resorted to in accordance with the usage (*vyavahārataḥ*) of the wise and learned people. An important rule (*YS*, II.12) is that a *dharmaśāstra* injunction is stronger than an injunction relating to *arthaśāstra* (contained in *smṛti*). For example, according to *dharmaśāstra*, continuous possession of a property for three successive generations constitutes right even if no valid mode of acquisition can be proved. This is a rule of *smṛti* relating to *dharmaśāstra*. Another *smṛti* rule, pertaining to *arthaśāstra*, is as follows: the king should punish him, like a thief, who possesses a property, without a valid mode of acquisition, even for many hundred years. In such a case, the former shall prevail. Again, *dharmaśāstra* ordains that a king, free from anger and greed, should administer justice according to *dharmaśāstra* (*YS*, II.1). But *arthaśāstra* provides — as it is better to gain a friend than the acquisition of gold and land, one should try to gain the former (*YS,* I.352). Now, in a judicial proceeding, if one party is caused to win, the king may gain a friend, but *dharmaśāstra* is violated. If, on the other hand, the other party is declared to be the winner, then *dharmaśāstra* is followed, but there will be no acquisition of friend. In such a case, the dictates of *dharmaśāstra* should be followed. For the significance of the word *arthaśāstra* in the dictum *arthaśāstrāttu balavad dharmaśāstramiti sthitiḥ* (*YS,* II.21), the reader is referred to R.C. Hazra's paper in Calcutta Govt. Sanskrit College Journal, *Our Heritage*, XII.1964.

Evidence, according to *YS,* II.22, is threefold, viz., *likhita* (document), *bhukti* (possession) and *sākṣin* (witness). In the absence of them, *divya* or ordeal is ordained. The first three are human, and the last one is divine. *Likhita* is twofold — *śāsana* (royal grant or decree) and *cīraka* (private document or a document of the common people). *Bhukti* is regarded as an evidence if there is continuous possession for three generations. Ordeals were of several kinds. According to *YS,* II.95 *Viṣṇu-dharmaśāstra,* IX-XIV and *Nārada,* IV.252, these are of five kinds, viz., *tulā* or *dhaṭa* (balance), *agni* (fire), *jala* (water), *viṣa* (poison) and *kośa* (consecrated water).

In all disputes, relating to money, the evidence as to the latter transaction is stronger. Supposing the pf proves that the dft borrowed money from him. If dft proves having repaid it, then he will win. In cases of mortgage, acceptance of gift or purchase, evidence as to the earlier transaction is stronger. The rule may, *prima facie*, appear to be meaningless, because the owner, by mortgaging, selling or giving away his property, loses the right of such a transaction again. But, when we consider that he can do so out of delusion or avarice, the rule appears to be meaningful.

The owner of a landed property loses his right over it if it is possessed by another person continuously for twenty years without any protest by him. In the case of money, adverse possession for ten years causes the owner's loss of right over it.

The law of adverse possession does not apply to the following: mortgage, boundary (*sīma*), *upanikṣepa* (an open deposit), property of an idiot or mentally retarded person, property of a minor, *upanidhi* (a sealed deposit), royal property, a woman's property, property of a Brahmaṇa versed in the Vedic lore.

Yājñavalkya declares (II.27) that a valid mode of acquisition is a stronger evidence than possession unless the latter is *pūrva-kramāgata* or for three generations. Valid modes of acquisition are, according to *Gautama* (X.39), inheritance, purchase, partition, seizure (e.g., appropriation of forest trees and other things having no owner) and by finding out (i.e., appropriation of lost property the owner of which does not exist or is unknown). *Gautama* (X.40-41) adds the following modes for the Brāhmaṇas, Kṣatriyas and Vaiśyas (also Śūdras) respectively: acceptance of a gift, conquest, gain by trade or labour. Even a correct mode of acquisition has no validity if there is not even slight possession over the property concerned. In the case of complaint in respect of a mode of acquisition, the person who acquired it will prove it. The onus of proving the mode of acquisition will not rest with his son or grandson; for them possession of the property is stronger than any other proof. The second generation will have to prove continuous possession in the presence of others without protest. The third generation will have to prove simply hereditary (*kramāgata*) possession.

If a person, accused in respect of the mode of acquisition of a property, dies before the dispute is settled, then the burden of proof will devolve on his heir; in such a case, possession without a valid mode of acquisition will not suffice.

Yājñavalkya (II.1) states that judicial proceedings will be 'seen' by the king accompanied by learned Brāhmaṇas. These associates (*sabhāsads*) of the king should be endowed with the following qualities: Vedic learning, versed in *dharma*, truthful, even attitude towards the enemy and the friend. This was the highest court of justice. There were other subordinate courts the formations of which were as follows, according to the *Mitākṣarā*:

Pūga — corporation of men of different castes and avocations, living at the same place.

Sreṇī — association of people of different castes, who earn their living by the same kind of work.

Kula — group of relatives, cognatic, of the litigants.

These were like tribuanls or *pancāyats*. In the dispensation of justice, each preceding one in the list is superior to the succeeding one.

As regards the recovered stolen property, *YS*, II.36, as interpreted in the *Mitāksarā*, means as follows: the recovered stolen property will be given by the king to the owner. If he fails to do so, he incurs the sin of both the owner and the thief. If the king remains indifferent to the article stolen, and does not take steps to recover it, then he is tainted by the sin of the owner. If, despite efforts, he fails to recover the thing, then he should pay its value to the owner.

Rāja-Dharma (Politics and Statecraft)

We shall briefly give an account of *rājadharma* dealt with in the *MS*, Chap. VII. In the interpretation of the verses, we have followed Kullūkabhatta.

ORIGIN OF KINGSHIP

According to the *MS* (VII.3-4), the king was created by God with the essential and eternal elements of various deities including Indra.

DANDA — ORIGIN, UTILITY AND APPLICATION

(*Danda* may mean also army. See Kullūka on *MS*, VII.65. We are not concerned with that meaning here).

For the king's use, God created *danda* (means of punishment). The functions of *danda* are as follows. Protection of all creatures; it is due to the fear of *danda* that all beings, mobile and immobile, become able to enjoy, and do not deviate from their own *dharma*. *Danda* chastises all the subjects; it is *danda* alone that protects (as stated above). *Danda* keeps awake (i.e., remains vigilant) when even the guards are asleep. If the king, free from sloth, does not punish those who should be punished, then *mātsya-nyāya* prevails; it is a chaotic condition in which the strong oppress the weak as, in the finny world, the strong fish devours the weak fish. In a society, devoid of *danda*, there is no ownership of any one over anything. All people are subdued by *danda*; a man (naturally) pure (*suci*) is rare. In the absence of *danda* or of the proper application of it, all the castes are polluted (by promiscuous inter-caste sexual intercourse), all Sāstric rules about the means to the attainment of the four ends of life are violated, all people become angry.

Manu warns against the arbitrary application of *daṇḍa* by an undisciplined king. The king, endowed with the following qualities, is stated to be fit for using *daṇḍa* properly: truthful, working with circumspection (*samīkṣyakārī*), wise, versed in matters relating to *dharma*, *artha* and *kāma*, pure, following the *śāstra*, assisted by good people.

Danda, if properly applied, pleases all subjects. If applied without circumspection, it brings about all-round destruction. If the king is attached to objects of sense, is irascible or a seeker of pretexts, then he is killed by that very *daṇḍa*. *Danda* kills a king who strays away from *dharma*, along with his son and friends. A king, who is without assistants, foolish, greedy, of uncultured intellect, and attached to material objects, is unable to apply *danda* justly.

So, *danda* should be duly applied to unlawful people after taking into consideration the place and time, correctly assessing the capacity and learning of the offender.

SACIVA, AMĀTYA

(*Amātya* may also denote *senāpati*. See Kullūka on *MS,* VII.65.

We are not concerned with that meaning here).

According to *Manu* (VII.54), the king should appoint seven or eight *saciva*s possessed of the following qualities:

> *Maula* (serving the king for generations, viz., father, grandfather), versed in *śāstra*s, heroic, *labdha-lakṣa* (who succeeded in hitting the target, i.e., skilled in the use of weapons), *kulodbhava* (born in a pure or untarnished family), *parīkṣita* (tested as to honesty in money-matters, character, ability, etc.).

Matters, on which they should be consulted by the king, are related generally to peace and war, *sthāna* (matters relating to *danda*, *kośa* or treasury, *pura* or capital city and the state), *samudāya* (sources of revenue like paddy-field, gold-mine, etc.), *gupti* (personal security as well as the security of the state) and *labdha-praśamanā* (right use of what has been acquired). The king has to consult them severally and jointly, and act for his welfare. A learned Brāhmaṇa *saciva* of special qualities appears to enjoy greater confidence of the king. It is only with such a *saciva* that the king should consult a matter of prime importance relating to the six political expedients, called *guna*s (see *infra*). Reposing confidence on him, the king should entrust him with all works; he should begin all work after ascertaining the mode with him.

Besides the *saciva*s, the king should also appoint as *amātya*s such men as are possessed of the following qualities: *śuci* (pure in financial matters), *prājña* (wise), *avasthita* (established), *samyaga-rtha-samāhartṛ* (earning money by proper means), *suparīksita* (well-tested). Kullūka takes *amātya* to denote *karma-saciva*, i.e., working or executive minister. Thus, the implication is that *saciva*s, mentioned above, were *dhī-saciva*s or *mati-saciva*s, i.e., advisory ministers. *En passant*, it may be noted that Kautilya makes (*Arthasāstra*, I.8, last verse) a clear distinction between *amātya* and *mantrin* by declaring—*amātyān kurvīta na tu mantrinah*.

MS, VII.61 provides that the king should engage as many men, energetic, skilled and wise, as are necessary for the completion of duties. It is not clear whether this provision relates to *saciva*s or *amātya*s or both. It, however, seems to be about *amātya*s; because these men are intended to perform duties for which *amātya*s are meant. *Saciva*s are meant only for giving counsel to the king. Of the above men, those, who are heroic, efficient and born in a good family, should be appointed for financial matters. Those, who are *suci* (pure in money-matters), should be engaged in mines and factories, while the timid ones should be engaged in the inner apartments, e.g., eating house, bed-chamber and harem, etc. The significance of the last provision is that if a heroic person is engaged at such places, then he, at the instigation of the enemy, can assassinate the king who may be alone or accompanied by women only.

Manu stresses the importance of secrecy of the king's deliberations with the ministers (VII.148). So, he recommends the following venues anyone of which may be selected: peak of a mountain, (secret place in the) palace, lonely forest (VII.147). The following persons and creatures are to be removed from such a place: idiots, dumb, deaf and blind persons, *tairyag-yona*s, too old persons, women, *mlecchas* (see Glossary), deceased person, deformed persons. *Tairyag-yona* denotes animal; but in this context, Kullūka takes it to denote talking birds like parrot. In VII.150, it is stated that neglected persons like idiots, talking birds and women (having a fickle nature) leak out counsel.

AMBASSADOR

Manu (VII.65) states that on the ambassador depend peace and war. It is he who brings about peace between two kings inimically disposed towards each other and rift between two kings living in amity, and engenders disaffection among the people.

An ambassador should be as follows: favourably disposed towards people (so that, even to the rival king, he may not be an object of hatred), pure in matters relating to money and women (so that he may not be won over by these two), clever, possessed of good memory, experienced about countries and proper and improper time, good-looking, fearless and capable of oratory. Through the rival king's attendants, their gestures and actions, the ambassador should ascertain his gesture and action in regard to his duties as well as what he intends to do about his employees (who are disgruntled, greedy and disgraced). Having correctly known what the other king wants to do, he should take care that he may not be subjected to suffering in that country.

CAPITAL CITY AND FORTIFICATION

The king should live in a region in which water and grass are not abundant, but which is full of wind and sunshine, rich in crops, mostly inhibited by cultured (pious, according to Kullūka) people, not infested by diseases, etc., charming (with fruits, flowers, trees, creepers, etc.), where the feudatory chiefs are loyal and the means of livelihood like agriculture and business, etc., are easily available. The king should live in a city protected by any of the following forts:

1. *Dhanva-durga* — surrounded by desert without water, extending over five *yojana*s (1 *yojana* = 8 or 9 miles).
2. *Mahīdurga* — built with stones or bricks and surrounded by a wall with height twice the width, minimum height being 12 cubits, on which soldiers can move for war, with covered windows.
3. *Abdurga* — surrounded by deep water.
4. *Vārkṣadurga* — surrounded outside, up to one *yojana*, by huge trees, thorny shrubs, etc.
5. *Nṛdurga* — guarded, on all sides, by many foot-soldiers equipped with elephants, horses and chariots.
6. *Giridurga* — situated on a mountain, very difficult to

climb and accessible only through a narrow pass, with river, spring, etc., within, with many corn-fields.

Of the above, the last one is stated to be the best.

WAR AND POST-WAR DUTIES

As we have seen, *daṇḍa* or war comes last in the list of political expedients, called *upāyas*. It is also the last means of dealing with a hostile king. *Manu* (VII.198) says that a king should never take recourse to war against a hostile king. This prohibition is not categorical, but conditional. It means that a king should never declare war so long as the other three means succeed. On failure of these three means, war has to be resorted to as *agatikāgati*. This is clearly stated in *MS,* VII.108.

GENERAL RULES REGARDING WAR

On a plain (not uneven) land, one should fight with chariots and horses. In a marshy place, one has to fight with boats and elephants. At a place, covered with trees and shrubs, one is to fight with bows. At a place, free from holes, thorns, stones, etc., one should fight with swords, shield and various weapons (*kunta* or lance, etc. — Kullūka).

Having placed the soldiers in array, one should cause delight (*praharṣayet*) to them, and test them thoroughly as to why they rejoice or become angry; the activities of the soldiers, fighting the enemies, should also be ascertained.

Even when the enemy is not engaged in battle, the rival king should besiege him and appear on his territory, and pollute the fodder, food, water and fuel there by mixing injurious things (*apadravya-miśraṇena* — Kullūka). In the enemy's kingdom, the tanks, ramparts and moats should be destroyed. At night, he should terrorise the enemy (with the sound of drums, etc). Those who are seducible in the enemy's kingdom, e.g., persons of the royal family desirous of getting the kingdom, greedy *amātya*s, should be seduced, and their activities ascertained. The stars being propitious for the king, he, wishing victory, should fearlessly start battle. As stated earlier, a king is advised to try to win over the enemy by political expedients, viz., *sāma* (conciliation) etc. War should, if possible, be avoided, because victory is uncertain and there is the likelihood of defeat.

Having conquered a kingdom, the victor should worship the deities there and honour the pious Brāhmanas. He should also give largesses for deities and Brāhmaṇas, and proclaim to these people who, out of loyalty to their king caused harm to the victor, freedom from fear in their pursuits.

The victor should instal, on the throne, a person of the family of the slain enemy, and enter into a contract about the do's and don'ts of the enthroned person and his *amātya*s.

As regards booty, the general rule is that chariots, elephants, umbrellas, money, corns, animals, women, base metal, all articles like molasses, salt, etc., will be the property of those who seize them individually (*MS*, VII.96). The soldiers, however, should make over to the king the best of the things obtained by them; like gold, silver, etc. The king should distribute, among all the soldiers, the booty that has been acquired collectively (*MS*, VII.97).

MORAL PRINCIPLES IN WAR

Manu is not an advocate of the maxim that nothing is unfair in war. Had he been alive, he would have condemned the kind of massacre in Hiroshima and Nagasaki as also the use of secret weapons and chemical means for decimating people. He did not prescribe indiscriminate killing of the people of the enemy's territory. He has clearly prohibited (VII.90) the use of secret weapons (e.g., a sharp weapon in a wooden case), arrows with ear-shaped blades, poisoned shafts and arrows with blazing blades. Among the persons, not to be killed, are the enemy on the ground (the attacker riding a chariot), a eunuch, one with folded hands (as a sign of submission), one with hairs let loose, one who is seated, one who says 'I am yours', one who is asleep, one devoid of armour, a non-combatant onlooker, one engaged in fight with another person, a naked person, an unarmed person, one with broken arms, a diseased person, one extremely injured, a terrified person, one who is fleeing (*MS*, VII.91-93).

MILITARY ARRAY

Such an array or positioning of soldiers in an expedition is called *vyūha* of which the following eight kinds are mentioned by Manu (VII.187-88). Kullūka describes them, and states the circumstances under which the particular *vyūhas* are to be formed.

1. *Danda — looking like a stick*

This is necessary when there is cause of fear on all sides. In it, the General is in front, the King in the middle, the Commander at his back; flanked by elephants near which remain horses and then infantry, it is uniformly arranged (*samavinyāsa*).

2. *Śakaṭa — looking like a cart*

It is tapering in the van, and wide in the rear. It is necessary when there is cause of fear at the rear.

3. *Varāha — looking like a boar*

It is narrow both in the van and the rear, but wide in the middle. It is necessary when there is cause of fear at the sides (*pārsva*).

4. *Garuda — like the huge mythical bird, said to be the mount of Lord Visnu.*

It is like *varāha-vyūha* with the difference that it is wider in the middle. These two are necessary when there is fear from the two sides.

5. *Makara — like shark*

It is just the reverse of Varāha.

It is necessary when there is cause of fear both in the van and the rear.

6. *Sūcī — like a needle*

In it, the soldiers are positioned like a row of ants; they are well-knit in the van and the rear, and swift and very heroic persons are placed in front. It is necessary when there is cause of fear ahead.

7. *Padma — like a lotus*

That is *padma-vyūha* in which a circle, uniformly wide all around, is formed by soldiers, and the king remains at the centre. *MS*, VII.191 mentions *vajra-vyūha*, but does not describe it.

Manu ordains (VII.188) that one should spread out the forces in the direction from which fear is apprehended. In the following verse the instruction is that a Commander and a General should be placed in each of the directions, and the battle front will be made in the direction from which fear is apprehended. Kullūka clearly explains the difference between Commander (*senāpati*) and General (*balādhyaksa*). Ten units of the army, each consisting of elephants, horses, chariots and infantry, are to be placed under one master who is designated as *pattika*. The head of ten *pattika*s is called *senāpati*. The leader of ten *senāpati*s is known as *balādhyaksa* or General.

ESPIONAGE

Spies are indispensable for the administration of a kingdom. Manu has not described the various types of spies. The mention of *pañcavarga* in *MS,* VII.154 appears to indicate the author's familiarity with five kinds of spies, according to Kauṭilya (I.11), who belonged to the *saṃstha* (staying at one place) class. Those five kinds of spies were, perhaps, too well-known in the society to need any description; this was probably the reason why Manu is silent about their characteristics and functions. Kullūka names and describes the five kinds as follows:

1. *Kāpaṭika* — a spy in the guise of a student. Such a person, knowing the minds of others and daring, seeking employment, should be won over by honour and money, and confidentially told by the king — you should at once report to me about a person whose wicked conduct is noticed by you.

2. *Udāsthita* — one fallen from mendicancy, who seeks means of livelihood, should be engaged as a spy and told in the above manner.

3. *Gṛhapati-vyañjana* — disguised as a householder, a cultivator, whose occupation is no longer paying and who is wise and pure, should be made to pursue agriculture and told in the aforesaid manner.

4. *Vaidehaka-vyañjana* — disguised as a merchant. A merchant, fallen from his profession, should be caused to take to trade and engaged after telling him in the above manner.

5. *Tāpasa-vyañjana* — distinguised as an ascetic. A man, with a shaved head or matted locks, desirous of earning livelihood, should be accommodated in a so-called hermitage, and told in the above manner.

In verse VII.153, one of the King's duties is stated to be ascertaining the activities of the informers. Kullūka explains that the king should enquire, through other spies about the activities of spies, engaged to gather information about the rival king, etc. It is one of the daily duties of the king to hear at night about the activities of spies (VII.223).

TAXATION

So far as merchants are concerned, before levying tax on their commodities, the king should consider the following factors: purchasing price, selling price, the distance covered in getting them, cost of meals incurred in this connexion, cost of security against theft, etc., and the profit derived (VII.127). The author illustrates the principle of taxation by a happy simile. As a leech, calf and bee suck or drink their food (blood, milk and honey respectively) little by little, so also the king should realise his annual revenue from the subjects (VII.129). He, however, warns the king against too liberal and too exacting attitudes in imposing taxes (VII.139). Total exemption of taxes out of affection for the subjects leads to the king's destruction, and the realisation of too much of taxes out of avarice causes oppression on the people (VII.139).

Regarding the king's dues, *Manu* (VII.130) perscribes 1/50th, 1/8th (or 1/6th or 1/12th) in the cases of cattle and gold, *dhānya* (not only paddy, but grain or corn in general) respectively. According to *MS,* VIII.39, the king is entitled to a half of the ore dug out of mines as he is the lord of the earth and gives protection. In the case of *dhānya*, the higher or lower rate will depend on the quality of the land and the labour involved in tilling the same (VII.130). It should be noted that this rate is meant for normal times. In emergency, the king may realise at the rate of one-fourth (X.118). Kullūka adds that the king, realising extra tax, which is meant for the maintenance of the people in distress, does not commit any fault. One-sixth of the profit is recommended in the cases of the following also: trees, meat, honey, ghee, *gandha* (fragrant substance or pounded sandalwood?), *oṣadhi* (it may mean herb, plant in general, a medicinal plant or a plant which dies after ripening of fruits), *rasa* (it may mean mercury, fluid substance, condiment, etc., which meaning is intended is not clear), flowers, roots, fruits, leaves, vegetables, grass, leather, bamboo, earthen vessels, all things made of stone (VII.131-32).

The main tax-payers appear to have been agriculturists and traders. It appears that everyone, excepting the *srotriyas* (Brāhmanas versed in the Veda), had to pay revenue or tax in some form or other. *MS,* VII.133 emphatically prohibits a king, even if dying, to realise *kara* from such Brāhmana. *MS,* VIII.394 exempts also the following: a blind man, an idiot, a crippled person, a seventy-year-old man (obviously, all old persons aged seventy or above are meant).

The common people, earning livelihood by dealing in cheap things like vegetables, leaves, etc., shall pay something as annual tax (VII.137) Each of the *kārukas* (*sūpakārādi* or cooks etc. — Kullūka) and *silpins* (pursuing slightly better vocations) and Śūdras living by manual labour, should be engaged by the king to work for him gratis one day in a month (VII.138).

RĀJAMANDALA — INTER-STATE RELATIONS

Manu conceives a circle of kings the relations among whom are defined. From VII.155 and 156, it is learnt that *vijigīṣu*, *madhyama*, *udāsīna* and *śatru* are the basic elements of the *rājamandala* (Circle of Kings). Manu does not define *vijigīsu*. Kullūka takes the term to denote a king who possesses wisdom, energy and the elements (*prakrti*). The kingdom is stated, in *MS,* IX.294, to consist of the following seven elements: *svāmī* (king), *amātya* (minister, etc.), *pura* (capital city), *rāṣṭra* (territory), *kosa* (treasury), *danda* (army) and *suhrt* (ally) *Madhyama* has been defined as the king whose territory is bordering on those of the *vijigīsu* and *satru* (enemy). *Madyama* king can favour these two when they are united; he can do harm to them when they are not united. Kullūka on *MS,* VII.158 states that, for the *vijigīsu*, the king whose realm is beyond those of the *ari* (enemy) and *mitra* (ally) is *udāsīna*.

Besides the above, there are eight others (*astau cānyāh samākhyātāḥ* — *MS,* VII.156). Kullūka, commenting on this verse clearly states the designations and realms of the kings constituting the *rājamandala* as follows.

Power towards the front of *vijigīsu* are as follows.

The king, whose realm is immediately next to that of the

vijigīṣu, is the latter's enemy (*ari*); the king of the next neighbouring territory is *vijigīsu*'s friend (*mitra*); the next king is *vijigīṣu*'s *ari-mitra* (enemy's friend); the immediately next king is *vijigīṣu*'s *mitra-mitra* (friend of the friend); the next neighbouring king is *vijigīṣu*'s *ari-mitra-mitra* (friend of friend of the enemy).

According to the same principle, towards the rear of the *vijigīṣu*, the hostile or friendly kings are to be determined. Their designations will be as follows: *pārsnigrāha*, *ākranda*, *pārṣṇigrāhāsāra*, *ākrandasāra*.

The concept of *rājamandala* can be made clear in the tabular form that follows:

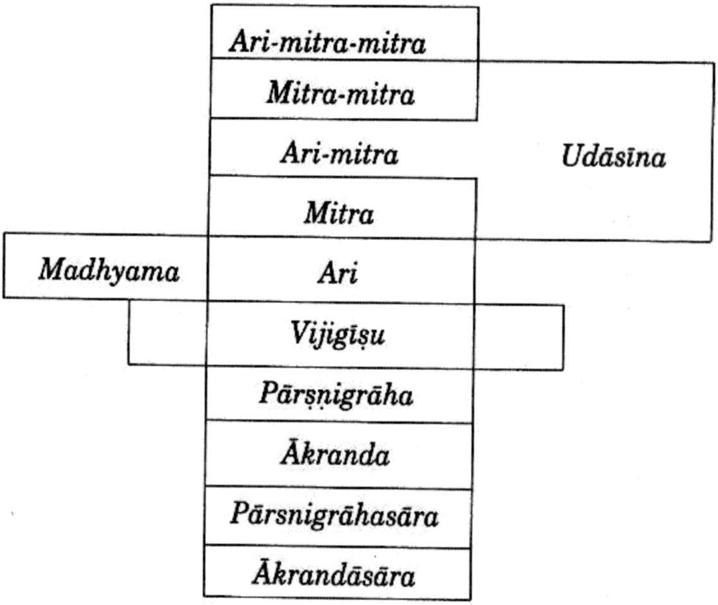

The general principle is that the *vijigīsu* should so act that the *udāsīna*, *mitra* and *satru* may not do any harm to him (*MS*, VII.180); Medhātithi, on *MS*, VII.171, says that even a friend or ally may be hostile if his interest so requires (*svārtha-gati-vasācca mitrama-pyarir bhavati*). Kullūka's warning is almost similar — even an ally may turn to be an enemy out of greed for money. Manu strikes a note on the balance of power when the king is asked (VII.177) to see, by all means, that a *mitra*, *udāsīna* or *śatru* may not be too powerful.

POLITICAL EXPEDIENTS

Manu formulates certain well-defined principles which should be followed by the king for the administration of the kingdom. Of these, four are called *upāyas*, and six *gunas*.

The *upāyas*, four in number, are as follows (*MS*, VII.107-9):

1. *Sāma* (Conciliation).
2. *Dāma* (Gift).
3. *Bheda* (Dissension).
4. *Danda* (It may mean punishment, punishing rod or army).

Of these, *sāma* and *danda* are commended for the prosperity of the state. Kullūka adds that *sāma* is commendable, because, in its application, not much effort is needed nor is it necessary for the king to spend much money or suffer loss in the slaughter of soldiers. *Danda* is praised because, despite loss of men and money, much is achieved. *MS*, VII.198 ordains that a king should try *sāma*, *dāna* and *bheda* separately or collectively, but should *never* resort to war. It is implied that war should be avoided so long as the three other *upāyas* serve the purpose. VII.200 clearly provides that the king should, in case of failure of the three other *upāyas*, fight by all means. VII.199 provides that, as a general rule, war should be avoided as long as possible, because victory is uncertain and defeat is possible.

The six *guṇa*s are (*MS*, VII.160): *sandhi* (mutual agreement), *vigraha* (hostility), *yana* (march, expedition), *asana* (attitude of indifference), *dvaidhībhava* (dividing the army into two parts, according to Kulluka), *samsraya* (taking shelter with a more powerful king). *Manu* (VII.169-74) clearly states the circumstances under which each of the above *guṇa*s should be adopted. When the king realises that, for the time being, he has to suffer a little but, after the war, he will certainly gain substantially, he should make *sandhi*. For *vigraha*, the proper time is when the king feels that ministers and all others in the kingdom are contented, and he is very well-equipped with elephants, horses and financial resources. The appropriate time for an expedition is when he thinks that his own army is joyful and nourished by the gift of money, etc., and reverse is the case with the enemy. When the king feels that he is weak in mounts and army, he should adopt *asana* while appeasing the enemy gradually by means of conciliation, presents, etc. The king should get his work accomplished by dividing the army into two parts, when he feels that the enemy is stronger in all respects. Kulluka explains that, in such a case, the king himself will remain in the fort with a part of the army, but the rest of his army would try to contain the enemy. Having done this, he will accomplish his work like the acquisition of an ally. When the king becomes extremely vulnerable to the enemy, he should quickly resort to a pious and powerful king.

RURAL ADMINISTRATION (*MS*, VII.114-20)

The king should appoint a headman for the village. One head should be appointed for each of the groups of ten, twenty, hundred and thousand villages. Offences like theft, committed in a village, should be reported to the head of the ten villages, if the village headman himself is incapable of remedy. Similarly, the head of ten villages should report to that of twenty villages, the head of twenty villages to that of hundred villages who, in his turn, should report to the head of thousand villages. The village headman will get, for his maintenance, all the food, drink, fuel, etc., which are to be offered by the villagers daily to the king. Kullūka makes it clear that the annual revenue, realised from a village, is not payable to the village headman. The heads of ten, twenty, hundred and thousand villages will get, for their maintenance, one *kula,* five *kula*s, a village and a city respectively. Here, *kula* means as much land as can be ploughed with two ploughs, each drawn by six bulls. A *saciva*, appointed by the king, for the purpose, will deal with the disputes of the villagers and with their offences of commission and omission.

As a measure of protection, a *gulma* is to be set up for units of two, three, five and one hundred villages. Here *gulma* means a troop of guards (*rakṣitṛ-puruṣa-samūha* — Kullūka); it seems to have been like a police outpost.

Moral and Ethical Principles in Smṛti-Śāstra

Indian Society, based on the four castes and four stages of life, is almost effete. Casteism, untouchability, etc., are being severely condemned. The rites and rituals, taught in *ṣmṛti* works, are mostly obsolete or obsolescent. Most of the practices, permitted and prohibited in these works, are losing their relevance. The spiritual overtone of the sacraments (*saṃskāra*s) like *upanayana*, *vivāha*, etc. is almost lost. Those, who try to cling to the age-old rules and regulations, have been reduced to a small coterie commanding scant regard of the people in general. Radhakrishnan aptly said that the society is wailing for a new *smṛti*.

Quick means of transport and emigration of young people to Western countries for career-making, education and in quest of lucrative jobs have resulted in a large number of non-resident Indians in foreign countries. The recent liberalisation of the Indian economy has given a fillip to the influx of foreigners into India. Thus, the free mixing of Indians with foreigners of different countries has brought about a cultural *melange*. This intimate contact has certainly produced some saltuary results, e.g., development of the scientific spirit, enterprise, industrial developments, etc. It cannot, however, be gainsaid that Indian culture has lost much of its Indianness. The Indians have, by and large, lost their moorings in religion and spirituality. *Artha* or material pursuit has ousted *dharma* as the principal end of life. The most dangerous effect is that people tend to earn and amass wealth by hook or by crook. As a result of the relegation of *dharma* to a junk-box, violence, broken marriage, promiscuous sex-relations, fraud, forgery, etc., are showing their ugly heads. General education is fast yielding place to technical training; in most cases, character-building of students is taking a backseat, and career-making has become the order of the day. Very often, we find the brain of man is being stuffed with technical knowledge, while their hearts are being neglected. This results in the production of human automatons or money-earning machines.

In these days of lack of idealism and erosion of values, it is worth our while to search for salutary principles-which have accumulated in the repertory of wisdom through ages. The principles, having a human face, adumbrated in our *śāstra*s, particularly in *dharmaśāstra*, hold good even today after the lapse of centuries. In fact, these are eternal verities which will endure as long as human civilisation lasts. This is why the renowned Indologist, Basham, declared in his treatise, *The Wonder that was India*, that the sages of India, who meditated in the jungles of the Gangetic valley six hundred years or more before Christ, are still forces in the world.

For the present, we shall take into consideration mainly some *Dharmasūtra*s, the *MS* and the *YS* as well as the *Mahābhārata*. As we have seen, the *Mahābhārata* contains a good deal of *smṛti* material.

Besides do's and don'ts for the different castes, we find precepts to be followed by all irrespective of caste. According to the *Mahābhārata* (*Śānti,* 60.7-8), the following virtues are to be cultivated by all:

> absence of anger, truthfulness, sharing possessions with others, forgiveness, raising issues on one's own wife, purity (perhaps denoting honesty in money matters), absence of spite, straightforwardness, maintenance of dependants.

Relation between Son and Parents

According to *Manu* (II.145), one's father is a hundred times more respectable than his *ācārya* (see Glossary). The mother is a thousand times more honourable than the father. *Manu* (VIII.299-300) does not allow the father to inflict on his son any heavier physical punishment than striking with a rope or a thin piece of bamboo.

The *Mahābhārata* declares (*Śānti,* 343.18) that the mother is one's greatest *guru*. According to the *Anuśāsana Parvan* (195.14-16) she deserves greater respect than the father.

The *Āpastamba-dharmasūtra* (I.10.28.9), *Baudhāyana-dharmasūtra* (II.2.48) and *Vaśiṣṭha-dharmasūtra* (13.47) also put the mother on a very high pedestal of honour.

Relation between the Teacher and the Taught

In ancient times, the student had to live in the preceptor's or teacher's house (*guru-gṛha*) during studenthood. According to the *Mahābhārata* (see S.C. Banerji, *Smṛti Material in the Mahābhārata*, pp. 52 ff.), the student must be very respectful towards not only his teacher, but also towards his (teacher's) wife and sons. He should serve the teacher to the best of his ability not only with money, but, if necessary, also with his life (*ācāryasya priyaṃ kuryāt prāṇairapi dhanairapi*). Before the commencement of study, he should salute his teacher and politely request him to give lessons. He should never speak ill of his teacher.

The *Gautama-dharmasūtra* (II.49) prohibits physical punishment of a student by his teacher. The next *sūtra* allows beating with a thin rope or cane when no other course is possible. *Manu* (II.199) forbids a student to mimic the gait, manner of speech or the action of his teacher. In the following verses, Manu asks a pupil to close his ears or to go away from the place where his teacher is criticised.

Relation between the Husband and the Wife

The *Mahābhārata* (*Ādi,* 68.40) declares that the wife is a man's half, his greatest friend, the root of his three ends of life (i.e., *dharma*, *artha* and *kāma*), and his (only) friend while he is dying. So, wives should always be honoured and nurtured (*Anuśāsana,* 46.5). The wife is Goddess Lakṣmī incarnate; when the wife is nurtured or tortured, Lakṣmī is also nurtured or oppressed (*Anuśāsana,* 46.14). Even when angry, a wise man should not utter unpleasant words to her; because, his enjoyment, love and *dharma* depend upon her (*Ādi,* 68.50).

That woman is pious who serves her husband, like her son, who is diseased, poor, tired by journey or reduced to a low position (*Anuśāsana,* 134.40). That woman is truly devoted to her husband, who even though looked at by him with cruel eyes or spoken to harshly by him, keeps a pleasant mien (*Anuśāsana,* 134.38). The good wife should be skilled in household work (*Ādi,* 68.39). The pious wife should be of good nature, pleasant speech, pleasing look, and have single-minded devotion to the husband (*Anuśāsana,* 134.33). She should not stay at the house of her father or other relatives for too long a time (*Ādi,* 68.11). In this connection, we may refer to Kālidāsa's remark (*Abhijñāna-śakuntalam,* V.17) that, though a married woman is chaste, she incurs blame by staying continuously in a kinsman's house.

The *Viṣṇu-dharmasūtra* asks the wife to be thrifty (*amuktahastā*). A woman is forbidden to practise *mūlakriyā*, i.e., magical rites like *vaśīkaraṇa,* etc., to decorate herself, and to go to the house of strangers in the absence of her husband. According to *Yājñavalkya* (II.285), a woman should avoid speaking to a man if she is forbidden to do so by her husband.

The *MS* (III.60) holds that constant well-being is sure in a family in which the husband is satisfied with the wife and the latter with the former. By the father, brother, husband, his younger brother, desiring much well-being, a woman should be honoured and adorned (*MS,* III.55), particularly in ceremonies and festivals (*Ibid.,* III.59).

Appendices

Appendix 1

Mahābhārata and Smṛti

THE great epic has been regarded as authoritative in the *smṛti-nibandhas* and the well-known commentaries on the *dharmasūtras* like those of Gautama, Baudhāyana, etc. and on the *dharmaśāstras* like those of Manu and Yājñavalkya.

We note below the principal *smṛti* digests citing the authority of the *Mahābhārata*. For the *Mahābhārata* passages, quoted in them, numbers of pages of the digests in which they occur, as also the location of the passages in the Poona critical edition of the epic, see the present author's *Smṛti Material in the Mahābhārata*, published by him in Calcutta, 1972.

Titles of Smṛti Digests
[In English alphabetical order]

Title	*Author*	*Place and year of publication, if any*
Ācārādarśa	Śrīdatta	Benares, Saṃvat 1936.
Brāhmaṇa-sarvasva	Halāyudha	Skt. Sāhitya Pariṣad, Calcutta.
Caturvarga-cintāmaṇi	Hemādri	Bibliotheca Indica, Calcutta.
Dānakriyā-kaumudī	Govindānanda	-Do-, 1903.
Dānasāgara	Ballālasena	- Do -, 1953.
Gṛhastha-ratnākara	Caṇḍeśvara	- Do -
Hāralatā	Aniruddha	Calcutta, 1909.
Kṛtya-cintāmaṇi	Vācaspati Miśra	Benares, Śaka 1814.
Kṛtya-kalpataru	Lakṣmīdhara	Baroda, 1948.

Title	*Author*	*Place and year of publication, if any*
Kṛtya-ratnākara	Caṇḍeśvara	Bib. Indica, Calcutta.
Kāla-viveka	Jīmūtavāhana	- Do -, 1905.
Madana-pārijāta	Attributed to Madanapāla. Composed by Viśveśvarabhaṭṭa.	Bibliotheca Indica, Calcutta.
Nirṇaya-sindhu	Kamalākara	Benares and Poona.
Pitṛdayitā	Aniruddha	Calcutta
Prāyaścitta-prakaraṇa	Bhavadeva	Rajshahi (Bangladesh), 1927.
Prāyaścitta-viveka	Śūlapāṇi	Calcutta, 1878.
Rājanīti-ratnākara	Caṇḍeśvara	
Śava-sūtaka-śauca-prakaraṇa	Bhavadeva	Calcutta, 1959.
Smṛti-tattva (in 2 vols.)	Raghunandana	Calcutta
Śrāddha-cintāmaṇi	Vācaspati Miśra	Benares, Śaka 1814.
Śrāddha-kriyā-kaumudī	Govindānanda	Calcutta, 1904.
Śrāddha-viveka	Rudradhara	Benares, Saṃvat 1920
-Do -	Śūlapāṇi	
Śuddhi-cintāmaṇi	Vācaspati Miśra	Benares, Śaka 1814.
Śuddhi-kaumudī	Govindānanda	Calcutta, 1905.
Tīrtha-cintāmaṇi	Vācaspati Miśra	Bibliotheca Indica, Calcutta.
Varṣa-kriyā-kaumudī	Govindānanda	Bibliotheca Indica, Calcutta.
Vīramitrodaya	Mitramiśra	Calcutta, 1875. Partly by Chowkhamba Skt. Series, Benares.

Title	*Author*	*Place and year of publication, if any*
Vivāda-ratnākara	Caṇḍeśvara	Bibliotheca Indica, Calcutta.
Vyavahāra-mātṛkā	Jīmūtavāhana	Asiatic Soc., Calcutta.

The *Mahābhārata* contains copious material which comes within the purview of *smṛti* or *dharmaśāstra*. As P.V. Kane states (*History of Dharmaśāstra*, Vol I, pt. 1, 2nd edn., p. 353), the *dharmaśāstra* material, contained in the great epic (Chitraśālā edn., with commentary of Nīlakaṇṭha) can be divided as

> *Abhiṣeka* — *Śānti* 40, *Arājaka* — *Śānti* 67, *Ahiṃsā* — *Ādi* II, *Anuśāsana* 115.1 ff.; *Āśvamedhika* — chs. 28, 43; *Śānti* 330, *Āśrama-dharma* — *Śānti* 61, 212-15; *Ācāra* — *Anuśāsana* 104, *Āśvamedhika* — 45; *Āpad-dharma* — *Śānti* 131 ff; *Upavāsa* — *Anuśāsana* 106-107, *Tīrthas* — *Vana Parva* 82 ff, *Anuśāsana* 25-26, *Śalya* 35-54; *Dāna* — *Vana* 186, *Śānti* 234, *Anuśāsana* 57-99, *Daṇḍa* — *Śānti* 15, 121; *Dāyabhāga* — *Anuśāsana* 45-47; *Putras* — *Anuśāsana* 48, 49; *Prāyaścitta* — *Śānti* 34, 35, 165/34 ff.; *Bhakṣyābhakṣya* — *Śānti* 36, 78; *Rājanīti* — *Sabhā* 5, *Vana* 150, *Udyoga* 33-34, *Śānti* 59-130, *Āśrama-vāsika* 5-7; *Varṇadharma* — *Śānti* 60 (mixed castes) *Śānti* 65, 297; *Anuśāsana* 48-49; *Vivāha* — *Anuśāsana* 44-46; *Śrāddha* — *Strī Parva* 26-27, *Anuśāsana* 87-92.

The author of the present work has collected the above portions of the *Mahābhārata* under the following main heads in his work, *Smṛti Material in the Mahābhārata*, (published by himself), Vol. I, Calcutta, 1972:

A. ĀCĀRA B. PRĀYAŚCITTA

C. VYAVAHĀRA D. RĀJADHARMA

Under each of these broad heads, the verses on the relevant topics have been collected. Based on the work is the author's *Indian Society in the Mahābhārata*. In the latter, the verses, collected in the former, have been rendered into English. The translation is followed by a study of the society reflected in the *Mahābhārata*.

Appendix 2

Purāṇa and Smṛti

We have seen, in the chapter on the historical background of the *smṛti* literature, how a number of *vrata*s arose in the Purāṇas. These were designed mainly for women and Śūdras, particularly for the former. The orthodox Brāhmaṇical society, in which women and Śūdras were denied freedom of performing religious practices and worship of deities, was jeopardised by the propagation of Buddhism and Tantras. Both these systems gave considerable latitude to the above repressed classes in religious observances. As a result, women and Śūdras were being alienated from the Brāhmaṇical society with its stranglehold on them. At such a juncture, the Brāhmaṇas composed or compiled a number of Purāṇas to stem the tide of the efflux. They afforded to the women and Śūdras opportunities to practise Purāṇic rites and rituals of which *vrata*s became very popular. The main reason of their popularity was that most of these *vratas* held out high prospects of material welfare, and the attainment of heaven in the other world. The very names of some of these *vrata*s indicate the purpose for which they were to be performed. For example,

> *Adāridrya-ṣaṣṭhī, Avaidhavya-śuklaikādaśī, Abhīṣṭa-tṛtīyā, Putrotpatti-vrata, Saubhāgya-śayana-vrata, Strī-putra-kāmāvāpti-vrata,* etc.

The Purāṇas concerned wax eloquent about the good effects of gifts to Brāhmaṇas. The gifts include even such things for daily use as rice, salt, sandals, umberlla, etc. It is said to be conducive to great merit to make gifts to a *kuṭumbī* Brāhmaṇa, i.e., one who has to maintain a big family. The carrying of the articles of gift to the donee's house, at the expense of the donor, is praised. Warning against *vitta-śāṭhya* (deceitful economy) has been sounded; this means that, in making gifts, one should spend to the limit of his capacity. All this betrays a wretched economic plight to which the Brāhmaṇas were reduced due to the efflux of people caused by Buddhism on the one hand and Tāntrism on the other.

The *vratas*, mentioned above, were devotional. Those of another kind were expiatory, designed to rid the people of sin; e.g., Cāndrāyaṇa, Prājāpatya, etc.

Smṛti looked upon Purāṇa as one of the sources of *dharma*. In *YS*, I.3, Purāṇa stands at the head of the list of the fourteen sources of *vidyās* and *dharma*. Naturally, therefore, *smṛti* attaches considerable importance to *vratas* which played a prominent rôle in the Purāṇas. Besides the works dealing with *vratas* as one of the topics, some treatises were devoted exclusively to this subject.

Śūlapāṇi of Bengal, in his *Vrata-kāla-viveka*, considers two things as the essential elements of a *vrata*; these are (1) *saṃkalpa* (vow, resolve) and (2) *dīrgha-kālā-nupālanīya* (to be observed or practised for a long time). The element of *saṃkalpa*, as the basis of *vratas*, is stressed also in the *MS*, II.3 (*vratāni yama-dharmāśca sarve saṃkalpajāḥ smṛtāḥ*).

The prominent works on *vrata* have been included in our Appendix on Classified list of *smṛti* digests.

Tīrtha (place of pilgrimage) is another topic in which Purāṇas appear to have influenced *smṛti*. Some *smṛti* digests deal solely with this topic.

The influence of Purāṇa on *Smṛti* was not a one-way traffic. *Smṛti*, in its turn, influenced Purāṇa. Many *smṛti* topics have been incorporated in some Purāṇas. For example, chapters 253-58 of the *Agni Purāṇa* reveal considerable similarity with the *vyavahāra* chapter of the *YS*.

Appendix 3

Tantra and Smṛti

As we have seen in our discussion about the background of *smṛtiśāstra*, *tantra* became very popular. Though in early times, *Tantra* was detested by the orthodox brāhmaṇas as *vedavāhya* (outside the ambit of the Veda), yet due to its pervasive popularity, the writers of *smṛti* digests felt compelled to recognise that much of *Tantra* which did not run counter to the Vedic religion. For example, in Bengal, which, according to some eminent scholars, was the original homeland of *Tantra*, Raghunandana (sixteenth century AD), the staunch upholder of the traditional *dharma*, for the first time, recognised Tāntric *dīkṣā* (initiation). In many rites and rituals, in vogue not only in Bengal but also in other regions, Tāntric *maṇḍala*s (figures), *mudrā*s (postures of hands and fingers), *yantra*s (diagrams) and the mystic *bīja-mantras* like *hrīṃ*, *hūṃ*, etc., are copiously used. Quite a number of Tāntric works have been cited or quoted from in different *smṛti* digests.

Appendix 4

Principal Schools of Navya-smṛti and Names of their Main Exponents

THE principal schools, into which the literature of the *smṛti*-digests on *smṛti-nibandhas* can be divided, are as follows. Under each school, we will mention the names of main authors. Their works have been dealt with in the chapter on WORKS. Brief biographical accounts of the authors have been given in the chapter on AUTHORS.

1. Gauḍīya or Bengal School

Aniruddha Bhaṭṭa, Ballālasena, Bhavadeva Bhaṭṭa, Bṛhaspati, Rāyamukuṭa, Govindānanda, Halāyudha, Jīmūtavāhana, Raghunandana, Śrīnātha Ācāryacūḍāmaṇi, Śūlapāṇi.

2. Maithila or Bihar School

Caṇḍeśvara Ṭhakkura, Harinātha, Rudradhara, Misarumiśra, Śaṃkaramiśra, Śrīdattopādhyāya, Vācaspati Miśra, Vardhamāna Upādhyāya, Vidyāpati.

3. Vārāṇasī School

Dalapatirāja, Kamalākarabhaṭṭa, Lakṣmīdhara, Mitramiśra, Nandapaṇḍita, Nārāyaṇabhaṭṭa, Viśveśvarabhaṭṭa.

4. Dākṣiṇātya or South Indian School

Devaṇṇabhaṭṭa, Haradatta, Hemādri, Kāśīnātha Upādhyāya, Mādhavācārya, Nīlakaṇṭhabhaṭṭa.

5. Kāmarūpīya or Assam School

Dāmodara Miśra, Nīlāmbarācārya (Mahāmahopādhyāya), Pītāmbara Siddhāntavāgīśa Bhaṭṭācārya, Vedācārya.

A Kāmarūpīya *nibandha* is mentioned by Raghunandana in different works, e.g., *Malamāsa-tattva*, *Prāyaścitta-tattva*, *Tithi-tattva* and *Ekādaśī-tattva*.

6. Orissa School

Gadādhara, Narasiṃha Vājapeyin, Pratāparudradeva, Vidyākara Vājapeyin.

Appendix 5

Inter-relations among Different Schools of Neo-smṛti

A COMPARATIVE study of the works of different schools reveals that they originated in widely apart regions which were, however, not in cultural isolation from one another. It is not surprising that the schools of Bengal and Bihar had the closest relation with each other. Apart from geographical contiguity, these two provinces had long been under a common administration. Besides, Navadvīpa, the academic metropolis of Bengal, attracted students from various regions of India, particularly from Bihar, the nearest neighbour. Likewise, the high reputation of Gaṅgeśa (thirteenth-fourteenth century AD) and other distinguished scholars of Bihar in *Navya-nyāya*, like Pakṣadhara Miśra (*c*. fifteenth century AD), attracted scholars of Bengal. For the influence of earlier authors and works on Raghunandana, see B. Bhattacharya's *Raghunandana*'s *Indebtedness to his Predecessors*.

Mithilā and Bengal

We find references to Maithila authors or their works in some of the works of the Bengal school. Sometimes, there are references to Maithilas without mentioning their names. The opinions of the Maithilas are often cited only to be refuted. The references to the authors and works of Mithilā are most numerous in the works of Govindānanda and Raghunandana. The prominent Maithila *nibandhas*, mentioned in those of Bengal, are as follows:

> *Ācāra-cintāmaṇi* (of Vācaspati Miśra), *Ācāra-candrikā* (of Padmanābha), *Āhnika-cintāmaṇi* (of Vācaspati Miśra), *Kṛtyacintāmaṇi* (both Caṇḍeśvara and Vācaspati Miśra have works of this title), *Kṛtya-mahārṇava* (of Vācaspati Miśra), *Kṛtya-ratnākara* (of Caṇḍeśvara), *Gaṅgāvākyāvalī* (of Vidyāpati), *Gṛhastha-ratnākara* (of Caṇḍeśvara), *Chandogāhnika* (of Śrīdatta), *Tīrtha-cintāmaṇi* (of Vācaspati), *Dānaratnākara* (of

Caṇḍeśvara), *Dāna-vākyāvalī* (of Vidyāpati), *Dvaita-nirṇaya* (of Vācaspati), *Mahā-dāna-nirṇaya* (of Vācaspati), *Ratnākara* (of Caṇḍeśvara), *Varṣa-kṛtya* (both Rudradhara and Vidyāpati wrote works of the title), *Vivāda-cintāmaṇi* (of Vācaspati), *Vivāda-ratnākara* (of Caṇḍeśvara), *Vyavahāra-cintāmaṇi* (of Vācaspati), *Śuddhi-cintāmaṇi* (of Vācaspati), *Śuddhi-ratnākara* (of Caṇḍeśvara), *Śrāddha-cintāmaṇi* (of Vācaspati), *Śrāddha-pradīpa* (of Śrīdatta), *Samaya-pradīpa* (of Śrīdatta), *Sugati-sopāna* (of Gaṇeśvara Ṭhakkura), *Smṛti-sāra* (of Harinātha), *Smṛti-ratnākara* (of Caṇḍeśvara), *Smṛti-paribhāṣā* (of Vardhamāna).

Bengal *smṛti* has been referred to in Maithila *smṛti* as *Gauḍa-nibandha, Gauḍa-smṛti, Gauḍa-grantha*, etc. The Bengal authors have been referred to as *Gauḍīyāḥ, Gauḍāḥ*, etc.

Among prominent Maithila writers, who appear to have been familiar with the Bengal school, are Śrīdatta (in *Samaya-pradīpa*), Rudradhara (in *Śrāddha-viveka, Varṣakṛtya*), Caṇḍeśvara (in *Kṛtyaratnākara*), Harinātha (in *Smṛtisāra*).

The prominent Bengal writers who or whose works are cited with approval or criticised by notable Maithila writers, are:

> Bhavadeva, Jīmūtavāhana, Aniruddha, Ballāla, Halāyuddha and Śūlapāṇi.

Bengal and South India

Of the South Indian writers, copious references are found to Mādhavācārya and Hemādri mainly in the works of Govindānanda and Raghunandana.

Bengal and Vārāṇasī School

The Vārāṇasī school of *smṛti* considerably influenced that of Bengal. Viśveśvarabhaṭṭa is referred to in Raghunandana's *Śuddhitattva* (p. 242). Viśveśvara's *Madana-pārijāta* has been copiously cited by him mostly in support of his own view. The references to this work are found mainly in the following works of Raghunandana:

> *Āhnika-tattva, Yajurvedi-vṛṣotsarga-tattva, Dāya-tattva, Jyotis-tattva, Śrāddha-tattva, Udvāha-tattva, Tithi-tattva, Malamāsa-tattva, Śuddhi-tattva.*

The *Madanapārijāta* is mentioned as an authoritative work also in Govindānanda's *Varṣa-kriyā-kaumudī, Śuddhi-kaumudī* and *Śrāddha-kriyā-kaumudī*. The *Madana-pārijāta* is referred to by Raghunandana's teacher, Śrīnātha Ācāryacūḍāmaṇi as well in his *Durgotsavaviveka*.

A *Mahārṇava*, presumably by Viśveśvarabhaṭṭa, is referred to or quoted from, always with approval, by Govindānanda in his *Varṣa-kriyā-kaumudī*.

Appendix 6

Theories on Creation in Manu-smṛti

Cosmogonical ideas have been haunting the inquisitive Indian ever since the Ṛgvedic times. Expectedly, the *Manu-smṛti*, the earliest and most authoritative *dharmaśāstra*, deals with the subject. What is interesting is that it contains three theories on creation. The first theory occurs in I.5-19. In the beginning, there was impenetrable darkness all around, nothing was perceived. There was no distinctive sign, nothing could be inferred, everything was unknowable, as if in deep slumber on all sides. Then the divine self-existent one, unmanifest to the external senses, possessed of irresistible power, the dispeller of darkness (or activator of *prakṛti* or destroyer of the state of dissolution), appeared making visible the gross elements (earth, water, fire, wind, ether as well as their subtle elements, viz., smell, taste, form, touch and sound). Wishing to produce beings of various kinds from his body, he at first produced water (*apa eva sasarjādau*) into which he cast his seed. That became a golden egg with the radiance of the sun. In it, he himself was born as Brahmā, the progenitor of the whole world. From that first cause, not yet unfolded, which was neither *sat* (existent) nor *asat* (non-existent) was produced a *puruṣa*, called Brahmā by the people. In course of time, the Divine Being split the egg into two parts. Out of the two halves, he created heaven and earth; between these two the middle region, the eight directions and the eternal receptacle of water (*apāṃ sthānaṃ ca śāśvatam*), i.e., the ocean. From Himself, he brought forth mind which was neither *sat* nor *asat*. From mind came *ahaṃkāra* (self-consciousness) and the *mahat-ātman*, all outcome of the combination of the three *guṇas* (*sattva*, *rajas*, *tamas*), the five sense-organs (eye, ear, tongue, nose and skin). All beings were created by him by joining the five subtle elements (*ṭanmātras*) and *ahaṃkāra* with the five great gross elements (*mahābhūtas*).

This theory is an echo of *Ṛgveda,* X.129 (particularly *Ṛks* 1-3 — *nāsadāsīnno sadāsīt-tadānīm, nāsīd rajo no vyomāparoyat* । *kimāvarīvaḥ kuha kasya śarman-nambhaḥ kimāsīd, gahanaṃ gabhīnam* ॥ *na mṛtyu-*

rāsīd-amṛtaṃ na ... na rātryā ahna āsīt praketaḥ .... taṁa āsīt tamasā gūḍhamagre 'praketaṃ salilaṃ sarvamā idam .... and *Chāndogya Upaniṣad,* III.19.1-2 about the golden egg. — *tat sadāsīt tat samabhavat tadāṇḍaṃ niravartata ... tannirabhidyata te āṇḍakapāle rajataṃ ca suvarṇaṃ cābhavatām tad yad rajataṃ seyaṃpṛthivi yat suvarṇaṃ sā dyauḥ.* Manu's theory also reminds one of *Sāṃkhya* theory of *tattvas* and *guṇas*. It should, however, be noted that Manu does not agree in the order in which *mahat, ahaṃkāra* and the five subtle elements arise.

Another theory of creation is stated in the *Manu-smṛti,* I.32-41. Brahmā split his own body into two halves, one of which was a male and the other a female. From the latter, he created Virāj who performed penance, and created a male. This male was Manu (propounded the *Manu-smṛti).* Urged by the intention of producing created beings, Manu at first created ten great sages, designated as Prajāpatis. They created seven Manus, Gods, certain classes of gods, great sages, *yakṣas, rākṣasas, gandharvas, apsarases*, serpents, birds, different classes of *pitṛs*, lightning, clouds, big and small stars, monkeys, fishes, cattle, deer, man, lions, worms, insects, flies, immovable things (like trees, etc.). This theory appears to be an echo of the *Puruṣa-sūkta* of the *Ṛgveda* (X.90), particularly of the following *ṛks*:

tasmād virāḍajāyata virājo adhipūruṣaḥ ।
sa jāto atyaricyata paścād bhūmimatho puraḥ ।। 5 ।।
tasmād yajñāt sarvahutaḥ saṃbhṛtaṃ pṛṣadājyam ।
paśūn tāṃścakre vāyavyānā-raṇyān grāmyāśca ye ।। 8 ।।
tasmād yajñāt sarvahuta ṛcaḥ sāmāni jajñire ।
chandāṃsi jajñire tasmād yajustasmāda-jāyata ।। 9 ।।
tasmād aśva ajāyanta ye ke cobhayādataḥ ।
gāvo hajajñire tasmāt tasmājjātā ajāvayaḥ ।। 10 ।।

The third theory is found in the *Manu-smṛti,* I.74-78. After awaking from sleep, Brahmā, with the intention of creation, applies his mind. It generates *ākāśa* with sound as its characteristic quality. Modifying itself *ākāśa* creates *vāyu* having the quality of touch. From *vāyu* emanates radiant light from which arises water. From water arises the earth with smell as its special quality. This theory appears to be a modified form of the *Sāṃkhya* doctrine according to which (*vide Sāṃkhya-kārikā,* 25) the five elements arise from *ahaṃkāra*. Manu, however, brings in God *Brahman* who is not recognised in the standard *Sāṃkhya*.

Appendix 7

Flora and Fauna in Manu-smṛti

THOUGH a *dharmaśāstra*, the *Manu-smṛti* contains interesting sidelights on Botany, Zoology, Ornithology and Ichthyology.

Flora

The following classification of trees and plants occurs in this work (I.46-48):

(1) *Oṣadhi* — trees of this class wither away after the ripening of fruits.

(2) *Vanaspati* — those which bear only fruits, but no flowers.

(3) *Vṛkṣa* — those which bear either flowers or fruits.

(4) *Guccha* — Fascicle.

(5) *Gulma* — Shrub.

(6) *Tṛṇa* — literally, grass. It is interesting to note that the bamboo belongs to this class, and is called *tṛṇa-rāja* (king of grass).

(7) *Pratāna* — plants with tendrils; low spreading plants.

(8) *Vallī* — creepers entwining a support.

It deserves special notice that Manu declares (I.49) that the trees and plants have consciousness within, and are capable of the feelings of pleasure and pain. This idea appears to be an echo of the *Ṛgveda,* X.97.21; this Veda is generally believed to have originated about 1500 BC.

The *Manu-smṛti* testifies (I.46) to the knowledge that of the trees and plants some grow from seeds (*bīja*) while others from branches (*kāṇḍa*).

Among the flora, the following are mentioned in this work:

Audumbara (from Udumbara) II.45 *Ficus glomerata*.

Bailva (from Bilva) II.45 *Aegle marmelos.*

Gṛñjana V.5 *Odina wodier*. Prohibited as food for Brāhmaṇas, Kṣatriyas and Vaiśyas.

Kavaka V.5 Mushroom. Prohibited as food for Brāhmaṇas, Kṣatriyas and Vaiśyas.

Khādira (from Khadira) II.45 *Areca catechu.*

Laśuna V.5 *Allium sativum*. Prohibited as food for Brāhmaṇas, Kṣatriyas and Vaiśyas.

Pailava (from Pilu) II.45 *Salvadora persica* or *S. olleoides*.

Palāṇḍu V.5 *Allium cepa*. Prohibited as food for Brāhmaṇas, Kṣatriyas and Vaiśyas.

Pālāśa (from Palāśa) II.45 *Butea frondosa.*

Śelu V.6 *Dilleni indica*. Prohibited as food.

Vāṭa (from Vaṭa) II.45 *Ficus bengalensis.*

Fauna

The *Manu-smṛti* (I.4) broadly divides worldly objects into two classes, viz., *sthāvara* (non-moving) and *jaṅgama* (moving). There is a broad division of the latter (I.43-45) into —

(a) *Jarāyuja* (viviparous) — comprising humans and animals.

(b) *Aṇḍaja* (oviparous) — birds, serpents, crocodiles, fish, tortoises, etc. The creatures of this class are sub-divided into *sthalaja* (terrestrial) and *audaka* (aquatic).

(c) *Svedaja* (born out of heat) — gad-flies, mosquitoes, lice, flies, bugs and others like ants.

The following creatures are mentioned in this work.

Animals

Manu does not separately mention different categories of animals. But, in different contexts, he names certain categories. For example, in verses XI.199; V. 9, 11, 13, 17, 18, 19; XI.199, the following categories of animals are mentioned:

Ekaśapha (having one hoof) V.8

Āraṇya (living in forest) V.9.

Kravyād (eating raw meat — carnivorous) XI.199.

Ekacara (moving about alone) V.17 (e.g., serpent),

Pañcanakha (five-toed) V.17, 18.

Ekatodat (having one row of teeth) V.18.

The milk of the animals of the *ekaśapha* class, mentioned above, should not be drunk. As regards the *āraṇya* animals, their milk, excepting that of the buffalo, should be avoided. One, bitten by carnivorous animals, becomes impure, and can be purified by *prāṇāyāma,* the three breathing exercises called *pūraka* (inhaling), *recaka* (exhalation) and *kumbhaka* (retention). The animals of the *ekacara* class are not edible.

So far as the animals of the *pañcanakha* class are concerned, the meat of the following is permitted as food:

Śvāvidh, śalyaka, godhā, kūrma, śaśa.

The meat of the animals having one row of teeth, excepting that of the camel, is edible.

Aja VIII.235, XI.136. The wild goat. *Capra hircus.*

Ākhu IV.126, XI.159. Mouse or Rat. *Mus boodug.*

Aśva IX.38, 136, 199. Horse. *Equus caballus.*

Avi V.8. Sheep. *Ovis ammon.*

Biḍāla XI.131, 159. Same as *Mārjāra* (q.v.).

Chuchundarī XII.65. Mole. *Talpa micrura.* Shrew. *Suneus caeruleus.* VIII.102

Dvipa VII.192. Elephant. *Elephas maximus.*

Gaja XI.136. Sameas *Dvipa* (q.v.).

Go VIII.146, 242. Cow. *Bos indicus.*

Godhā V.18, XI.131. Iguana. *Varanus* sp.

Gomāyu XI.154. Same as *Sṛgāla* (q.v.).

Haya XI.136. Same as *Aśva* (q.v.).

Kapi XI.154. Same as *Vānara* (q.v.).

Khaḍga V.18. Rhinoceros. *Rhinoceros unicornis.*

Khara XI.154, 199. Ass. *Equus hemionus.*

Mahiṣa V.9. Buffalo. *Bubalus bubalis.*

Maṇḍūka IV.126, XI.131. Frog. *Rana tigrina* and other species and *Bufo melanostictus* and other species.

Mārjāra IV.126. Cat. *Felis domestica.*

Mrabhra XI.136. Ram, *Ovis ammon, Ovis orientalis.*

Mṛga I.39. Deer.
(1) Musk-deer — *Moschus moschiferus.*
(2) Spotted deer or *Cītal* — *Axis axis.*
(3) Barking deer — *Muntiacus muntiak.*
(4) Black antelope, Blackbuck or Indian antelope — *Antelope cervicapra.*
(5) Swamp deer or *Bārāsiṅghā* — *Cervus duvauceli.*
(6) Sambar — *Cervus unicolor.*

Nakula XI.131, 159.·Mongoose.
(1) *Herpestes auropunctatus.*
(2) *Herpestes edwaarsii.*

Śalyaka V.18. Probably procupine. *Hystrix indica.*

Śaśa V.18. Hare. *Lepus nigricollis.*

Śṛgāla XI.199. Jackal. *Canis aureus.*

Śūkara VIII.239. Boar. *Sus scrafa.*

Śvan IV.126, VIII.239, XI.131, 199. Dog. *Canis familiaris*

Śvāvidh V.18 ?

Uṣṭra V. 8, 18, VIII.146, 239, XI.137, 154, 199. Camel.
(1) *Camelus dromedarius* (One-humped Arabian camel).
(2) *Camelus bactrianus* (Two-humped Bactrian camel of Central Asia).

Vānara I.39, XI.135, 154. Monkey.
(1) *Macaca mullatta.*
(2) *Hylobates* sp.
(3) *Prestytis entellus.*

Varāha V. 14, 19; VIII. 239; XI.134, 154, 199. Same as *śūkara*(q.v.).

Vṛka VIII. 235, 236. Wolf. *Canis lupus.*

Birds

Manu does not specifically mention any classification of birds. But several categories of them are incidentally mentioned in different contexts. These categories are as follows:

Pratuda V.13. Those which peck their food with beaks before eating.

Jālapāda V.13. Web-footed.

Nakhāviṣkira V.13. Those which scatter their food with their foot before eating.

Matsyāda V.13. Those which feed on fish.

Kravyāda V.11. Feeding on raw meat.

Grāmya V.19. Living in rural areas.

The following birds are mentioned.

Athene brama. Its killing is as sinful as the killing of a Śūdra.

Baka V.14, XI. 135. Heron. There are three species, viz., Purple heron (*Ardea purpurea*), Grey heron (*Ardea purpurea*, the common heron) and the one called egret (*Bubulus ibis*). Its meat is not edible.

Balākā V.14. Common teal. *Nettion crecca*. Its meat is not edible.

Barhiṇa (*Mayūra*) XI.135. *Pavo cristatus*. The killing of it is as sinful as the killing of a Śūdra.

Bhāsa XI.135. The white-backed vulture. *Gyps bengalensis*. Its killing is sinful.

Cakravāka V.12. The ruddy sheldrake or Brahminy Duck. *Tadorna ferruginea*. Its meat is prohibited as food.

Cāṣa XI.131. Blue Jay. *Coracias benghalensis*. Its killing is as sinful as the killing of a Śudra.

Dātyūha V.12. Gallinule (Moorhen) *Gallinula chloropus*. Its meat is prohibited as food.

Haṃsa V.12. XI.135.

(1) Grey-leg goose. *Anser anser*.
(2) Bar-headed goose. *Anser indicus*.
Its meat is prohibited as food.

Kāka XI.131, 154, 159. Crow.

(1) *Corvus splendeus*
(2) *Corvus macroarhynchus*
Its killing is as sinful as the killing of a Śudra.

Kākola V.14. Raven. *Corvus corax*. Its meat is prohibited as food.

Kalaviṅka V. 12. Indian house-sparrow. *Passer domesticus*.

Khañjarīṭa V.14. Grey wagtail. *Mota cilla cinurea*. Large pied wagtail. *Motacilla* sp. Its meat is prohibited as food.

Kukkuṭa V.12, 19; XI.156. Cock (Domestic fowl). *Gallus domesticus*. The meat of the village cock is prohibited as food.

Plava V.12. According to Monier-Williams, a kind of aquatic bird. Some identify it as *Rosy pelican*.

Rajjuvāla V.12. A kind of wild fowl. *Gallus* sp. Its meat is prohibited as food.

Sārikā V.12. Common myna. *Acridotheres tristis*. Its meat is prohibited as food.

Śuka V.12. Parrot or Rose-ringed Parakeet. *Psittaculo krameri*. Its meat is prohibited as food.

Śyena XI.135. Hawk, falcon. *Falco peregrinator*. Its killing is sinful.

Ṭiṭṭibha V.11. Its meat is prohibited as food.

Tittiri XI.134. Francoline partridge. (1) *Francolinus* sp. (Grey partridge). (2) *Francolinus francolinus* (Black partridge). Its killing is sinful.

Ulūka XI.131. (1) Barn owl *Tyato alba*. (2) Spotted owlet.

Fish and other Aquatic Creatures

Manu appears (V.16) to have divided fish into two broad classes, viz. *saśalka* (with scales) and *aśalka* (without scales). The following fish and other aquatic creatures are mentioneed by Manu.

Kacchapa I.44. Tortoise. *Kachuga* sp., *Testudo* sp., *Trionyx* sp. Stated to be *aṇḍaja* or born out of egg.

Kumbhīra V.18. Crocodile. *Crocodylus* sp.

Madgura V.13. *Clarius batrachus*.

Mīna XI.68. Fish in general. *Wallago, Mystus, Pangasius*.

Nakra I.44. From the description, it appears that it is either Sword-fish or Saw-fish. *Pristis* sp.

Pāṭhīna V.16. It is the same, as *Vodāla*, mentioned in Monier-Williams' *Skt.-Eng. Dictionary*. From Kullūka's commentary, it appears to have been a large fish preying upon small ones. *Wallago attu*.

Rājīva V.16.

Rohita V.16. Pink-coloured. Probably so-called because of its reddish tinge; in Sanskrit, sometimes *R* and *L* become interchangeable. *Labio fimbriatus*.

Siṃhatuṇḍa V.16. Lion-faced (fish). *Bagarius bagarius*.

Appendix 8

Geographical Information in Manu-smṛti

[*N.B.* : Here we set forth only as much information as can be gleaned from the text of the *Manu-smṛti* and its commentary, *Manvartha-muktāvalī*, by Kullūka. For details about the entries in this list, the curious reader may consult D.C. Sircar's *Studies in the Geography of Ancient and Medieval India,* Delhi, 1971, and N.L. Dey's *The Geographical Dictionary of Ancient and Medieval India*, New Delhi, 1971.]

Āryāvarta (II. 22)

Name of that part of India, which lies in between the mountains, Himālaya and the Vindhya, and extends up to the eastern and western oceans.

Brahmarṣideśa (II. 19)

The land, beyond Brahmāvartta, comprising Kurukṣetra (Thāneśvar), Matsya (territory of Jaipur), Pañcāla (Rohilkhaṇḍa; according to Kullūka — Kānyakubja), Śūrasena (Mathurā).

Brahmāvartta (II. 17)

The part of India lying between the rivers Sarasvatī and Dṛṣadvatī.

Madhyadeśa (II. 21)

That part of India, in between the Himālaya and the Vindhya, lying on the east of *Vinaśana* (q.v.) and the west of Prayāga (Allāhābād).

Mleccha-deśa (II. 23)

The region, lying beyond the Yajñiyadeśa (q.v.), is so-called.

[*Note* : According to *Bālakrīḍā* commentary of Viśvarūpa (*c.* ninth cent.) on *Yājñavalkya-smṛti,* III. 256, *mleccha* was the name of the tribe *Pulinda* as well as of the Tājikas or Arabs.

***Vinaśana* II.21**

Vinaśanāt sarasvatyntardhānadeśāt — Kullūka. It means the place where the river Sarasvatī disappeared.

Yajñiyadeśa (II. 23)

The region in India, which is the natural habitat of the species of deer, called Kṛṣṇasāra (spotted antelope).

Appendix 9

Mixed Castes and Tribes Mentioned in Manu-smṛti

[In Devanāgarī alphabetical order]

[*N.B.* We have followed Kullūka's commentary.]

Antyāvasāyin (X.39)

A mixed caste sprung from the union of a Caṇḍāla (q.v.) male and a Niṣāda (q.v.) female.

Ambaṣṭha (X.8, 13, etc.)

One sprung from the union of a Brāhmaṇa male and a Vaiśya female.

Ābhīra (X.15)

One sprung from the union of a Brāhmaṇa and an Ambaṣṭha (q.v.) female.

Āyogava (X.12, 15, etc.)

One born of the union of a Śūdra with Vaiśya female.

Āvantya (X.21)

Offspring of a vrātya (q.v.) Brāhmaṇa from a Brāhmaṇa woman.

Āvṛta (X.15)

One sprung from a Brāhmaṇa male and an Ugra (q.v.) female.

Āhiṇḍika (X.37)

Offspring of a *Niṣāda* (q.v.) male by a *Vaideha* (q.v.) female.

Ugra (IV.212, X. 9, 13 etc.)

According to an authority, quoted by Kullūka on IV.212, one born of the union of a Kṣatriya and a Śūdra female. This is confirmed by *Manu,* X.9, 13.

Karaṇa (X.22)

One born of the union of a Kṣatriya and a *vrātya* (q.v.) woman of the same caste.

Kārāvara (X.36)

A sub-caste sprung from the union of a *Niṣāda* (q.v.) with a *Vaideha* (q.v.) woman.

Kāruṣa (X.23)

A sub-caste sprung from the union of a *vrātya* (q.v.) *Vaiśya* and a woman of the same caste.

Kukkuṭaka (X. 18)

One born of the union of a Śūdra and a *Niṣāda* (q.v.) female.

Kaivarta (X.34)

One born to a *Niṣāda* (q.v.) by an *Āyogava* (q.v.) woman.

Khasa (X.22)

One born of the union of a *vrātya* (q.v.) Kṣatriya and a woman of the same caste.

Kṣattā (X. 12, 13, etc.)

One born of the union of a Śūdra male and a Kṣatriya female.

Jhalla (X.22)

One born of the union of a *vrātya* (q.v.) Kṣatriya and a female of the same caste.

Tunnavāya (IV.214)

Offspring of a *Vaideha* (q.v.) from a Kṣatriya woman.

Draviḍa (X.22)

One born of the union of a vrātya (q.v.) Kṣatriya and a woman of the same caste.

Nicchivi (X.22)

Parentage same as that of a Draviḍa above.

Niṣāda (X.8, 18, etc.)

Offspring of a Brāhmaṇa by a Śūdra woman.

Pāṇḍusopāka (X.37)

Offspring of a *Cāṇḍāla* (q.v.) male from a *Vaideha* (q.v.) female.

Pāraśava (IX.78, X.8)

Another name of *Niṣāda* (q.v.).

Puṣpadha (X.21)

Same as Bhūrjakaṇṭaka (q.v.).

Bhūrjakaṇṭaka (X.21)

Offspring of a *vrātya* (q.v.) Brāhmaṇa from a woman of the same caste.

Malla (X.22)

Parentage same as that of *Jhalla* (q.v.).

Māgadha (X.11, 17, etc.)

One born of the union of a Vaiśya male and Kṣatriya female.

Mārgava (X.34)

Parentage same as that of Kaivarta (q.v.).

Meda (X.36, 48)

Offspring of a *Vaideha* (q.v.) male and a *Niṣāda* female.

Maitreyaka (X.33)

Offspring of a *Vaideha* (q.v.) male and an *Āyogava* (q.v.) female.

Mleccha (X. 45)

Kullūka designates *mleccha* as *dasyu* (demon). According to him, it denotes those among the members of the four castes who have become outcast due to the non-performance of their duties irrespective of whether they speak the *mleccha* tongue or the Aryan language.

It may be noted that Viśvarūpa, in his *Bālakrīḍā* commentary on *Yājñavalkya*, III.256, explains *mleccha* as (the tribe called) Pulinda and (the Arabs called) Tājika.

According to some, the word denotes a Persian and the like. Others take it to stand for those who live in Ceylon and such other places as are devoid of *varṇāśrama-dharma*.

Rañjaka (IV.216)

Offspring of clandestine union of a Śūdra male and a Kṣatriya female.

Veṇa (X.19, 49)

One born of the union of a *Vaidehaka* (q.v.) male and an *Ambaṣṭha* (q.v.) woman.

Vaideha(ka) (X.11, 13, etc.)

Offspring of the union of a Vaiśya male and a Brāhmaṇa female.

Vrātya (VIII.373, X. 20-23, etc.)

1. One born to a member of *dvija* (twice-born) class, by a wife of the same caste, on whom or on whose ancestors the sacrament of *upanayana* has not been performed.
2. Any one born of the mixture of *varṇas* or castes.

Śaikha (X.21)

Same as Āvantya (q.v.).

Śvapaca (X.51)

Neither Manu nor Kullūka defines it. From various other *smṛti* works, the following descriptions can be gathered:

(1) Offspring of an *Ugra* (q.v.) male from a female of the *Kṣatṛ* (q.v.) caste.

(2) Offspring of a *Kṣatṛ* (q.v.) male from an *Ugra* female.

(3) Offspring of a *Caṇḍāla* (q.v.) male from a Brāhmaṇa female.

Śvapāka (X.19)

One born of the union of a *Kṣatṛ* (q.v.) male and an *Ugra* female.

Appears to be the same as Śvapaca above.

Sūta (X.11, 17, etc.)

One born of the union of a Kṣatriya male and a Brāhmaṇa female.

Sairindhra (X.32)

"A kind of menial or domestic servant (in the caste-system born from a *dasyu* and an *āyogavī*.)" — Monier-Williams.

Sopāka (X.38)

Offspring of the union of a *Caṇḍāla* male and *pukkasa* (q.v.) female.

Appendix 10

Manu Abroad

[FOR a detailed account, see *Manu Dharmaśāstra* by K. Motwani.]

The influence of Manu spread far beyond the limits of India. We shall briefly describe his influence in different countries of the East and the West.

In some law books of Myānmār (Burma), indebtedness to Manu has been acknowledged. The well-known Ceylonese work, *Cūlavaṃśa* often mentions the *Rājadharma* of Manu. Some countries of south-east Asia testify to the deep impact of the *Manu-smṛti*. The Indonesian treatises on law appear to be based on it. Among such works, the *Kutara Mānava* is the oldest, the major portion of which follows the work of Manu. Based entirely on the *Manu-smṛti* is the *Dawagama*. The *Svarajambu* is mostly influenced by Manu.

Manu appears to have influenced the laws of Mālaya. The legal literature of Jāvā appears to have drawn considerably on the *Manu-smṛti*. The code of law, called *Kramaning Sākṣī*, reveals the impact of Manu.

Some Balinese works testify to the influence of Manu.

The Siamese legal system seems to be based on the *Manu-smṛti*. A work on law is entitled *Phra Dhamaśāstra*.

The high esteem, in which Manu was held, is indicated by the establishment of his statue in the Art Gallery of the Senate Chamber of the Philippine Republic.

R. Lingat deals (*Annals of Bhandarkar Oriental Res. Inst.*, Poona, vol. XXX) with the spread of Hindu law in Hīnayānist Indo-China and Bali (See *S.K. Āiyangār Pres. Vol.*, pp. 445 ff). Manu, perhaps, played a considerable part in this matter.

Some Aryans established colonies in Japan long before the advent of the Buddha (*c.* 500 BC). They appear to have introduced several scriptures there including the *Manu-smṛti* (*vide* H. Kimura, "Sanskrit Studies in Japan", *Jour. of Oriental Research*, Madras, 1956-57).

The worship of Manu and the study of his *smṛti* were introduced, through the followers of Zoroaster, in West Asia and Western countries.

It is interesting to note that Vaivasvata Manu figures as a deity in the pantheon of Persia. Iranian culture reveals the great influence of the *Mañu-smṛti*. It is said that, for the administration of the Persian empire under Darius (sixth-fifth centuries BC), laws were formulated according to Manu's treatise.

It deserves notice that, among the wandering Gypsies, we find traces of professions ordained by Manu for outcastes.

Appendix 11

A Classified List of Smṛti Works

SUCH a list is necessary for those who want to study a particular aspect of ancient Indian society, e.g. *Saṃskāra, Śrāddha, Prāyaścitta, Vyavahāra, Udvāha* or *Vivāha, Rājadharma, Durgāpūjā, Vrata, Dāna, Tīrtha, Dattaka, Aśauca*. By *Rājadharma* here we mean politics and statecraft, as dealt with in some *smṛti* works. We shall set forth the titles of the noteworthy works in the English alphabetical order, under appropriate heads, with the names of the respective authors. As the bibliography of editions of texts and studies as also of the authors has been given under Authors and Works as well as in the general bibliography, we do not repeat them here.

Saṃskāra
(including marriage which is a *saṃskāra*)

Title	*Author*	*Remarks*
Brāhmaṇa-sarvasva	Halāyudha	
Chandoga-paddhati		Same as *Karmānuṣṭhāna-paddhati* (q.v.).
Daśa-karma-paddhati		Same as *Karmānuṣṭhāna-paddhati* (q.v.).
Karmānuṣṭhāna-paddhati	Bhavadeva Bhaṭṭa	On the performance of *saṃskāras*
Karmopadeśinī		Same as *Brāhmaṇa-sarvasva* (q.v.).
Madana-pārijāta	Madanapāla	Portion on *saṃskāra*.
Nirṇaya-sindhu	Kamalākara	Portion on *saṃskāra*.

Title	*Author*	*Remarks*
Nṛsiṃhaprasāda	Dalapati	Portion on *saṃskāra*.
Sambandha-cintāmaṇi	Vācaspati Miśra	On marriage.
Sambandha-viveka	Bhavadeva Bhaṭṭa	On marriage.
Saṃskāra-paddhati		Same as *Karmānuṣṭhāna-paddhati* (q.v.).
Saṃskāra-tattva	Raghunandana	Included in author's *Smṛtitattva*
Smṛti-candrikā	Devaṇabhaṭṭa	Portion on *saṃskāra*.
Smṛtikaustubha	Anantadeva	Portion on *saṃskāra*.
Udvāha-candrāloka	Candrakānta Tarkālaṃkāra	
Udvāha-tattva	Raghunandana	Included in author's *Smṛti-tattva*.
Vivāha-tattvārṇava	Śrīnātha Ācāryacūḍāmaṇi	

Aśauca

Title	*Author*	*Remarks*
Hāralatā	Aniruddha	Deals with *aśauca*.
Madana-pārijāta	Madanapāla	Portion on *aśauca*.
Nirṇaya-sindhu	Kamalākara	Portion on *aśauca*.
Pitṛdayitā	Aniruddha	Portion on *aśauca*.
Smṛti-candrikā	Devaṇabhaṭṭa	Portion on *aśauca*.
Smṛti-ro'nākara	Caṇḍeśvara	Portion on *aśauca*.
Śuddhi-kaumudī	Govindānanda	
Śuddhi-tattva	Raghunandana	

Śrāddha

Title	Author	Remarks
Karmopadeśinī-paddhati		Same as *Pitṛ-dayitā* (q.v.).
Kṛtya-kalpataru	Lakṣmīdhara	Portion on *śrāddha*.
Madana-pārijāta	Madanapāla	Portion on *śrāddha*.
Pitṛdayitā	Aniruddha	A portion on *śrāddha*.
Nirṇaya-sindhu	Kamalākara	Portion on *śrāddha*.
Nṛsiṃhaprasāda	Dalapati	Portion on *śrāddha*.
Pitṛdayitā	Aniruddha	Portion on *śrāddha*.
Sāma-śrāddha-tattva	Raghunandana	Included in author's *Smṛti-tattva*.
Smṛticandrikā	Devaṇabhaṭṭa	Portion on *śrāddha*.
Śrāddha-kriyā-kaumudī	Govindānanda	
Śrāddha-viveka	Śūlapāṇi	
Śrāddha-viveka	Rudradhara	
Yajur-vṛṣotsarga-tattva	Raghunandana	Included in author's *Smṛti-tattva*.
Yajus-śrāddha-tattva	Raghunandana	Included in author's *Smṛti-tattva*.

Dāna

Title	Author	Remarks
Caturvarga-cintāmaṇi	Hemādri	A portion on *dāna*.
Dāna-kriyā-kaumudī	Govindānanda	
Dāna-ratnākara		A part of Caṇḍeśvara's *Smṛti-ratnākara*.

Title	Author	Remarks
Dāna-sāgara	Vallālasena	
Kṛtyakalpataru	Lakṣmīdhara	Portion on *dāna*.
Nṛsiṃhaprasāda	Dalapati	Portion on *dāna*.
Pitṛdayitā	Aniruddha	Portion on *dāna*.
Smṛti-kaustubha	Anantadeva	Portion on *dāna*.
Smṛti-ratnākara	Caṇḍeśvara	Portion on *dāna*.

Prāyaścitta

Title	Author	Remarks
Baudhāyana-dharmasūtra	Baudhāyana	*Prāyaścitta* discussed among other topics.
Gautama-dharmasūtra	Gautama	*Prāyaścitta* discussed among other topics.
Madana-pārijāta	Madanapāla	Portion on *prāyaścitta*.
Manu-smṛti		Ch. XI *prāyaścitta*
Nṛsiṃhaprasāda	Dalapati	Portion on *prāyaścitta*
Parāśara-smṛti	Parāśara	Portion on *prāyaścitta*
Prāyaścitta-prakaraṇa	Bhavadeva Bhaṭṭa	
Prāyaścitta-viveka	Śūlapāṇi	
Prāyaścitta-tattva	Raghunandana	Included in author's *Smṛti-tattva*.
Yājñavalkya-smṛti	Yājñavalkya	Portion on *prāyaścitta*

Tīrtha

Title	*Author*	*Remarks*
Caturvarga-cintāmaṇi	Hemādri	A portion on *tīrtha.*
Kṛtyakalpataru	Lakṣmīdhara	Portion on *tīrtha.*
Nṛsiṃhaprasāda	Dalapati	Portion on *tīrtha.*
Tīrtha-cintāmaṇi	Vācaspati Miśra	
Tristhalīsetu	Nārāyaṇabhaṭṭa	

Vrata

Title	*Author*	*Remarks*
Caturvarga-cintāmaṇi	Hemādri	A portion is on *vrata.*
Kṛtya-ratnākara	Caṇḍeśvara	Portion on *vrata.*
Nirṇaya-sindhu	Kamalākara	Portion on *vrata.*
Nṛsiṃhaprasāda	Dalapati	Portion on *vrata.*
Smṛti-ratnākara	Caṇḍeśvara	Portion on *vrata.*
Vrata-kāla-viveka	Śūlapāṇi	
Vrata-tattva	Raghunandana	Included in author's *Smṛti-tattva.*

Durgotsava

Title	*Author*	*Remarks*
Durgā-bhakti-taraṅgiṇī	Vidyāpati	
Durgotsava-tattva	Raghunandana	Included in author's *Smṛti-tattva.*
Durgotsava-viveka	Śūlapāṇi	

Dattaka

Title	*Author*	*Remarks*
Dattaka-candrikā	Kubera	
Dattaka-mīmāṃsa	Nandapaṇḍita	

Vyavahāra

Title	*Author*	*Remarks*
Baudhāyana-dharmasūtra	Baudhāyana	*Vyavahāra* discussed among other subjects.
Daṇḍaviveka	Vardhamāna	
Dāyabhāga	Jīmūtavāhana	
Dāya-tattva	Raghunandana	Included in author's *Smṛti-tattva.*
Gautama-dharmasūtra	Gautama	*Vyavahāra* discussed among other topics
Kṛtyakalpataru	Lakṣmīdhara	Portion on *vyavahāra.*
Madana-pārijāta	Madanapāla	Portion on *dāyabhāga* which comes under *vyavahāra.*
Manu-smṛti		Chs. VII, IX *Vyavahāra*
Nārada-smṛti	Nārada	
Nṛsimhaprasāda	Dalapati	Portion on *vyavahāra.*
Parāśara-smṛti	Parāśara	Mādhava's commentary introduces a discussion on *vyavahāra.*
Sarasvatī-vilāsa	Pratāparudradeva	Portion on *vyavahāra.*
Smṛticandrikā	Devaṇabhaṭṭa	Portion on *vyavahāra.*
Smṛti-ratnākara	Caṇḍeśvara	Portion on *vyavahāra.*
Viṣṇu-dharmasūtra (or, *-smṛti)*	Viṣṇu	Portion on *vyavahāra.*

Title	*Author*	*Remarks*
Vivāda-bhaṅgār-ṇava	Jagannātha Ta-rkapañcānana	
Vivādārṇava-setu	Bāṇeśvara Vid-yālaṃkāra and others	
Vyavahāra-cintā-maṇi	Vācaspati Miśra	
Vyavahārā-mātṛkā	Jīmūtavāhana	
Vyavahāra-mayūkha	Nīlakaṇṭha	
Vyavahāra-tattva	Raghunandana	Included in author's *Smṛti-tattva*.
Yājñavalkya-smṛti	Yājñavalkya	Portion on *vyavahāra*.

Rājadharma

Title	*Author*	*Remarks*
Baudhāyana-dharmasūtra	Baudhāyana	*Rājadharma* discussed among other topics.
Kṛtyakalpataru	Lakṣmīdhara	Portion on *rājadharma*.
Manu-smṛti		Chapter VII on *rājadharma*.
Rājanīti-ratnākara	Caṇḍeśvara	
Smṛti-kaustubha	Anantadeva	Portion on *rājadharma*.
Viṣṇu-dharmasūtra	*Viṣṇu*	Portion on *rājadharma*.
Yājñavalkya-smṛti	*Yājñavalkya*	Portion on *rājadharma*.

Appendix 12

Manu's Recipe for Health and Hygiene

THE attitude of the wise people of ancient India, regarding health, is aptly expressed by Kālidāsa in the following oft-quoted line — *śarīram ādyaṃ khalu dharma-sādhanam* (*Kumāra-sambhava*, V). It means that the first means for performing *dharma* or pious acts is the body. *MS,* V.4 (with Kullūka's commentary thereon) attributes premature death to the following four causes : non-practice of Vedic study, avoidance of *ācāra* or (rules of) good conduct, laziness and fault of food. Here, we shall set forth the views of the *MS* on the principal things permitted and prohibited as food. The obscurantists will, perhaps, say that all the rules about this matter are gospel truth, whereas the iconoclast may reject all the injunctions as having no relevance after lapse of centuries. The balanced view seems to be to avoid the above two extremes. Human body has certain inherent characteristics which are similar in all ages. The wisdom of the ancient Indians, especially in the realm of *Āyurveda*, is well-known. Dietetics plays an important rôle in *Āyurveda*. The sagacity of Manu has been recognised not only in India, but also in several other countries. So, it seems reasonable to examine scientifically Manu's prescriptions regarding food before accepting or rejecting them.

As regards food, there is a time-honoured tradition that purity of food leads to the purity of spirit (*āhāra-śuddhau sattva-śuddhiḥ*). That food is an essential factor for health has been recognised in all times and climes. Modern medical science also lays stress on food in the treatment of patients. There is increasing importance of dieticians in modern medical treatment.

Before taking up the do's and don'ts, prescribed by Manu in respect of food, it should be noted that he, like all other ancient Indian authors of *śāstras*, strongly emphasises the restraint of one's senses, viz., the five sensory organs (eye, ear, tongue, nose and skin), the five motor organs (speech, hand, foot, anus and penis) and the eleventh organ, called mind. As regards food, he indirectly advises restraint of the tongue when he condemns *atibhojana* or over-eating as *anārogya* (causing disease), *anāyuṣya* (causing loss of longevity) and *loka-vidviṣṭa* (hated by people), *MS*, II.57.

Chapter five of the *MS* deals with food permitted as well as prohibited for the three upper castes.

Vegetables

Prohibited (*MS*, V.5)

> Laśuna (garlic, *Allium sativum*); *Gṛñjana* (*Odina wodier*) — according to Apte's *Skt.-Eng. Dictionary*, it may mean a small red variety of garlic of turnip; *Palāṇḍu* (onion, *Allium cepa*); *Kavaka* (mushroom).

Besides the above, everything grown on impure things like excreta, etc. (*taṇḍulīyādi* — Kullūka; the botanical name of *taṇḍulīya*(*ka*) is *Amarantus spinosus*) is prohibited.

Fruits

Prohibited (*MS*, V.6)

> *Śelu* (*bahu-vāraka-phalam* — Kullūka. Does it mean a fruit which grows several times in a year? Its botanical name is *Dillenia indica*).

Liquid Substances

Prohibited (*MS*, V.6).

> Red exudations of trees (according to Kullūka, such things, when solidified, are prohibited), any kind of exudation appearing as a result of cutting, *gavya peyūṣa* (milk of a cow that has calved recently). The next verse prohibits the milk of a cow within ten days of calving. Also prohibited are the milk of camels and of non-hoofed animals, of sheep, of a cow in heat desiring crossing, of a cow which is *vivatsā* (of which the calf is dead or not present). Excepting the milk of a buffalo, that of all other wild animals is forbidden. The milk of women is also to be avoided.

Meat

BIRDS

The meat of the following birds is prohibited: *carnivorous* (e.g., vulture), rural (e.g., pigeon), *ṭiṭṭibha* (a kind of partridge?), *kalaviṅka* (Indian house-sparrow, *Passer domesticus*), *plava* (*Pelecanus onocrotalus* — it is mainly a winter visitor). The resident species is spotted billed Pelican (*Pelecanus philippensis*), *haṃsa* (grey-leg goose — *Anser anser* or bar-headed goose — *Anser indicus*), *cakrāhva*, i.e., *cakravāka* (ruddy sheldrake or brahminy duck — *Todorna ferruginea*), *grāma-kukkuṭa* (village fowl — *Gallus domesticus*), *sārasa* (kind of crane — *Grus antigone*), *rajjuvāla* (a kind of wild fowl), *dātyūha* (gallinule moorhen or white-breasted water hen — *Gallinula chloropus*), *śuka* (parrot or rose-ringed parakeet — *Psittacula krameri*), *sārikā* (common myna — *Acridotheres tristes*).

It is interesting to note that to orthodox Hindus, the fowl-meat in general is a taboo. But, the above prohibition of *grāma-kukkuṭa* clearly implies that *vanya-kukkuṭa* or forest-fowl is not prohibited.

Also prohibited are the following birds:

Pratuda (a class of birds which eat food after pecking it with their beaks); *dārvāghāṭādi* — Kullūka; *dārvāghāṭa* is, perhaps, wood-pecker, *jālapāda* (web-footed bird; *śarāri prabhṛti* — Kullūka). *Śarāri* is heron — *Ardea cineria*), *Koyaṣṭi* (Siberian or great white crane (*Grus eucogeranus*), *nakha-viṣkira* (a class of birds which eat food after scattering it with their claws), *nimajjataḥ* (that which dives and eats fish); *Madgu-prabhṛti* — Kullūka. *Madgu* is little cormorant), *baka* (purple heron — *Ardea purpurea*, or grey heron — *Ardea cinerea* or cattle egret — *Bubulcus ibis*), *balākā* (common teal — *Nettion crecca*), *kākola* (raven — *Corvus corax*), *khañjarīṭa* (grey wagtail — *Motacilla cinurea* or large pied wagtail — *Motacilla* sp.).

BEASTS

Manu, V.56 declares that there is no fault in eating meat; creatures are naturally inclined to do so, but abjuration leads to great result. V.50 states — one who does not eat meat, not sanctioned by the *śāstra*, endears himself to people, and does not suffer from diseases. Verse V.48 gives reason for the categorical prohibition of meat. Meat cannot be obtained without killing creatures; slaughter of creatures does not lead to heaven, so meat should be avoided. Kullūka gives a proviso to this general rule; according to him, meat as such is not forbidden, what is forbidden is meat of creatures which are not allowed to be eaten. V.39 states that animals have been created by the Self-born Lord for sacrifice; so, killing of animals for that purpose is tantamount to non-slaughter. V.41 allows the slaughter of animals only for the following specific purposes:

madhuparka, sacrifice like *Jyotiṣṭoma* and rites in honour of the manes and gods.

Madhuparka is a special offering to distinguished guests, and consists generally in curd, ghee, water, honey and sugar. Kullūka, however, quotes the authority of a *Gṛhyasūtra* which declares that *madhuparka* should not be devoid of meat.

The meat of the following animals is prohibited (V.14, 17):

> that which feeds on fish (e.g. crocodile), boar (according to Kullūka, wild boar is not prohibited), *ekacara* (moving alone, e.g. serpent), an animal of which the name and genus are not known.

V.17 categorically prohibits five-toed animals. But, the next verse allows the following among them:

> *śvāvidh* (*sedhā*—Kullūka), *śalyaka* (probably procupine; *Hystrix indica*), *godhā* (iguana; *Varanus* sp.), *Khaḍga* (*Rhinoceros unicornis*), *Kūrma* (tortoise; *Kachuga* sp.), *Śaśa* (hare; *Lepus nigricollis*).

Also allowed are animals with one row of teeth, excepting camels.

FISH

MS, V.14, 15 categorically ban fish. But, V.16 permits the eating of the following species of fish: *pāṭhīna* (*Wallago attu*; appears to be the same as *Vodāla*), *rohita* (*Labeo fimbriatus*), *rājīva* (?), *siṃhatuṇḍa* (lit. lion-faced; *Bagarius bagarius*), *saśalka* (all kinds of fish having scales).

Miscellaneous things (V.7-10)

The following are prohibited :

> *Kṛsara* (rice cooked with sesame), *saṃyāva* (ghee, milk, molasses, crushed wheat, boiled together), *pāyasa* (rice with sugar, boiled in milk), *āpūpa* (cake)—all these prepared for one's own self, but not for offering to a deity; meat of an animal not consecrated; food meant for a deity, before offering; articles meant for *homa*, before offering. All kinds of *śukta*, excepting curd, curd-products and those which are mixed with flowers, roots and fruits, are prohibited. Kullūka explains *śukta* as those things which are naturally sweet, but, due to lapse of time as also by the mixing of water, become sour.

Glossarial Index of Smṛti Literature*

(The terms, marked with asterisks, indicate sub-castes or mixed castes.)

Abbreviations

M = Manu-smṛti *Y = Yājñavalkya-smṛti.*

Abdurga : Fort surrounded by deep water. (*M*, VII.70)

Abhicāra : Magic spell or rite for malevolent purposes. (*M*, IX.290, XI.63, 197)

Abhijit : (1) Name of Soma sacrifice (part of the great sacrifice *Gavāmyana*). (2) Name of a constellation. (*M*, XI.74)

*Ābhīra : A sub-caste sprung from the union of a Brāhmaṇa male and an Ambaṣṭha (q.v.) female. (*M*, X.15)

Abhiśasta : Used to denote (i) murderer of a Brāhmaṇa, (ii) murderer of a woman who is *Ātreyī* (q.v.), (iii) one guilty of a grave sin, (iv) murderer of a person of a Brāhmaṇa or a Kṣatriya who had studied the Veda or had been initiated for Soma sacrifice, (v) one who destroys the

---

* Based on *Manu-smṛti*, ed. by J.L. Shastri (Delhi, 1983) and *Yājñavalkya-smṛti*, ed. by V.L.S. Pansikar (Bombay, 1926).

foetus of a Brāhmaṇa. (*Y*, II.70)

Ācārya : (1) One who, having performed the *upanayana* (q.v.) of his pupil, teaches him the Veda along with the *Kalpa-sūtras* and *Upaniṣads*.

One from whom the pupil learns his duties (*M*, II.140 and other places; *Y*, I.34, 49, etc.)

Adhamana : Mortgaging. (*M*, VIII.165)

Ādhāna : Pledging or mortgaging. (*Y*, II.247)

Ādhi : "Pledge or mortgage of a chattel or mmovable property to the creditor himself with or without possession." (P.V. Kane, *History of Dharmaśāstra*, III, p. 419, fn. 681). (*M*, VIII.144, 145, etc.; *Y*, II.23, 25, etc., II.90)

Ādhivedanika : A kind of *strīdhana* (q.v.), presented to a woman by her husband on his marrying another woman. (*Y*, II. 143, 148)

Adhyāvāhnika : A kind of *strīdhana* (q.v.), obtained by a woman while taken from her father's house to that of the bridegroom. (*M*, IX.194)

Adhyagni : A kind of *strīdhana* (q.v.), given to a girl, at the time of her marriage, before the nuptial fire. (*M*, IX.194; *Y*, II.143)

Āgama : Valid mode of acquisition of a property; e.g. purchase, gift, etc. (*M*, VIII.200, 401; *Y*, II.2. 27-29, etc.)

Aghamarṣaṇa : A kind of expiation consisting in the recital of the Vedic hymn of this name (*Ṛ̥V*, X.190-1-3); name of a *vrata* in which one has to fast for three days, remain standing by day and sitting up by night and to donate a milch cow at the end. (*M*, XI.259; *Y*, III.301)

Agniṣṭut : Laudatory of Agni; the first day of *Agniṣṭoma* sacrifice. (*M*, XI.74)

Āgrayaṇa : An *iṣṭi* (sacrifice) in which fresh corns are first offered to gods. (*M*, IV.4, 5)

**Ahiṇḍika* : Offspring of a *Niṣāda* (q.v.) male by a *Vaideha* (q.v.) female. (*M*, X.37)

Ākranda : The king ruling over a territory just beyond that of *Pārṣṇigrāha* (q.v.). (*M*, VII.207)

Āmayāvī : One who cannot digest rice. (*Y*, III.210)

Ambaṣṭha : One sprung from the union of a Brāhmaṇa male and a Vaiśya female. (*M*, X.8, 13, etc.; *Y*, I.91)

Amṛta : (1) Food obtained without begging.

(2) Remnant of what is offered in a sacrifice. (*M*, IV.4, 5)

*Andhra : One sprung from the union of a *Vaidehaka* (q.v.) male and a *Kārāvara* (q.v.) female. (*M*, X.36, 48)

Anirdaśā : A cow within ten days of calving. (*Y*, I.170)

Annaprāśana : Name of the ceremony in which a child is fed with rice for the first time after birth. It is to be held in the sixth month from the child's birth. (*Y*, I.12)

*Antyāvasāyin : A mixed caste sprung from the union of a *Caṇḍāla* male and a *Niṣāda* (q.v.) female. (*M*, X.39)

Anūcāna : One who has mastered the Vedas and the

Vedāṅgas. (*M*, II.154; *Y*, III.24)

Anuloma : In regular order. Generally applied to marriage between a man of a higher caste and a woman of a lower one. (*M*, X.25)

Anvādheyaka : A kind of *strīdhana* (q.v.), obtained by a woman, after her marriage, from her husband or parents. (*Y*, II.144)

Anvāhita : Sub-mortgage, i.e., mortgage of a property by the mortgagee. (*Y*, II.67)

Anvaṣṭakā : The ninth day in the latter half of the three (or four) months following the full moon in *Agrahāyaṇa, Pauṣa, Māgha* (and *Phālguna*). (*M*, IV.150)

Ānvīkṣikī : (1) *Tarka-vidyā* or logic.

(2) *Ātma-vidyā* or spiritual knowledge. (*M*, VII.43; *Y*, I.311)

Aparāntika : A kind of song. (*Y*, III.113)

Apasada : Designation of children of six kinds of degrading marriag — of a Brāhmaṇa with a woman of any of the three lower castes, of a Kṣatriya with a woman of any of the two lower classes and of a Vaiśya with one of the Śūdra class. (*M*, X.10, 16, 17)

Apātrīkaraṇa : A class of sins which renders the perpetrator unworthy of receiving gifts. Acceptance of money from condemned persons, trade, service of Śūdras, utterance of an untruth — these are sins of this class for a Brāhmaṇa. (*M*, XI.69, 125)

Apaviddha : One cast off by one's parents, and accepted by another person as his son. (*M*, IX.159,

171; *Y*, II.132)

Ardha-sīrin : A cultivator entitled to half the agricultural produce raised from the land entrusted to him by the owner. (*Y*, II.10)

Ārṣa (Vivāha) : The kind of marriage in which a girl is given away after taking a pair or two of cattle as a matter of form, and not as the price of the girl. (*M*, III.21, IX.196; *Y*, I.59)

Artha-dūṣaṇa : Theft of money or not to give a person his due. (*M*, VII.48, 51)

Arthin : Plaintiff, suitor. (*Y*, II.6)

Āryāvarta : (1) That part of India, which lies between the Himālayas and the Vindhya mountain, and extends up to the eastern and western oceans.

(2) The region between the river Gaṅgā and Yamunā.

(3) That region of India, where spotted antelopes roam about naturally. (*M*, II.22)

Asat-pratigraha : Acceptance of the gift of prohibited articles or of any article from a prohibited person. (*M*, XI.194; *Y*, III.289)

Asipatravana : A kind of hell. (*M*, XII.75)

Aṣṭakā : The eighth day after full moon (especially that in *Hemanta* or dewy season and *Śiśira* or winter), on which the progenitors or manes are worshipped. There are three kinds of *aṣṭakā-śrāddha*, viz.,

(i) *Pūpāṣṭaka* — in which cakes are offered;

(ii) *Māṃsāṣṭaka* — in which meat is offered;

(iii) *Śākāṣṭaka* — to be performed with vegetables. (*Y*. I.217)

Āsura (vivāha) : A form of marriage in which a girl is given away, at the father's will, after the bridegroom gives as much wealth as he can afford to the relatives of the girl and to the girl herself. (*M*, III.21, IX.197; *Y*, I.61)

Aśvamedha : Name of a sacrifice in which a horse was immolated. The horse was to be placed by a king in charge of military men, and then let loose. On its return after a year, the sacrifice was to be performed. It was believed to destroy sin, and ensure the attainment of heaven and salvation, in the other world, by the performer. (*M*, XI.74, 260; *Y*, III.244, 333)

Asyavāmīya : Name of the hymn beginning with the words *asya vāmasya* (*Ṛgveda*, I.164). (*M*, XI.250)

Ātatāyin : The following hostile persons are so-called : an incendiary, a poisoner, one armed with a weapon, a robber, one who wrests a field or carries away one's wife. (*M*, VIII.350, 351)

Atikṛcchra : A form of expiation in which the sinner has to eat merely one morsel of food for three days in the morning only, for three days in the evening only, one morsel each for three days without asking for it, and has to fast for three days. (*M*, XI.208, 213; *Y*, III.264, 292, 319)

Ātreyī : A woman who has bathed after her monthly impurity. (*M*, XI.87; *Y*, III.5, 251)

Aurasa : A son begotten by a man on his wife. (*Y*, II.

128, 141)

Auveṇaka : A kind of song. (*Y*, III.113)

Avabhṛtha : Ablution after the conclusion of a sacrifice. (*Y*, III.244; *M*, XI.82)

Avakīrṇī : A *brahmacārī* who has had sexual union with a woman. (*M*, III.155, XI.118, 121; *Y*, I. 222, III.280)

Avakraya (Avakrīta) : (1) "A transaction whereby a bailee (e.g., a washerman) transfers an article bailed to him (for washing, etc.) to another for hire." (P.V. Kane, *History of Dharmaśāstra*, III, p. 494, fn. 874)

(2) Purchase of an article the price of which is unpaid or partly paid. (*Y*, II.238)

**Āvantya* : Offspring of a *vrātya* (q.v.) Brāhmaṇa by a woman of the same caste. (*M*, X.21)

Avaṭa : Any depressed part of the body, a sinus. (*Y*, III.98)

Avīra : (1) A woman having neither husband nor son.

(2) A woman who is independent, but not gone astray. (*M*, IV.213; *Y*, I.163)

**Āvṛta* : One sprung from the union of a Brāhmaṇa male and *Ugra* (q.v.) female. (*M*, X.15)

**Āyogava* : (1) One born of the union of a Śūdra male and a Vaiśya female.

(2) One born of the union of a Vaiśya male and a Kṣatriya female. (*M*, X.12, 15, etc.; *Y*, I. 94)

Bandhaka : Pledge or mortgage. (*Y*, II.37)

Bāndhava : The following three classes of relatives:

(1) *Ātma-bandhu* — son of one's father's sister, mother's sister and of one's maternal uncle.

(2) *Pitr̥-bandhu* — son of one's father's father's sister, father's mother's sister and of one's father's maternal uncle.

(3) *Mātr̥-bandhu* — son of one's mother's mother's sister, mother's father's sister and of one's mother's maternal uncle. (*M,* V.81, 101, etc.; *Y,* I.108, 220, etc.)

Bandhu-dāyāda : Same as *Dāyāda-bāndhava* (q.v.). (*M,* IX.158.)

Bhāṣā : Plaint in a lawsuit. (*M,* VIII.164)

Bhauta-yajña : Same as *Bhūta-yajña.* (q.v.). (*M,* III. 70. *Y,* I. 102)

Bheda : A political expedient by which seeds of dissension are sown in the territory of a hostile king. (*M,* VII.198; *Y,* I.346)

Bhīṣā : The act of frightening, coercion. (*M,* VIII. 264)

Bhrāmarin : Affected with Vertigo or Epilepsy. (*M,* III. 161)

Bhrūṇa : (1) A Brāhmaṇa, versed in the Veda, who has performed Soma sacrifices.

(2) Foetus.

(3) Any Brāhmaṇa.

(4) A Brāhmaṇa who has studied the Veda with its six accessories. (*M,* IV.208, VIII.

317, etc.; *Y*, I.64)

Bhukti : Possession. (*Y*, II.29)

Bhūrjakaṇṭaka : Offspring of a *vrātya* Brāhmaṇa by a similar woman. Sometimes also called *Āvantya* or *Vāṭadhāna*, *Puṣpadha* or *Śaikha*. (*M*, X.21)

Bhūta (Bhauta)-bali : Offering to birds, animals, etc. (*Y*, I.103)

Bhūta (Bhauta)-yajña : Same as *Bhūtabali* (q.v.). (*M*, IV.21)

Bhujiṣyā : A woman, dependant on or working for others; a slave girl. (*Y*, II.24, 290)

Bhūtātmā : The individual soul. (*M*, V.109, XII.12; *Y*, III. 34)

Bījin : "The owner or giver of seed, the real progenitor (as opposed to *kṣetrin*, the nominal father or merely the husband of a woman)". — Monier-Wliams. (*M*, IX.52, 53)

Bradhna : Sun. (*M*, IV.201, IX.137)

Brāhma (vivāha) : The form of marriage in which the daughter, decked with valuable garments and honoured with jewels, etc., is given away to a man, versed in the Vedas and having good conduct and invited by the girl's father himself. (*M*, III.21, IX.196. *Y*, I.58, II.145)

Brahmadeyā : A woman married in the *Brāhma* (q.v.) form of marriage. (*M*. III. 185)

Brahma-gītikā : A kind of song. (*Y*, III.114)

Brāhmaṇa-bruva: One who refers to himself as Brāhmaṇa without having the requisite qualifications; a Brāhmaṇa only in name. (*M*, VIII.20)

Brahmāñjali : Hands folded by a pupil as a preliminary to Vedic study with the teacher. (*M*, II.71)

Brahma-rākṣasa : The ghost of a Brāhmaṇa who used to lead an unholy life. (*M*, XII.60; *Y*, III.212)

Brahma-satra : Sacrifice in the shape of devotion or meditation; constant repetition of Vedic texts. (*M*, II.106, IV.9)

Brahma-tīrtha : Designation of the root of the thumb. (*Y*, I. 19)

Brāhma-tīrtha : Same as *Brahma-tīrtha* (q.v.). (*M*, II. 58, 59; *Y*; I.18)

Brahmāvarta : The part of India between the rivers Sarasvatī and Dṛṣadvatī. (*M*, II.17)

Brahma-yajña : Study and teaching of the Vedas. (*M*, III.70; Y I.102)

Brahmodya : (1) Such riddles, questions and answers as are found in *Taittirīya Saṃhitā*, VII.4.18, and *Vājasaneyī Saṃhitā*, XXIII.9-12, etc.

(2) Legends narrated in the Veda.

(3) Talks relating to the exposition of *Brahman*. (*M*, III.231)

Cailāsaka : Name of an evil spirit. (*M*, XII.72)

Cakravṛddhi : Compound interest, i.e., interest on interest. (*M*, VIII.153)

Caṇḍāla (*Cāṇḍāla*) : It generally denotes a man outside the Aryan society. It also denotes the following:

(1) The caste sprung from the union of a Śūdra male and a Brāhmaṇa female.

(2) Offspring of an unmarried woman.

(3) One born as a result of a man's union with a *sagotrā* girl.

(4) Son of one who, after becoming an ascetic, returns to the householder's life. (*M*, X.12, 16, etc.; *Y*, I.93, 103, II.61)

Cāndra-vratika : A king who acts in a manner of the moon, i.e., in whom the subjects take as much delight as in the moon. (*M*, IX. 309)

Cāndrāyaṇa : A form of penance in which the sinner is required to eat fifteen morsels of food on the Full Moon day, reduce the morsels by one on each day of the dark fortnight, and to fast completely on the New Moon day. This is of many kinds; e.g. *Pipīlikāmadhya*, *Yavamadhya*, etc. (*M*, XI.41, 106 etc; *Y*, III. 287, 325, etc.)

Cara (Cāra) : Spy. (*Y*, I.328)

Caritra-bandhaka : "A kind of *ādhi* (q.v.) which occurs either when the creditor being known to be very honest, the debtor gives as security a property of very great value for a small debt or where the debtor being known to be very honest a property of very small value is accepted as security for a large debt." (P.V. Kane, *Hist. of Dharmaśāstra*, III, p. 435).

**Carmakāraka (-kāra, Carmāvakartin, Carmopajīvin)* : (1) Offspring of a Śūdra by a Kṣatriya girl.
(2) One sprung from the union of a *Vaidehaka* (q.v.) male and a Brāhmaṇa famale.
(3) Offspring of an *Āyogava* (q.v.) by a Brāhmaṇa female. (*M*, IV.218)

Cīrin : Name of an insect making loud noise. (*M*,

XII.63. *Y*, III.215.)

**Cuñcu* : Offspring of a Brāhmaṇa by a *Vaidehaka* (q.v.) woman.

Cūḍākarman (Cūḍākaraṇa, Cūḍā, Cūḍa) : A sacrament in which the hairs on a child's head are cut for the first time. *Cūḍā* means the tuft of hair kept on the head when the major part is shaved off. (*M*, II.35; *Y*, I.12, III.23)

Daiva-tīrtha : Same as *Divya-tīrtha* (q.v.). (*M*, II.59; *Y*, I.19)

Daiva-vivāha : The form of marriage in which the father gives away his daughter after decking her with ornaments, etc., to a priest who duly officiates at a sacrifice, during the course of its performance. (*M*, III.21, IX.196; *Y*, I.59)

Daiva-yajña : Same as *Deva-yajña* (q.v.). (*M*, III.70, *Y*, I. 102)

Dakṣavihitā : A kind of song. (*Y*, III.114)

Dambhī : One who acts merely for pleasing people. (*Y*, I.130)

Dāna : Name of a political expedient (*upāya*) in which a king pleases a hostile king by gifts. (*M*, VII.198)

Daṇḍa : (1) Staff, especially that held by one at the time of *upanayana* (q.v.).

(2) Punishment, sometimes personified.

(3) Fine.

(4) Sceptre as the symbol of royal power.

(5) A political expedient by which a king invades an enemy's country. (*M*, VII.14, 17,

etc.; *Y,* I.346, 353, etc.)

Daṇḍadāsa : One enslaved for non-payment of fine. (*M,* VIII.415)

Danda-nīti : (1) Judicature as a science.

(2) *Arthaśāstra.* (*M,* VII.43; *Y,* I.311, 313)

Dandaśuka : Serpent. (*Y,* III.197)

Daṇḍa-vyūha : A kind of soldiers' array looking like a stick. (*M,* VII.187)

Darśa : "New Moon or a sacrifice performed at that time; the day on which the moon is seen only by the sun and by no one else." (P.V. Kane, *Hist. of Dharmaśāstra*, II, p. 1009). (*M,* IV.25)

Dāsa(śa) : Same as *Kaivarta* (q.v.). (*M,* VIII.408, 409, 415, 416; *Y,* I.166)

Dattaka : A boy who, being given by his parents, is adopted by a person as a son. (*M,* IX.159; *Y* II. 130)

Dattātmā : A boy who, either bereft of parents or forsaken by them, offers himself to a person as his son. (*Y,* II.131)

Dattrima : Same as *Dattaka* (q.v.). (*M,* VIII.415; IX. 141, 142, 168)

Dāyāda : One who is entitled to inheritance. (*Y,* II. 118, 119)

Dāyāda-bāndhava (bandhu) : Such *bandhus* or *bāndhavas* (q.v.) as are entitled to inheritance. (*M,*IX.158;160;*Y,*II. 264)

Devala(ka) : (1) "A brāhmaṇa who performs the worship of an image for wage for three years, and who thereby becomes unfit to officiate at *śrāddhas*".

(2) "One who maintains himself on the treasury of a shrine".

(3) "Worshipper of Śiva for wages". (Kane, *Hist. of Dharmaśāstra*, III, p. 951). (*M,* III. 152, 180)

Deva-yajña : "Sacrifice to gods, especially the *homa*, one of the five great oblations". (Monier-Williams). (*M,* IV.21)

Dhanvadurga : A kind of fort, surrounded by deserts, and devoid of water for five *yojanas*. (1 *yojana* = 8 or 9 miles). (*M,* VII.70)

Dharaṇa : "A sort of weight variously reckoned as = 10 *palas* = 16 silver *māṣakas* = 1 silver *purāṇa* = 1/10 *śatamāna* = 19 *niṣpāva* = 2/3 *karṣa* = 1/10 *pala* = 24 *rattikās*." (Monier-Williams). (*M,* VIII.134-137; *Y,* I. 364)

Dhāraṇaka : A debtor. (*Y,* II.63)

**Dhigvana* : Offspring of a Brāhmaṇa by an *Āyogava* (q.v.) female. (*M,* X.15, 49)

Didhiṣu(u) : An elder sister before whom her younger sister has been married. (*M,* III.173)

**Divākīrti*: (*-kīrtya)* : (1) *Caṇḍāla* (q.v.).
(2) Barber. (*M,* V.85)

Divya : Divine proof; e.g., ordeal by fire, water, etc. (*Y,* II. 22, 95, 97)

Divya-tīrtha (or, *Daiva-*) : The tips of fingers, supposed to be sacred for offering articles to gods. (*M,* II.59)

Dvaidha (Dvaidhībhāva) : One of the six kinds of royal policy (*guṇa*). According to some, it means double-dealing, keeping apparently friendly relations with the enemy. According to others, it means splitting one's army into two parts. (*M*, VII. 160; *Y*, I.347)

**Draviḍa* : Same as *Karaṇa* (q.v.). (*M*, X.22)

Ekārāma : A mendicant unaccompanied by any other person. (*Y*, III.58)

Gaja-cchāyā : Name of a particular constellation. (*Y*, I. 218)

Gaṇa : (1) An association of merchants, etc.

(2) A guild of horse-dealers.

(3) An association of men living in a village, etc.

(4) An association of warriors, etc. who pursue the same vocation. (*M*, I. 118; *Y*, I. 361, II.187, 192)

Gāndharva : The form of marriage in which the bride and the groom marry with mutual consent. (*M*, III.21, IX.196; *Y*, I.61)

Garuḍa : Name of a particular array (*vyūha*) of soldiers, resembling *Varāha-vyūha* (q.v.), with the only difference that, in *Garuḍa*, the middle part is wider. (*M*, VII.187)

Gauḍī : Wine distilled from molasses. (*M*, XI.94)

Giridurga : A kind of royal fort, situated on a hill, very difficult to climb, accessible through a narrow path, with a supply of water from rivers and falls, and many productive lands and trees. (*M*, VII.70, 71)

Glaha : Wager mutually agreed upon by gamblers. (*Y*, II.199)

Golaka : An illegitimate son of a widow. (*M,* III.156, 174; *Y,* I.222)

Gosava : Name of a one-day Soma sacrifice in which, according to some, the performer has to act like cattle, e.g., drinking water like them, cutting grass with his teeth, and so on. (*M,* XI.74)

Gotra : "All persons who trace descent in an unbroken male line from a common male ancestor". (P. V. Kane, *History of Dharmaśāstra* (*M,* III.5; *Y,* I.53)

Gṛhabali : Domestic oblation; offering of the remnants of a meal to all creatures. (*M,* III.265)

Gūḍhaja (*Gūḍhotpanna*) : A son, born to a woman, as a result of clandestine union, in the absence of her husband, the real father being unknown. (*M,* IX.159; *Y,* II. 129)

Gulma : (1) A troop or guard of soldiers.

(2) Shrub. (*M,* VII.114, 190, VIII.247, 330; *Y,* II.229, III.208, 276)

Gurutalpa : (1) Mother or step-mother belonging to the same caste as the father.

(2) Wife of a Vedic teacher. (*M,* IX.63, 235, etc.; *Y,* III.209. 227, etc.)

Haituka : A rationalist, sceptic, heretic. (*M,* IV.30; *Y,* I. 130)

Haviṣpāntīya : The Ṛgvedic hymn beginning with *Haviṣpāntam* (X.88). (*M,* XI.251)

Havya : A sacrificial food or gift. (*M,* III.128, 133, etc.)

Hayamedha : Same as *Aśvamedha* (q.v.). (*M*, XI.82; *Y*, I.181)

Iṣṭāpūrta : *Iṣṭa* may mean:

(1) Whatever is offered in the *gṛhya* fire and the three *śrauta* fires, and gifts made inside the *vedī* in the *śrauta* sacrifices.

(2) "Honouring a guest and performance of *Vaiśvadeva*." (Kane, *History of Dharmaśāstra*).

(3) Oblation to fire, penance, truthfulness, Vedic study, hospitality, performance of *Vaiśvadeva*.

Pūrta has been defined as:

(1) "Dedication of deep wells, oblong large walls and tanks, temples, distribution of food and maintaining public gardens." (Kane, *Hist. of Dharmaśāstra*)

(2) To the above are added, by some, gifts made at the time of eclipse or on the sun's passage into a zodiac or on the twelfth day of a month.

(3) Nursing of those who are ill. (*M*, IV. 227)

Jāmi : (1) Sister, (2) a lady of the family, (3) a lady with her husband alive. (*M*, III.57, 58, IV. 180, 183; *Y*, I.157)

Jāṅgala : (1) A place, with scanty water and grass, where there are sufficient sunshine, air and corns, etc.

(2) A place with water, trees and hills. (*M*, VII.69; *Y*, I.321)

Jātakarman (*Jātakriyā*) : A sacrament performed after the birth of a son to ensure his well-being. (*Y*, I.11)

Jātibhraṃśakara: A class of sins, believed to cause loss of caste to the sinner. (*M*, XI.67)

**Jhalla* : Same as *Karaṇa* (q. v.).

Dimbāhava : (1) A battle where no king is present.

(2) A quarrel wherein no weapons are used. (*M*, V.95)

Jñāti : Agnatic relations. (*M*, III.31, 264, IV.179; *Y*, II.149)

Jyeṣṭhasāmaga : Chanter of the *mantras*, referred to under *Jyeṣṭhasāman. Jyeṣṭhasāmāni āraṇyake gīyante, teṣāṃ gātā* (Kullūka). (*M*, III.185)

**Kaivarta* : One born to a *Niṣāda* (q. v.) by an *Āyogava* (q.v.) woman. (*M*, X.34; *Y*, III.52)

Kalā : A measure of time equal to three *Kāṣṭhās* (q.v.). (*M*, I.64)

Kālasūtra : A kind of hell. (*M*, III.249)

Kālikā (*Kāla-vṛddhi*) : Interest accruing and payable every month. (*M*, VIII.153)

Kalka : Crooked. (*Y*, III.312)

Kānīna : Son of an unmarried woman. (*M*, IX.160, 172; *Y*, II.129)

Kaṇṭaka : A harmful person. (*M*, IX.252)

**Karaṇa* : (1) One born of the union of a Vaiśya male and a Śūdra female.

(2) Offspring of a Kṣatriya *vrātya* (q. v.) and a Kṣatriya woman. (*M*, VIII.154, X.22; *Y*, I.92)

**Kārāvara*	:	A sub-caste that springs from the union of a *Niṣāda* (q.v.) with a *Vaideha* (q.v.) woman. (*M*, X.36)
Kāritā	:	The interest stipulated by the debtor himself. (*M*, VIII.153)
Karmānta	:	(1) A place where sugarcanes and paddy, etc., are gathered. (2) Conclusion of a work. (*M*, VII.62, VIII. 419)
Kārmika	:	A piece of cloth on which various designs like wheel and *svastika* are made with line. (*Y*, II.180)
Kārṣāpaṇa	:	A coin or weight of different values (if of gold = 16 *māṣas*; if of silver = 16 *paṇas* or 1280 *kowries*; if of copper = 80 *rattikās* or about 176 grains; but, according to some = only 1 *paṇa* of *kowries* or 80 *kowries*). (*M*, VIII. 136, 274, 336, etc.)
Kārṣika	:	Same as *kārṣāpaṇa* (q.v.). (*M*, VIII.136; *Y*, I.365)
**Kāruṣa*	:	A sub-caste sprung from the union of a *vrātya* (q.v.) Vaiśya and a Vaiśya woman. (*M*, X.23)
Kāṣṭhā	:	A measure of time equal to eighteen winks. (*M*, I.64)
Kaṭapūtana	:	A kind of *pretas* (evil spirits) whose form is supposed to be assumed by a deceased Kṣatriya who neglected his duties when alive. (*M*, XII.71)
Kavaka	:	Mushroom. (*M*, XI.155; *Y*, I.171)
Kavya	:	Oblation of food offered to deceased

ancestors. (*M,* III.128, 133, IV.31; *Y,* III.39)

Kāyatīrtha : The root of the little finger. (*M,* II.59)

Kāyavivāha : The form of marriage, called *prājāpatya* (q. v.) (*Y,* I.60)

Kāyikā : (1) Interest of a *paṇa* or quarter *paṇa* (q. v.) to be paid everyday without the principal being liable to be reduced whatever interest may have been recovered.

(2) Interest received from the body; e. g., milk received from a cow pledged or the work put in by a slave or by a bull pledged. (*M,* VIII.153)

Keśānta : The ceremony of tonsure, also called *godāna*, performed in the sixteenth year of age of a Brāhmaṇa, twenty-second year of a Kṣatriya and twenty-fourth year of a Vaiśya. (*M,* II. 65. *Y,* I.36)

Khala : Threshing floor for paddy, etc. (*M,* XI.17; *Y,* II.282)

Kharvaṭa : (1) "Mountain-village" (Monier-Williams)

(2) *Kharvaṭasya pracura-kaṇṭaka-santānasya grāmasya — Mitākṣarā.* (*Y,* II. 167)

Khasa : One born as a result of the union of a *vrātya* (q. v.) Kṣatriya and a Kṣatriya woman. (*M,* X. 22)

Kīnāśa : Cultivator. (*M,* IX.150)

Kitava : One who, having no experience of gambling, makes others gamble for self-interest. (*M,* III.159)

Kloma (Kloman) : Right lung. (*Y*, III.94)

Kokundara : A cavity of the loins. (*Y*, III.96)

Kṛcchra : (1) Bodily mortification, penance.

(2) A particular kind of penance. For an incapable person, one cow is substituted for this penance. (*M*, V.21; *Y*, III.264, etc.)

Kṛcchrātikṛcchra : (1) A penance in which only water is drunk on those days on which food is allowed.
(2) A penance in which one has to subsist on water alone for 21 days. Four cows are substituted by some for this purpose when the sinner is incapable of undergoing it. (*M*, XI. 208; *Y*, III. 222, 320)

Krīta(ka) : One who is purchased, from his parents, to be treated as a son. (*M*, IX.160, 174; *Y*, II. 131)

Kriyā : Evidence in a lawsuit. (*Y*, II.23)

Kṛsara : Rice boiled with sesame. (*M*, V.7)

Kṛṣṇala : (1) The black berry of the plant *Abrus precatorius*, used as a standard of weight (= 1 or 2 grains on an average).

(2) A coin of the same weight. (*M*, VIII.134, etc.; *Y*, I. 363, 364)

Kṛtrima : A parentless boy adopted by a person as his son after alluring him with money, land, etc. (*M*, IX.159, 169; *Y*, II.131)

Kṛtyā : A magical rite designed to cause harm to a person. (*M*, IX.290)

**Kṣattā* : A *pratiloma* (q. v.) caste sprung from a

Sūdra father and Kṣatriya mother. (*M,* X.12, 13, etc.; *Y,* I.94)

Kṣema : Preservation and protection of what has been obtained. (*M,* VIII.230, IX.219; *Y,* I. 100)

Kṣetra : Wife. (*M,* IX.33, 36, 54; *Y,* III.178)

Kṣetraja : A kind of son, begotten by a person by means of *niyoga* (q. v.), on the wife of a sonless man. (*M,* IX.159, 162, etc.; *Y,* I.69, II.128, 141)

Kṣetrajña : "Knowing the body, i.e., the soul, the conscious principle in the corporeal frame." —Monier-Williams. (*M,* VIII. 96, XII.12, 14; *Y,* III.178)

Kṣetrin : (1) The husband of a woman on whom a son is begotten by another person, called *bījin*, according to *niyoga* (q.v.).

(2) Owner of a field. (*M,* IX.32, 51, 52; *Y,* II. 161)

Kṣupa : A short tree like the *karavīra* (*Y,* II.229)

**Kukkuṭaka* : (1) A particular *pratiloma* (q. v.) caste.

(2) Offspring of the union of a Śūdra with a *Niṣāda* (q. v.) woman.

(3) Offspring of a Vaiśya by a *Niṣāda* woman. (*M,* X.18)

Kula : (1) As much land as can be tilled with two ploughs, each drawn by six bulls.

(2) A multitude of kinsmen. (*M,* VII.119; *Y,* II: 30)

Kumbhīdhānya-(ka) : One who has a store of corn, in an earthen vessel, sufficient for six or ten days or, according to others, for one year or six months. (*M,* V.7; *Y,* I.128)

Kumbhīpāka : Name of a hell where the wicked are believed to be baked like potter's vessels or cooked like the contents of a cooking pot. (*M,* XII. 76)

Kuṇḍa : Offspring of the clandestine union of a man with a woman whose husband is alive. (*M,* III.156, 158, 174; *Y,* I.222, 224)

Kupya : Base metal; any metal but gold and silver. (*M,* VII.96, X.113, *Y;* III.237)

Kuśīlava : A professional dancer. (*M,* III.155)

Kuṣmāṇḍī : Name of the verses XX.14 ff. of the *Vājasaneya-saṃhitā*. (*Y,* III.303)

Kusūladhānyaka : A householder who has grain stored for three years' consumption. (*M,* IV.7; *Y,* I.128)

Kūṭasākṣin : A perjurer. (*Y,* II.77)

Lepa-bhāgin (-bhuj) : Paternal ancestors in the fourth, fifth and sixth degrees, who are entitled to *lepa*, i.e., particles or remnants wiped from the hand after offering oblation to the three ancestors. (*M,* III.216)

Likṣā : Young louse, the egg of a louse (as a measure of weight = 8 *trasareṇus*). (*M,* VIII.138)

Liṅgastha : A religious student. (*M,* VIII.65)

Madhuka : One who speaks sweetly. (*M,* X.33)

Madhuparka : A mixture of certain delicious substances offered to deities in religious rites and to distinguished guests. Opinions of some authorities, who differ on the ingredients, are as follows:

(1) Mixture of curd and honey.

(2) Mixture of water (or milk) and honey.

(3) Meat.

Now-a-days, used in the worship of deities only, it consists of a mixture of curd, ghee, water, honey and sugar. (*M,* III.120, V.41)

Mādhvī : A spirituous liquor distilled from the flowers of *Madhuka* plant (*Madhuka longifolia*). (*M,* XI.94) (See Kullūka's comments also)

Madraka : A kind of song. (*Y,* III.113)

**Magadha* : (1) A caste sprung from the union of a Viśya male and a Kṣatriya female.

(2) Offspring of a Vaiśya male and a Brāhmaṇa female.

(3) Offspring of a Śūdra male and a Kṣatriya female. (*M,* X.11, 17, etc.; *Y,* I.94)

Mahāpātaka (-pāpa) : A class of grave sins, comprising murder of a Brāhmaṇa, drinking wine of the *surā* (q.v.) type, theft of a Brāhmaṇa's gold, incestuous relation with one's mother and association with one who has committed any one of the above sins. (*M,* IX. 235, 243, etc.; *Y,* I.77, II.73, etc.)

Mahāsāntapana : An expiatory rite about the nature of which the divergent opinions are as follows:

(1) Lasting for seven days. One has to drink cow's urine, dung, milk, curd, ghee and water in which *kuśa* grass has been soaked, one each in the successive days and to fast on the last day.

(2) Of twenty days' duration. Each of the above six substances is to be taken for three successive days and fast undergone for the last three days.

(3) It spreads over fifteen days. Cow's urine, dung, milk, curd and ghee — each of these is to be taken for three days consecutively. (*Y*, III.315)

Mahāvyāhṛti : Name of the mystical formula — *bhūr-bhuvaḥ-svaḥ* (*M*, XI.222; *Y*, I.15)

Mahāyajña : The five great sacrifices (See *Pañca-yajña*). (*M*, IV.22, VI.5, etc.; *Y*, I.102)

Mahīdurga : A kind of fortress which is surrounded by a wall made of stone or brick, twice the width in height, which will not be less than twelve cubits, provided at the top with sufficient space for the movement of troops, and fitted with covered windows. (*M*, VII.70)

Māhiṣa : One who acquiesces in the conduct of one's wife who has gone astray. (*Y*, III.26)

**Māhiṣya* : A caste sprung from the marriage of a Kṣatriya male with a Vaiśya female. (*Y*, I.92, 95)

Māhitra : Name of the Ṛgvedic hymn X.185 beginning with the words *mahi triṇām*. (*M*, XI.249)

Maitra : Same as *Kāruṣa* (q.v.).

Maitrākṣa-jyotika : Name of a class of evil spirits. (*M*, XII.72)

**Maitreyaka* : Offspring of a *Vaidehaka* male and an *Āyogava* (q.v.) female. (*M*, X.33)

Makara : A military array which is the reverse of

Varāha-vyūha (q.v.). (*M*, VII. 187)

Malāvaha : A class of sins comprising killing of birds, acquatic creatures, worms and insects, eating things similar to intoxicating drinks. (*M*, X. 70)

Malinīkaraṇīya : Same as *Malāvaha* (q.v.).

**Malla* : Same as *Jhalla* (q.v.). (*M*, X. 22)

Maṇḍala : The circle of a king's near and distant powers. (*M*, VII.156; *Y*, I.345)

**Mārgava* : Same as *Kaivarta* (q.v.).

Māruta-vrata : According to Kullūka, it means — As the wind, called *prāṇa*, enters into all creatures, and moves about, so also the king should penetrate, through spies, all the places in his own territory as well as in that of another, in order to collect the intended information; this is *māruta vrata*. (*M*, IX. 306)

Māṣaka (Māṣa) : "A particular weight of gold (= 5 *kṛṣṇalas* = 1/10 *suvarṇa*, the weight in common use is said to be about 17 grains troy)." — Monier-Williams.

Maula : One holding office from previous generation; hereditary. (*M*, VIII.62, 259; *Y*, I.312)

Meda : Offspring of a *Vaidehaka* (q.v.) male and a *Niṣāda* (q.v.). female. (*M*, X.36, 48)

Mleccha : (1) Persians and the like.

(2) Those who live in Ceylon, and such other places as are devoid of the caste-system and the four stages of life. (*M*, X.45)

It is interesting to note that Viśvarūpa (ninth

century), in his *Bālakrīḍā* commentary on Y, III. 256, explains this word as *Pulinda*s and *Tājika*s (Arabs).

Mlecchadeśa : According to Manu, the land beyond the region which is the natural habitat of spotted antelopes. (*M*, II. 23)

Mṛta : Food obtained by begging. (*M*, IV. 5.).

Muhūrta : "A particular division of time, the 30th part of a day, a period of 48 minutes." — Monier-Williams. (*M*, I.64)

Mūlakarman : "Employment of roots for magical purposes." — Monier-Williams. (IX.290, IX.63)

**Mūrdhāvasikta* : (1) A caste sprung from the marriage of a Brāhmaṇa with a Ksatriya woman.

(2) Offspring of the clandestine union of a Brāhmaṇa with a Kṣatriya woman. (*Y*, I. 91)

Naigama : The *Pāśupata*s, etc., who accept Vedic authority.

Nāṇaka : A coin or anything stamped with an impression. (*Y*, II.20, 240, 241)

Naraka : Hell in general, a kind of hell. The following 21 kinds are enumerated by Manu:

(1) *Tāmisra*, (2) *Andhatāmisra*, (3) *Mahāraurava*, (4) *Raurava*, (5) *Naraka*, (6) *Kākasūtra*, (7) *Mahānaraka*, (8) *Saṃjīvana*, (9) *Mahāvīcī*, (10) *Tāpana*, (11) *Saṃpratāpana*, (12) *Saṃghāta*, (13) *Sakākola*, (14) *Kuḍmala*, (15) *Pratimūrtika*, (16) *Lohaśaṅku*, (17) *Ṛjīṣa*, (18) *Panthā*, (19) *Śālmali*, (20) *Asipatravana*, (21) *Lohadāraka*. (*M*, IV.87-90; *Y*, III.222-24).

Y, does not mention 3, 5, 9, 15, 17, 18, 21, but gives instead *Pūtimṛttikā, Lohitoda, Saviṣa, Avīcī, Kumbhīpāka, Mahāniraya, Mahāpatha*; for 13, *Y,* reads *Kākola*.

Nārāśaṃsī : Relating to praise of man. (*Y,* I. 45)

Nāstika : (1) Atheist or unbeliever.

(2) Denying the consequence of deeds.

(3) One who speaks ill of the Vedas, Brāhmaṇas, *dharma,* etc.

(4) Denying the existence of future life in the other world. (*M,* II.11, III.65, VIII.309; *Y,* III.139)

Naṣṭika : Owner of a lost thing. (*M,* VIII. 202)

**Naṭa* : Same as *Karaṇa* (q.v.). (*M,* X. 22)

Nibandha : (1) "A periodic payment or allowance in cash or kind permanently granted by a king, a corporation or a village or a caste to a person, family or a temple."

(2) "Delivery or payment of so many leaves of betel (or the like) on each bundle of leaves or so many betelnuts on each load of betelnuts."

(3) "The wealth to be obtained under the order or direction of a king or other authority that dealers in commodities should pay every year or month a certain amount to a certain Brāhmaṇa or shrine."

(4) "What is granted by a king or the like to be obtained at fixed times and the like."

(See P.V. Kane, *Hist. of Dharmaśāstra,* III,

p. 575, fn.). (*Y*, I.318, II.121)

**Nicchivi* : Same as *Karaṇa* (q.v.). (*M* X.22)

Nidhi : Treasure-trove, i.e., gold, etc., lying underground for a long time. (*Y*, II.34, 35)

Nikṣepa : "A deposit entrusted to a man after counting the articles in his presence."

(2) "Deposit of one's articles with another through confidence."

(3) "Delivery of one's articles to another for handing it over to a third."

(P.V. Kane, *Hist. of Dharmaśāstra*, III, p. 454).

It differed from *adhi* in that the former was not given by way of security for a debt or for collecting interest, but in confidence for safe custody. (*M*, VIII.4, 149, etc.; *Y*, II.67, III. 230)

Nirākṛti : (1) One who does not perform the five *Mahāyajñas* (q.v.).

(2) One who has not studied his own Veda or does not perform *vratas*. (*M*, III.154)

Nirdhūta : One deserted by friends. (*Y*, II.71)

Nirhāra : (1) Setting aside or accumulation of private store, hoard.

(2) Expense (see Kane, *Hist. of Dharmaśāstra*, III, p. 788, f.n.). (*M*, IX.199)

Nirṛti : Name of a malevolent goddess. (*M*, XI.118)

**Niṣāda* : Offspring of the marriage of a Brāhmaṇa with a Śūdra woman, such an offspring being called *Pāraśava* (q.v.) by some. (*M*,

X.8, 18, etc.; *Y*, I.91)

Niṣeka : The ceremony of impregnation. (*M*, II.16)

Niṣka : A coin (of silver, according to the *Mitākṣarā*) equivalent to four *suvarṇas* (q.v.). (*M*, VIII. 137, 220; *Y*, I.365)

Niṣkrama(ṇa) : The sacrament by which a child is taken out for the first time after birth. (*M*, II.34. *Y*, I.12)

Niṣkraya : Price, hire, ransom. (*Y*, II.182)

Nivītin : One wearing the sacred thread round the neck like a garland. (*M*, II.63)

Niyoga : Appointment of a sonless wife or widow to procreate a son from intercourse with an appointed male, usually her brother-in-law younger than her husband. (*Y*, II.127)

Niyukta : A male appointed for the purpose set forth under *niyoga* (q.v.). (*M*, IX.58, 60)

Nṛdurga : A kind of royal fort, guarded, on all sides, by infantry with elephants, horses and chariots. (*M*, VII.70)

Nṛ-yajña : Entertainment of guests. (*M*, III.70, IV.21)

Nyāsa : (1) An open deposit for safe custody.

(2) "Handing over to some member of the house an article in the absence of the head of the house for delivery to the head of the house." (Kane, *Hist. of Dharmaśāstra*, III, p. 455)

(3) Mental appropriation or assignment of various parts of the body to tutelary deities. (*Y*. II.67)

Pāda-kṛcchra : A form of penance in which the sinner takes food on one day only once by day, only once at night, then once only (by day or at night) but without asking for it, and observes total fast for one day. (*Y*, III.318)

Padma-vyūha : A kind of military array in which the king remains at the centre, and spreads the army on all sides. (*M*, VII.188)

Paiśāca : The basest and most sinful form of marriage in which a man has sexual intercourse with a girl stealthily while she is asleep. (*M*, III. 34; *Y*, I.61)

Paiṣṭī : Spirituous liquor distilled from rice or other grains. (*M*, IX.94)

Pāka-yajña : A sacrifice in which cooked offerings are given. According to some, the following are the *Pāka-yajñas* — *vaiśvadeva*, *bali*, *śrāddha*, entertaining guests. (*M*, II.143, III.70, etc.)

Pākhaṇḍin (*Pāṣaṇḍin*) : Heretic; e.g., a Buddhist. (*M*, IV.30, 61; *Y*, I. 130, II.70, etc.)

Pakṣiṇī : The period of one night with one day immediately preceding it and one day immediately following. (*M*, IV.97; V.81)

Pala : A particular weight (= 4 *karṣa*s = 100 *tolā*s). (*M*, VIII.135, 397; *Y*, I. 363-65, II.178, 179, III.215, etc.)

Paṃkti-dūṣaṇa (*-dūṣaka*) : One who defiles society, and, as such, should not be associated with. (*Y*, III.33)

Paṃkti-pāvana (*-pāvaka*) : One who sanctifies society. (*M*, III. 183, 184 186)

Paṇa : (1) "A weight of copper, used as a coin (= 20 *māṣas* = 4 *kākinīs*)". — Monier-Williams

(2) A bet or wager. (*M*, VIII.136, 138, etc.; *Y*, I.366)

Pañcagavya : The five products of the cow, viz., milk, curd, ghee, cow's urine and cowdung. (*M*, XI.105, 211; *Y*, III.319)

Pañcāgni : The five sacred fires, viz., *anvāhārya-pācana* or *dakṣiṇa, gārhapatya, āhavanīya, sabhya* and *āvasathya*. (*M*, III.185)

Pañca-nakha : Five-toed animal. (*M*, V.17, 18; *Y*, I.177)

Pañcasūnā : The five things in a house, by which the lives of creatures may be accidentally destroyed; viz., fire-place, slab for grinding condiments, broom, pestle and mortar, water-pot. (*M*, III.68)

Pañcavarga : The five classes of people appointed as spies, viz., a pilgrim or a rogue, an ascetic who violated his vows, an agriculturist in distress, a decayed merchant and a fictitious devotee. (*M*, VII.154)

Pañcayajña (*-makha, -satra*) : The five religious acts to be performed by a householder of any of the three upper classes, viz., *Brahmayajña* (study and teaching of the Veda), *pitṛyajña* (offering libation to the manes), *daivayajña* (= *homa*), *bhūtayajña* (offering food, etc., to birds, beasts, etc.) and *Nṛyajña* (hospitality). (*M*, III.67, 70; *Y*, I.121, III.310)

Paṇḍaka : Eunuch. (*Y*, III.273)

**Pāṇḍusopāka* : Offspring of a *Caṇḍāla* by a *Vaidehaka* (q.v.) woman. (*M*, X.37)

Pāṇika : A kind of song. (*Y*, III.114)

Parāka : An expiatory rite consisting in a fast for twelve days and control of the senses. (*M*, XI.215, 258; *Y*, III.265, 320)

**Pāraśava* : Offspring of a Brāhmaṇa by a Śūdra woman, sometimes designated as *Niṣāda*. (*M*, IX.78, 8; *Y*, I.91)

Pariṇāha : A space of 100 *dhanus* (1 *dhanus* = 4 cubits) between a village and a field. (*Y*, II.10.167)

Pāriṇāhya : Household furniture and utensils. (*M*, IX. 11)

Pariṣat (Parṣat) : An assembly of learned men for the removal of doubts about *dharma*. (*M*, XII. 111, 112; *Y*, I.9, III.300)

Parivedana : The act of one's marrying before his elder brother. (*M*, IX.60; *Y*, III.234)

Parivettā : Same as *Parivindaka* (q.v.). (*M*, III.154, 171, 172)

Parivindaka : The younger brother who has married before the elder. (*Y*, I.223, III.238)

Parivitti : The unmarried elder brother whose younger brother is married. (*M*. III.154, 171)

Parṇakūrca (*-kṛcchra*) : An expiatory rite in which *palāśa*, *udumbara*, lotus and *bilva* are boiled separately on each day in succession, and the decoction of each is drunk on each day separately, and then water in which *kuśa* grasses have been dipped is drunk. Thus, *parṇakṛcchra* is a penance of five days' duration. According to some authorities, its duration is six days, the leaves of *aśvattha* being added to the above five. (*Y*, III.316)

Pārṣṇi : Heel. (*Y*, II.213, III.86)

Pārṣṇigrāha : A king whose territory is just behind that of another. (*M*, VII.207)

Pāṣaṇḍa : Heresy, heretic. (*M*, I.118, V.90, IX.225)

Paunarbhava : Son or daughter of a girl called *punarbhū* (q.v.) (This word is sometimes used synonymously with *punarbhū*.). (*M*, III.155, IX.160; *Y*, I.222, II.130)

Pauruṣasūkta : Name of the Ṛgvedic hymn X.90. (*M*, IX. 251)

Peyuṣa : Beestings (*M*, X. 6)

Pitṛ-tīrtha (Pitrya-) : The root of the finger, called *ādeśinī*. (*Y*, I. 19; *M*, II.59)

Pitṛ-yajña : Offering of libation to the manes. (*M*, III.70)

Pracāra : Pasture-ground. (*M*, IX.219)

Prajāpati-tīrtha : Same as *kāya-tīrtha* (q.v.). (*Y*, I.19)

Prakarī : A kind of song. (*Y*, III.113)

Prakṛti : Constituent element of a Political Circle (*Rājamaṇḍala*) or State. It is chiefly of two kinds—*mūla-prakṛti* and *śākhā-prakṛti*. In the former are *vijigīsu, madhyama, udāsīna* and *śatru*. The latter includes *mitra, ari-mitra, mitra-mitra, ari-mitra-mitra, pārṣṇigrāha, ākranda, pārṣṇigrāhā-sāra* and *ākrandāsāra*. Each of the *śākhā-prakṛtis* has five *dravya-prakṛtis*, viz., minister, territory, fortress, treasury and army. (*M*, VII.156, IX.294, 295; *Y*, I.353)

Praṇava : The mystical and sacred syllable *oṃ*. (*M*, VI. 70, X.248; *Y*, I.23)

Praṇidhi : Spy. (*M,* VII.153, 223, VIII.182)

Pratāna : A plant with tendrils. (*M,* I.47)

Pratibhū : Surety. (*Y,* II.54, 55, etc.)

Prātibhāvya : Suretyship. (*Y,* II.53)

Pratiloma : The reverse order, usually applied to marriage between a male of a lower caste and a female of a higher one. (*M,* X.25)

Pūga : Any combination or body of persons; an association, corporation, union. (*M,* III. 151; *Y,* II.30, 211)

Pukkasa : (1) Offspring of a *niṣāda* (q.v.).

(2) Offspring of a Śūdra by a Kṣatriya female.

(3) Offspring of a Vaiśya male from a Kṣatriya female. (*M,* X.18, 49, etc.)

**Pulkasa* : Same as *pukkasa* (q.v.). (*Y,* III.207)

Puṃsava(na) : A sacrament performed, before the throbbing of the foetus in the womb, for obtaining a male child. (*Y,* I.11)

Punarbhū : Generally means a remarried widow. *Punarbhūs* are of seven kinds:

(1) A girl who had once been promised to be given away in marriage.

(2) A girl round whose wrist the auspicious band was tied by the husband.

(3) A girl already intended to be given in marriage.

(4) A girl who had been given by her father with water.

(5) A girl whose hand was held by the bridegroom.

(6) A girl who circumambulated the nuptial fire.

(7) A girl who bore a child after marriage.

Regarding the different classes of *punarbhūs*, authorities differ. (*Y*, I.67. Also see *paunarbhava*)

Purāṇa : A *karṣa* or measure of silver (= 16 *paṇa*s of cowries) (*M*, VIII.136)

**Puṣpadha* : Same as *Bhūrjakaṇṭaka*. (*M*, X. 21)

Putrikā or Putrikā-putra (-sūta) : (1) A sonless man's daughter's son, appointed to be his own son.
(2) A sonless man's daughter, appointed as his son. (*Y*, II.128)

Raivata : (1) Name of the fifth Manu.

(2) Name of various *Sāmans*. (*M*, I.62)

**Rajaka* : (1) Offspring of a *Pulkasa* (q.v.). or *Vaideha* (q.v.) by a Brāhmaṇa woman.

(2) Offspring of a *Pulkasa* (q.v.) by a Vaiśya girl. (*Y*, II.48)

Rāja-sarṣapa : "Black mustard, *Sinapis ramosa* (the seed used as a weight = 3 *likṣās* = 1/3 of a *gaura-sarṣapa*". —Monier-Williams. (*M*, VIII.133; *Y*, I.362)

Rākṣasa : The form of marriage in which a maiden is forcibly abducted. (*M*, III.21; *Y*, I.61)

**Rañjaka* : Offspring of the clandestine union between a Śūdra male and a Kṣatriya female. (*M*, IV. 216)

**Rathakāra* : (1) Offspring of the marriage of a Vaiśya by

a Śūdra female.

(2) Offspring of a *Māhiṣya* (q.v.) by a *Karaṇa* (q.v.) woman.

(3) Offspring of the clandestine union of a Kṣatriya male and a Brāhmaṇa woman. (*Y*, I.95)

Riktha (Ṛktha) : Any property, wealth, especially that left by one at death, inheritance. (*M*, VIII.27, 30; *Y*, II.51)

Rikthin : An heir. (*Y*, II.29, 45, 127)

Ṛktha : See *Riktha*.

Ṛṣi-yajña : Same as *brahma-yajña* (q.v.). (*M*, IV.21)

Ṛta : (1) True, truth.

(2) Gleaning of corns as a means of a Brāhmaṇa's obtaining livelihood. (*M*, IV.5, VIII.61, 82, etc.)

Ṛtvik : Priest, usually of four kinds, viz., *hotā*, *adhvaryu*, *brahmā* and *udgātā*. (*Y*, I.35)

Sada : Agricultural produce. (*M*, VIII.241)

Ṣaḍguṇa : The six measures of royal policy, viz., *sandhi*, *vigraha*, *yāna*, *āsana*, *dvaidhībhāva* and *saṃśraya*. (*M*, VII.160)

Ṣāḍguṇya : Same as *ṣaḍguṇa* (q.v.). (*M*, VII.58, 167)

Sāhasa : (1) "Punishment, fine regarded as of three kinds, the highest being called *uttama*, half of that *madhyama* and half of that *adhama*". — Monier-Williams.

(2) Violence, rape, felony. (*M*, VIII.6, 72; *Y*, I. 366, II.12, 230 ff.)

Sahoḍha (Sahoḍhaja) : A kind of son, born to a married woman, pregnant before marriage. (*M*, IX.160, 173; Y, II.131)

**Śaikha* : Same as *Āvantya* (q.v.). (*M*, X.21)

Śailūṣa : Actor. (*M*, IV.214; *Y*, II.48)

Sairindhra : "A kind of menial or domestic servant, born from the union of a *dasyu* and an *Āyogavī*." (See *Āyogava*)—Monier-Williams. (*M*, X.32)

Sakulya : The three paternal ancestors above the paternal great grandfather, and the three male descendants beyond the great grandson. (*M*, IX.187)

Sāma (Sāman) : Policy of conciliation being one of the four *upāyas* or means of success against the enemy. (*M*, VII.107, 109, 159, 198, VIII.187; *Y*, I.345, 346)

Samāhvaya : Betting, especially on animals. (*M*, IX.221-24; *Y*, II.203)

Samānodaka : "Having only libation of water to ancestors in common, distantly related (the relationship, according to some, extending to the 14th degree, the first seven being both *sapiṇḍas* (q.v.) and *samānodakas*, while the remaining seven are *samānodakas* only)." — Monier-Williams (*M*, V.60, IX.187)

Samaya : (1) Agreement, contract.

(2) Contract by association. (*M*, VIII.218, 220, 221; X.53)

Saṃayādhyuṣita : The time when the sun has not yet appeared, and the stars are invisible. (*M*, II.15)

Saṃdātā : One who ties up or fetters. (*M*, VIII.342)

Saṃgrahaṇa : Adultery. (*M*, VIII.356-59; *Y*, II.5-72, 283, 285)

Saṃprapada : Moving about. (*Y*, III.51)

Saṃśraya : One of the six *guṇas* (see *Ṣaḍguṇa*) or political expedients; according to it, a king, pressed hard by the enemy, takes the help of a more powerful king. (*M*, VII.160-62, 168; *Y*, I.347)

Saṃsṛṣta (*Saṃsṛṣṭin*) : One re-united with the coparceners after the partition of a property. (*M*, IX.212, 216. *Y*, II.138, 139)

Samudaya : Sources of revenue; i.e., the places from which paddy, gold, etc., are raised. (*M*, VII. 56)

Saṃvit : Contract. (*Y*, II.187, 259)

Saṃyāva : A sort of cake. (*M*, V.6; *Y*, I.173)

Sanābhi : Kinsman on the paternal side. (*M*, V.72, 84, IX.192)

Sandhi : A treaty of peace as one of the six measures of royal policy. (*M*, VII.56, 65, etc.; *Y*, I.346)

Sandhinī : (1) A cow in heat.

(2) A cow that gives milk while big with young.

(3) A cow that is milched with the calf of another's animal.

(4) A cow that is milched every alternate *velā* (time) of milching (?). (*M*, V.8; *Y*, I.170)

Sandhyā : 400 years at the beginning of *satya-yuga*. (*M*, I.69)

Sandhyāṃśa : 400 years towards the end of *satya-yuga*. (*M*, I.69)

Sāntapana : A form of penance. "It is of five kinds; the first is for two days, the second for seven days, the third for twelve, the fourth for fifteen days and the fifth for twenty-one days." (P.V. Kane, *History of Dharmaśāstra*, III, p. 151). (*M*, V.20, XI.124, etc.; *Y*, III.314, 315)

Sapiṇḍa : Two persons are said to be *sapiṇḍa* of each other when they are connected by the offering of *piṇḍa* (rice-ball offered to the manes of certain relations in *śrāddha*).

On connotation of *piṇḍa*, authorities differ. *Sapiṇḍa* generally means one's —

(1) ancestors up to the sixth degree from one's father and descendants down to the sixth degree from oneself.

(2) ancestors up to the fourth degree from mother and descendants down to the fourth degree from father. (*M*, III.5, V.59, 60, etc.; *Y*, I.52, 68)

Sapiṇḍīkaraṇa : Name of the *śrāddha* performed after one year from one's death. It is supposed to unite the deceased with the bodies of his ancestors. (*Piṇḍa* means body; Cf. *ekānta-vidhvaṃsiṣu madvidhānāṃ piṇḍeṣvanāsthā khalu bhautikeṣu*—*Raghuvaṃśa* II.57). (*Y*, I.254, 255)

Sarobindu : A kind of song. (*Y*, III.114)

Sarvauṣadhi : Certain herbs together are so called. Authorities differ on the names of the herbs. The *Aparārka* commentary gives a list of such herbs. (*Y*, I.278)

Śāsana : A royal edict. (*M*, IX.232; *Y*, I.320)

**Sātvata* : Same as *Kāruṣa* (q.v.). (*M*, X.23)

Satyānṛta : Trade and commerce. (*M*, IV.6)

**Śaudra* : "The son of a man of either of the three classes by a Śūdra woman (the last of the 12 kinds of sons acknowledged in ancient Hindu law)." — Monier-Williams. (*M*, IX.160)

Śaulkika : "Superintendent of tolls or custom duties." (P.V. Kane, *History of Dharmaśāstra*, III, p. 1005). (*Y*, II.173)

Saumya-kṛcchra : Authorities differ on its nature. According to *Y*, it is a penance lasting for six days, in the first five of which one subsists in succession on oil-cake, foamy scum of boiled rice, butter-milk, water and *saktu* (pulverised grain), and on the last day total fast is observed. (*Y*, III.321)

Sāvitrī : (1) The verse *Ṛgveda*, III.62.10, also called *Gāyatrī*.

(2) "Initiation as a member of the three twice-born classes, by reciting the above verse and investing with the sacred thread". — Monier-Williams. (*M*, II.81, XI.191, 194, 215; *Y*, I.24)

Sāvitrī-patita : Same as *vrātya* (q.v.). (*Y*, I.38)

Śelu : The plant *Dillenia indica*. Kullūka says: *Bahuvārakaphalam*; that which yields fruits many times (a year ?) (*M*, V.6)

Śila : Gathering stalks or ears of corns. (*M*, III. 100, IV.10, VII.33, X.112; *Y*, I.128)

Sīmantonnayana: The parting or dividing of the hairs; name of

(*Sīmanta*) one of the sacraments observed by a woman in the fourth, sixth or eighth month of pregnancy. (*Y*, I.11)

Śiśu-cāndrāyaṇa : A form of *Cāndrāyaṇa* (q.v.). In it, a Brāhmaṇa eats, for a month, four mouthfuls in the morning and four after sunset. (*M*, XI. 219)

Snātaka : One who has performed ablution marking the end of studenthood. (*M*, IV.13, 34, etc.; *Y*, I.110)

Somaraudra : Name of a sacred text (*Ṛgveda*, VI.74). (*M*, XI. 251)

**Sopāka* : Son of a *Caṇḍāla* (q.v.) by a *Pulkasa* (q.v.) woman. (*M*, X.38)

Sphic : Buttock, hip. (*Y*, III.97)

Śreṇī : A guild or association of traders, dealing in the same articles. (*Y*, I.361, II.30, 192)

Sthāla(ka) : The hollow of a tooth. (*Y*, III.85)

Sthāna : Prop of kingdom, viz., army, treasury, capital city and territory. (*M*, VII.56)

Sthānapāla : Appears to be the same as the *sthānika* who "had to keep a register of the caste, *gotra*, name and occupation of the men and women in their districts and also of their income and expenditure". (P.V. Kane, *History of Dharmaśāstra*, III, p. 149). (*Y*, II.173)

Strīdhana : A woman's exclusive property. Certain special kinds of property, given to a woman by relatives on certain occasions or in different stages of her life, over which she has absolute right. Authorities differ on the various kinds of *strīdhana*. According to Manu, it is of the following varieties :

What is given before the nuptial fire (*adhyagni*), what is given in the bridal procession (*adhyavāhnika*), what is given as a token of love (*dattaṃ ca prīti-karmaṇi*) and what is received by the girl from her parents and brothers (*bhrātṛmātṛ-pitṛ-prāptam*). (*M*, IX.194; *Y*, II.143, 145, etc.)

Sūcī : A kind of military array in which the van and the rear are compact like a row of ants. (*M*, VII.187, 191)

Sudhanvācārya : See *Kāruṣa* (q.v.). (*M*, X.23)

Śukriya : Name of the *Pravarga* section or *Vājasaneyi-saṃhitā*, 39-40. (*Y*, III.308)

Śukta : (1) Sweet substance which has become sour through staleness.

(2) Harsh word. (*M*, V.9, 10, XI.153; *Y*, I.33)

Śulka : (1) Bride's price, i.e., money paid by the bridegroom's party to the bride's guardian.

(2) Toll, tax, especially money levied at ferries, passes and roads. (*M*, VIII.159, 204, etc., IX.93, 97, etc., X.120; *Y*, II. 47, 144, etc.)

Sūnā : See *pañcasūnā* (q.v.). (*M*, XI.155)

Surā : Spirituous liquor, distilled from rice, molasses and flowers of the *madhuka* plant. See *Mādhvī*. (*M*, XI.90, 92-95)

Sūrmī : A hollow metal column made red-hot for burning a criminal (especially, adulterers) to death. (*M*, XI.103)

**Sūta* : One sprung from the union of a Kṣatriya male and a Brāhmaṇa female. (*M*, X.11, 17, etc.; *Y*, I.73)

Sūtaka : Child-birth; impurity of parents consequent upon the birth of their child or miscarriage. (*Y*, III.19)

Suvarṇa : A particular weight of gold (= *karṣā* = 16 *māṣas* = 80 *raktikās* = about 175 grains troy). (*M*, VIII.134, 135, etc.; *Y*, I.363-65)

**Śvapaca* : (1) Offspring of an *Ugra* (q.v.) male and a female of the *Kṣatṛ* sub-caste.

(2) Offspring of a *Kṣatṛ* male and an *Ugra* female.

(3) Offspring of a *Caṇḍāla* (q.v.) by a Brāhmaṇa female.

(4) Offspring of a *Caṇḍāla* by a Vaiśya female. (*M*, X.51)

**Śvapāka* : Same as *Śvapaca* (q.v.). (*M*, X.19)

Svarjit : A kind of sacrifice. (*M*, XI.74)

Svayaṃdatta (Svayamupāgata) : A kind of son who, bereft of parents or forsaken by them, voluntarily offers himself to a person as his son.

**Takṣaka (Takṣa)* : (1) One born to a *Sūcaka* (offspring of the union of a Vaiśya male and a Śūdra female) by a Brāhmaṇa female.

(2) Offspring of a *Cūcuka* (offspring of the marriage of a Vaiśya male with a Śūdra woman) by a Brāhmaṇa female. (*M*, IV.210)

Tāmisra : A kind of hell. (*M*, XII.75)

Taptakṛcchrā : (1) A form of expiation in which the sinner has to subsist on hot water, hot milk, hot ghee for three days each, and to fast for the last three days when he should inhale hot vapour or atmosphere.

(2) A form of penance of four days' duration when the sinner has to take hot milk, hot ghee and hot water for one day each, and to fast on the fourth day.

(3) A penance of two days' duration.

(4) A penance of 21 days' duration. (*M*, XI. 214; *Y*, III.317)

Tara : (1) Crossing a river or ocean.

(2) Toll payable by a merchant before crossing a river with merchandise. (*M*, VIII.404, 406, 407)

Tarat-samandīya: (*Tarat-samandi*) Name of the Ṛgvedic hymn beginning with *tarat-samandi dhāvati* (IX.58). (*M*, XI.253)

Tarika : Officer-in-charge of tolls payable by boats. (*Y*, II.263)

Tīrtha : (1) A holy place, (2) Parts of some fingers, e.g. (*Brāhma-tīrtha*, *Daiva-tīrtha*. (*M*, IV. 214)

Trasareṇu : "The mote or atom of dust moving in a sunbeam, considered as an ideal weight of the lowest denomination."—Monier-Williams. (*M*, VIII.132; *Y*, I.362)

Tridaṇḍa : Control over speech, mind and body. (*M*, XII. 11)

Tridaṇḍin : (1) Carrying the three staves together, a wandering mendicant.

(2) A triple commander, (i.e., controlling one's thought, word and deed. (*M*, XII.10; *Y*, III. 58)

Trimadhu : Knowing or reciting three verses beginning with *madhu* (*Ṛgveda*, I.90. 6-8). (*Y*, I.219)

Triṇāciketa : (1) One who has thrice kindled the *Nāciketa* fire or studied the *Nāciketa* section of the *Kāṭhaka*. — Monier-Williams.

(2) Name of three *anuvāka*s of the *Kāṭhaka*. (*M*, III.185; *Y*, I.220)

Triṣavaṇa : The three ablutions at dawn, noon and sunset. (*M*, XI.123; *Y*, III.48, 325)

Trisuparṇa(ka) : (1) Name of the Ṛgvedic hymn X.114, 3-5.

(2) Familiar with or reciting the above verse. (*M*, III.185)

Trisuparṇika : One who recites the verses referred to under *Trisuparṇa* above. (*Y*, I.219)

Triviṣṭapa : Heaven. (*Y*, III.329)

Tulā-puruṣa : (1) Gift of gold, etc. equal to the weight of the donor's body.

(2) A ten-day penance. (*Y*, III. 322)

**Tunnavāya* : Same as *Sūcika* (offspring of a *Vaidehaka* (q.v.) by a Kṣatriya woman). (*M*, IV.214)

Udakī (*Udakyā*) : A woman in her monthly impurity. (*M*, IV. 57, V.85, etc.; *Y*, I.168, III.30, etc.)

Udāsīna : A king who is able to help the *vijigīṣu* (q.v.) and the *madhyama* (q.v.) when united, or to harrass them when separated from each other. (*M*, VII.155, 211; *Y*, I.345)

Udaya : Interest, gain, increase, etc. (*Y*, II.67, 254)

Uddhāra : (1) The best part of things obtained in a conquest.

(2) That which is set aside, e.g., for the eldest brother, in the partition of patrimony among brothers. (*M,* VII.97, IX.112, 115, etc.)

Ugra : (1) Child of a Ksatriya male by a Śūdra female.

(2) One born of the union of a Brāhmaṇa male and a Śūdra female.

(3) Offspring of the union of a Vaiśya male with a Śūdra woman. (*M,* IV.212, X.9, 13, etc.)

Ullopya : A kind of song. (*Y,* III.113)

Uñcha : Gathering of abandoned corns, one by one. (*M,* IV.10; VIII.260, etc., *Y,* I.128)

Upadhi : Fraud, circumvention. (*M,* VIII.165, IX.258; *Y,* II.89, 202)

Upādhyāya : One who teaches a pupil a portion of the Veda or the *Vedāṅga*s for livelihood. (*Y,* I. 35, III.15)

Upagata : "A receipt passed by the creditor to a debtor on payment of the whole or part of a debt."

(P.V. Kane, *Hist. of Dharmaśāstra,* III, p. 311). (*Y,* II.93)

Upākarma : Commencement of Vedic study. (*M,* IV.119)

Upanayana : Initiation of a pupil, by the preceptor, to Vedic studies. (*M,* II.36; *Y,* I.14)

Upanidhi : Sealed deposit, i.e., an article deposited with a person in a sealed receptacle without disclosing the contents. (*M,* VIII.145, 149, etc.; *Y,* II.25)

Upanikṣepa : Open deposit, i.e., an article, kept by one with another for safe custody, after showing the latter the nature of what is deposited. (*Y,* II.25)

Upapātaka : A class of sins lighter than *mahāpātaka* (q.v.), comprising such sins as incest, giving up Vedic study, allowing the time for initiation to Vedic study to pass, following the profession of dancing, singing, acting, cow-killing, fornication, etc. (*M,* XI.66, 108; *Y,* II. 210, III.225, etc.)

Upavītin : One who wears the sacred thread (*yajñopavīta*) in the regular way, i.e., allows it to hang over the left shoulder and under the right arm. (*M,* II.63)

Upāya : Expedient of royal policy. The four expedients are *sāma* (conciliation), *dāna* (gift), *bheda* (dissension) and *daṇḍa* (war). (*M,* VII.108, 109, etc.; *Y,* I.346)

Vaiḍāla-vratika : Acting like a cat, hypocritical, a religious impostor. (*M,* IV.30, 192, 195)

**Vaideha(ka)* : (1) A caste sprung from the union of a Vaiśya and a Brāhmaṇa female.

(2) Offspring of a Śūdra by a Kṣatriya woman.

(3) Offspring of a Śūdra by a Vaiśya female. (*M,* X.11, 13, etc.; *Y,* I.93)

Vaiṇa : Same as *Veṇa* (q.v.). (*Y,* I.161)

Vaiśvānarī : A sacrifice performed at the beginning of every year. (*Y,* I.126, III.250)

Vajra : A kind of military array in which the soldiers

are arranged in three ways. (*M*, VII.191)

Vākovākya : Vedic texts in the form of catechism. (*Y*, I.45)

Vaṅkhana : Thigh-joint. (*Y*, III.97)

Varāha : A form of military array in which the soldiers are so arranged that it is tapering at the van and rear, but wide in the middle. (*M*, VII. 187)

Vārdhuṣi(ka) : Usurer. (*M*, III.158, 180; *Y*, I.132, 161)

Vārkṣa : A kind of fortress which is surrounded, up to one *yojana* (= 8 or 9 miles), by huge trees, thorny shrubs, creepers, etc. (*M*, VII.70)

Vārtā : Agriculture, cattle-rearing, trade, etc. (*M*, VII.43, IX.326, X.80; *Y*, I.311)

**Vāṭadhāna* : Same as *Āvantya* (q.v.). (*M*, X.21)

**Veṇa* : (1) Offspring of a *Vaidehaka* (q.v.) by an *Ambaṣṭha* (q.v.) female.

(2) Offspring of the union of different castes in the reverse order (*pratiloma* — q.v.), subsisting by cutting bamboo, cane, etc. (*M*, X.49; *Y*, III.207)

Vighasa : This is what is left after Brāhmaṇas and guests have partaken. (*M*, III.285)

Vigraha : War as one of the six *guṇas* (see *Ṣaḍguṇa*) or measures of royal policy. (*M*, VII.56, 160, etc.; *Y*, I.347)

Vinaśana : The place where the river Sarasvatī disappeared; regarded as a holy place. (*M*, II. 21)

Vinna : Married. (*Y*, I.92)

Viṣṭapa : (1) A world, region.

(2) Heaven.

(3) *Brahman* who is free from pain. (*M*, IV. 231, IX.137)

Viśvajit : Name of a sacrifice in which one has to give away one's all as sacrificial fee. (*M*, IX.74)

Vṛddhi : (1) Usury, interest.

(2) A kind of *śrāddha* performed, on an auspicious occasion, e.g., birth of a son, marriage of son or daughter, in honour of *pitṛs*; this *śrāddha* is also designated as *Nāndī-mukha*. (*Y*, I.217)

Vṛkkaka : A lump of flesh near the heart. (*Y*, III.94, 97)

Vyāhṛti : The mystical utterance of the names of the seven worlds, viz., *bhūḥ*, *bhuvaḥ*, *svaḥ*, *mahaḥ*, *janaḥ*, *tapas*, *satya*. (*M*, VI.70, XI. 248; *Y*, I.23, 239)

Vyatipāta : The day of new moon when it falls on Sunday, and when the moon is in certain *nakṣatras*. (*Y*, I.218)

Vyavahāra : (1) Legal procedure.

(2) Administration of justice.

(3) Contract.

(4) Competency to manage one's own affairs, majority. (*M*, VIII.7, 45, etc.; *Y*, I.360, II.1, etc.)

Yama : It means *brahmacarya*, kindness, forbearance, truthfulness, *ahiṁsā*, etc. (*Y*, III. 312)

Yama-vrata : Punishing the subjects, like Yama, without respect for persons and without partiality, as one of the duties of the king. (*M*, IX.307)

Yāna : One of the six *guṇas* (see *Ṣaḍguṇa*) to be resorted to by a king; marching against the enemy. (*M*, VII.160-63, 165, 181)

Yati-cāndrāyaṇa : "A penance where the sinner eats only eight mouthfuls of food only once in the noon for a month and exercises control over himself." (P.V. Kane, *History of Dharmaśāstra*.) (*M*, XI.218)

Yautuka (-taka) : A kind of *strīdhana* (q.v.). The various opinions about its nature are: (1) Wealth received, as a gift from anybody, by a woman while seated together with the bridegroom at the time of marriage.

(2) Separate property of a woman.

(3) Wealth obtained from the family of the woman's father, which is separate in its characteristics. (*M*, IX.131, 214; *Y*, II.149)

Yava : A particular weight = 6 or 12 mustard seeds = 1/2 *guñjā*. (*M*, VIII.134)

Yava-madhyama (-madhya) : A kind of *cāndrāyaṇa* (q.v.). The word literally means — large in the middle like a grain of *yava*. (*M*, XI.217; *Y*, I.363)

Yoga : (1) Acquisition of what has not been acquired.

(2) A trick.

(3) Connexion, relation.

(4) Power, zeal. (*M*, VII. 44, VIII.165, 230, IX. 219; *Y*, I.100)

Select Bibliography

[The important editions and translations of the *Smṛti* works, included in the present work, have been mentioned under the respective texts. So, we have not mentioned them here again.]

Altekar, A.S. : *Position of Women in Hindu Civilisation.*

Ambedkar, B.R. : *Who were the Shūdras*, Bombay, 1946.

Apte, V.M. : *Sacrament of Marriage in Hindu Society from Vedic Period to Dharmaśāstras*, Delhi, 1978.

Banerjee, G. : *Marriage and Strīdhana*, Calcutta.

Banerji, S.C. : *Dharmasūtras*, etc., Calcutta, 1962.

———, *The Castaway of Indian Society —Prostitution in Vedic Times*, Calcutta, 1989.

———, *Society in Ancient India*, New Delhi, 1997.

———, *Crime and Sex in Ancient India,* Calcutta, 1981.

———, *A Glossary of Smṛti Literature*, Calcutta.

Bhattacharya, B. : *Studies in Nibandhas.*

Bhattacharya, P.S. : *Conceptualisation in the Manu-smṛti.*

Brough, J. : *Early Brahmanical System of Gotra and Pravara*, Cambridge, 1953.

Bühneman, G. : *Pūjā, A Study in Smārta Ritual.*

Chatterjee, H. N. : *Studies in Some Aspects of Hindu Saṃskāras in Ancient India*, vols. I & II, Calcutta, 1967.

———, *The Law of Debt in Ancient India*, Calcutta, 1971.

———, *Studies in the Social Background of the Forms of Marriage in Ancient India*, vols. I & II, Calcutta.

Chatterjee, G.K. : *Studies in the Rites and Rituals of Hindu Marriage in Ancient India*, Calcutta.

Crawford, S.G. : *Evolution of Hindu Ethical Ideals*, Calcutta, 1974.

Das, B. : *The Science of Social Organisation or the Laws of Manu*, Madras, 1932-35.

Derrett, J.D.M. : *Hindu Law, Past and Present*, Calcutta, 1957.

———, *Dharmaśāstras and Juridical Literature*, Wiesbaden, 1973.

Gharpure, J. : *Sāpiṇḍya*.

———, *Teachings of Dharmaśāstra*.

Goswami, K.G. : *Intercaste Marriage in Ancient India*, Calcutta.

Goswami, H.G.: *Hindu Ethics — Purity, Abortion and Euthanasia*, Delhi.

Jolly, J. : *Recht und Sitté*, Strassbürg, 1896. (Trs. into Eng. by B.K. Ghosh with the title *Hindu Law and Custom*, Calcutta, 1928).

Kane, P.V. : *History of Dharmaśāstra*, vols. I-V, Poona.

Karandikar, S.V. : *Hindu Exogamy*, Bombay, 1929.

Leslie, J. : *Roles and Rituals for Hindu Women*, Delhi, 1992.

Mookerjee, R.K. : *Education in Ancient India*.

Om Prakash : *Food and Drink in Ancient India*, Delhi, 1961.

Pandey, R.B. : *Hindu Saṃskāras*, Benares, 1949.

Pendse, S.N. : *Oaths and Ordeals in Dharmaśāstra*, Vadodara, 1985.

Sastri, D. : *Origin and Development of the Rituals of Ancestor-worship in India.*

Senart, E. : *Les castes dans Inde*, Paris, 1896. [Eng. tr. by E.D. Ross under the title *Caste in India*, London, 1930.]

Sharan, M.K. : *Court-procedure in Ancient India.*

Sharma, K. *et al.* : *Satī.*

Sharma, N.R. : *The Kāmarūpa School of Dharmaśāstra*, 1993.

Sharma, R.N. : *Brahmins through Ages.*

Sharma, R.S. : *Śūdras in Ancient India*, Patna, 1958.

Singh, S.D. : *Polyandry in Ancient India.*

Singh, S. : *Evolution of the Smṛti Law*, Varanasi, 1972.

Smith, B.K. : *Classifying the Universe, the Ancient Indian Varṇa System and the Origin of Caste.*

Sternbach, L.: *Juridical Studies in Ancient Indian Law Texts*, Delhi, 1996.

———, *Bibliography of Dharma and Artha in Ancient and Medieval India.*

Supakar, S.: *The Law of Evidence in Ancient India*, vol. I, Calcutta, 1990.

Upadhyaya, G.P. : *Brāhmaṇas in Ancient India*, New Delhi, 1979.